NDON

JACK THE RIPPER
The Bloody Truth

Books by Melvin Harris

Strange to Relate 1 and *2*
Critics' Gaffes (with Ronald Duncan)
Sorry You've Been Duped!
Investigating the Unexplained

JACK THE RIPPER

The Bloody Truth

Melvin Harris

*

Columbus Books
London

First published in Great Britain in 1987 by
Columbus Books Limited
19-23 Ludgate Hill
London, EC4M 7PD

Designed by Ronald Clark

British Library Cataloguing in Publication Data

Harris, Melvin
Jack the Ripper: the bloody truth.
1. Jack, *the Ripper*   2. Whitechapel murders, 1988
I. Title
364.1′523′0924   HV6535.G6L65

ISBN 0-86287-328-2

Set in Linotype Century Schoolbook by
Facet Film Composing Limited, Leigh-on-Sea, Essex

Printed and bound in Great Britain by R. J. Acford Limited,
Chichester, Sussex

All illustrations are from the author's own collection
except the following:
Between pages 24–5, 'Sir James Whitehead's Procession,
9 November 1888' by William Logsdail,
courtesy of The Bridgeman Art Library.
Pages 55 and 74, illustrations by R. G. Trow.
Pages 96–7, the Whitechapel Club,
courtesy of the *Chicago Tribune*.
Page 113, the Duke of Clarence,
courtesy of The BBC Hulton Picture Library.
Opposite page 144, 'St Martin-in-the-Fields'
by William Logsdail,
courtesy of Tate Gallery Publications.
Page 156, 'A Man with Secrets' by Walter Sickert,
courtesy of The Central Reference Library.

For indomitable Mo, who battled courageously
with many dragons; stalked over battlefieds littered
with the wreckage of wordprocessors
and golf-ball machines; and finally conquered
with the aid of an antique manual.

Contents

Foreword

Something *new* on the Ripper? Is it possible? It certainly is. In this book I provide the answers to many of the problems raised by the Whitechapel mystery. I disclose for the first time the pyramid of hoaxes that led to the involvement of the Freemasons and the Royal Family in bogus solutions to the murders. It is a sorry but intensely intriguing tale of self-deception, skullduggery and worse.

But to do justice to these new insights has meant paring away the details of the murders themselves to the bare essentials. The anecdotes and minutiae beloved of other writers have been discarded. I avoid line-by-line transcripts of the coroners' inquests. I am sparing with lengthy quotes from the press. I even ignore the in-fighting at Scotland Yard and the clashes between Home Secretary Matthews and Sir Charles Warren. As I see it, such information is relatively easy to come by, but the revelations I have to make are on a different plane altogether. They need space to allow them to expand naturally, to carry conviction and above all to satisfy and entertain you, the reader.

Acknowledgements

My eternal thanks to Richard Whittington-Egan who insisted that I write this book – and wouldn't take no for an answer!

Special thanks to Simon Welfare, who has been telephonically pinioned with fearsome regularity.

And thanks to Francis King, author of *The Magical World of Aleister Crowley*, etc. etc., for his cheerful chats.

To Librarians everywhere in the UK, especially the Local History Section at Hull. In the USA, thanks to the Chicago Historical Society; to Dr Joan Healy, New York; and to dear Dr Leona Bayer in San Francisco.

Finally, to the acknowledged First Lady of Crime, Camille Wolff, of Grey House Books, Chelsea.

Map of the Whitechapel Murders

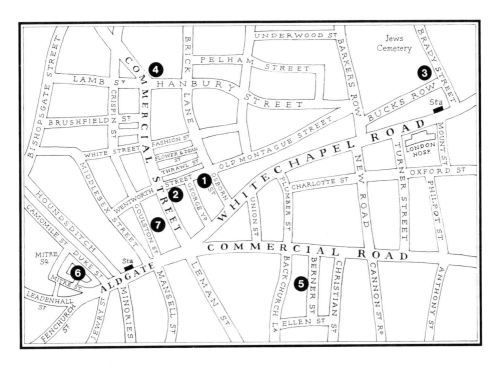

1. Emma Smith
2. Martha Turner
3. Mary Ann Nichols
4. Annie Chapman
5. Elizabeth Stride
6. Catherine Eddowes
7. Mary Kelly

After Kelly's death in November 1888, the *Police News* logged these seven 'Ripper' killings. Was this the right conclusion?

The Nemesis of Neglect.

1
The Man in the Shadows

A terrified woman is on her knees. An ape-like creature yanks at her long hair. With his other hand he slashes her throat with an awesomely huge knife. Look again: there alongside are two madmen butchering two women. One strangles with a thick rope. The other attacks with knife and axe.

This is *Punch*, in grim mood, protesting at the spate of aggressive posters that jarred on the walls and hoardings of London. But few took notice, for the year was 1887 – Jubilee Year. No time for solemn strictures, the mood was one of organized rejoicing. Brass medallions were showered on ragged schoolchildren, the streets were festooned with streamers and flags. And presiding over London's celebrations was the rigid, slightly comic figure of Sir Charles Warren.

Sir Charles is the first character to meet in the Whitechapel drama. He was precipitated into office in March 1886, when Chief Commissioner of Police Henderson resigned, and he entered that office knowing he'd been chosen over the heads of more than four hundred applicants. Warren's confidence was unbounded. Henderson had been pushed out of office by his inept handling of labour unrest, but that wouldn't happen to him. Good military discipline was the answer. Firmness above all – with justice, of course.

His marshalling of the Jubilee processions brought glowing praise, and Warren loved that. But his handling of the next confrontation with the Great Unwashed that year was much more contentious: it became known as Bloody Sunday. By his order, Trafalgar Square was closed to all rallies, but the Reds, the Radicals and the Unemployed claimed the right to protest there. Warren answered with a show of force, platoons of police to ring the square, the Grenadier Guards to clear the roadways. And the hated cavalry to intervene if needed. The inevitable clashes led to the death of Alfred Linell, and Warren's name was no longer uttered with a smile. He started 1888 with a loss of good will, yet soon he would need every fragment of good will he could glean. A sickening drama was about to be set in motion, and all of Warren's planning and techniques were due to be tested to their very limits.

The scene of the drama was the Whitechapel area of London's East End, a place where violence was endemic and expected. But nothing prepared it for the interlinked killings of 1888.

It was an area of filth and despair, jam-packed by people without a future, people grubbing along from day to day, toiling when they could, starving when they couldn't. And for many, the toil was remorseless, like the tasks of the matchbox makers. Each box demanded fourteen or more operations and when the quota was met, it was tuppence or less for a gross of boxes. Little wonder that many women turned their backs on such slavery and took to the streets.

East End whores were rarely enticing minxes, but those in Whitechapel counted as the worst of the lot. Here's how an eagle-eyed reporter from the London office of the *New York Herald* saw them:

> You can see them any evening, a dozen at least, on the pavement in front of the big old Spitalfields church. They are all over the adjacent district, but this is a sure place to find a group. They are old, actually or prematurely, as the case may be. Their dress holds together but would not stand daylight. Their shoes are full of holes. Their bonnets would be rejected with nausea by a respectable rag-bag. They wear little, if any underclothing for several reasons, one of which is that it costs money. They are all bent, and walk slowly, the tottering gait of a wreck. And in all the scale of zoology there is nothing that can compare with the faces that look at you in the flickering lights of the street.

One hundred and forty-four matchboxes brought in twopence, or less.
To some the streets seemed more inviting.

They are seamed and seared and wrinkled and bloated. Their eyes are dull like those of dead fish. They sit on the little shelf of stone, their backs against the iron fence palings of the churchyard, too sodden to talk – too torpid for anything save an occasional quarrel. A ha'penny buys 'em a drink, and when they get one they stagger to the nearest 'pub', and sit down to linger over it. There is no slum character in any city of earth except London which furnishes this type. It is an Anglo-Saxon result produced by the slum constitution, the slum traditions, and the rawest of strong spirits. The Latin peoples, more nervous by constitution, do not go to pieces in this way. The paternal relations of the German cities and the German character itself prevent it there. In America, in every city of the United States, every one of these creatures and all the women of the Strand and Regent-street as well would be arrested instantly and sent to prison as vagrants or worse.

They are not vicious. They do not know the meaning of vice, because they have never had any definition of virtue. Depravity is a feeble word, degradation a familiar and inadequate expression to describe their condition. The French alone could suggest it in *la misère*. There is nothing in the menagerie of the wilds to equal them, because even the beasts and the savages have a kind of self-respect which in these beings, without the vestige of moral sense, is absolutely lacking.

These were the pathetic creatures soon to be terrorized. Some of them would meet stark horror on their beats. For in the shadows a twisted and depraved man watched and waited. He studied their movements. He noted the places that attracted them. He trod through the alleys and courts they used, etching a map of the area onto his fevered brain. His satanic plan – to rule these sordid streets with his invisible, omniscient presence.

'Their heritage a sunless day'.

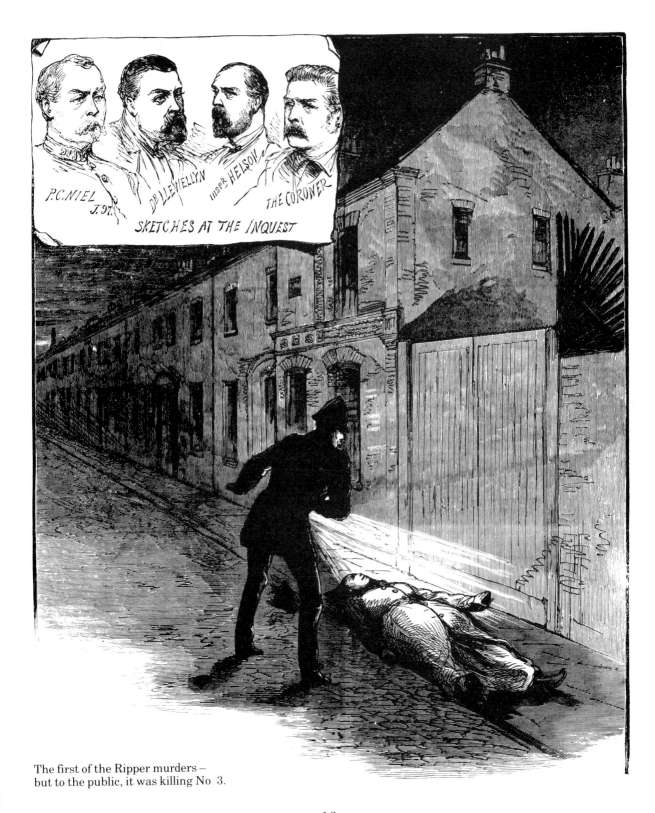

The first of the Ripper murders –
but to the public, it was killing No 3.

2

The Bundle at Buck's Row

Friday 31st August 1888

It looked like a discarded tarpaulin, just a grey bundle lying near the wooden gateway. Pickford's carman Charles Cross was curious, but the light was dim and unhelpful – only one feeble, yellow gas-lamp sputtering away at the far-off street corner. But the bundle might be worth something. So he crossed the street and peered down at the greyness. He saw a woman lying silently on her back, her skirt pushed up, suggesting rape. Nothing warned him that the woman was neither drunk nor unconscious; in fact, when he heard John Paul approaching, he called on him to help lift her.

Fellow carman Paul behaved quite sensibly. He made no attempt to raise the body. He felt the chilly hands and face and guessed that she was dead. But then he felt unsure. Had there been a trace of a heartbeat? The safest move was to locate the nearest bobby. So both men set off in search and met a patrolling constable at Baker's Row.

In the meantime, Police Constable John Neil had strolled through Buck's Row and discovered the body. His bull's eye lantern disclosed all: the woman's throat had been slashed deeply, but was it suicide or murder? Neil was joined within minutes by Constables Mizen and Thain. Thain then ran to fetch the nearest doctor in Whitechapel Road.

When Dr Llewellyn reached Buck's Row he estimated that the woman had been dead for less than half an hour. He had taken some fifteen minutes to arrive, so the woman had expired not long before the two carmen had viewed her. The time then had been close to 3.45 a.m.

The doctor ordered the body removed to the mortuary; later on he would go there to make a thorough examination. At the mortuary – a make-shift annexe to the workhouse – the police found the woman had been disembowelled. When Dr Llewellyn heard this news, he hurried to the sordid outbuilding and began his preliminary post-mortem.

Inspector Spratling's report states that the doctor found: '. . . her throat had been cut from left to right, two distinct cuts being on the left side, the windpipe, gullet and spinal cord being cut through, a bruise apparently of a thumb being on the right lower jaw, also one on the left cheek. The abdomen had been cut open from centre of bottom of ribs on the right side, under pelvis to left of the stomach; there the wound was jagged . . . two small stabs on private parts appeared done with a strong bladed knife, supposed to have been done by some left handed person, death being almost instantaneous.'

There was nothing on the body to identify it. The woman's flannel petticoats carried the stencilled brand 'Lambeth Workhouse', but the workhouse matron couldn't help: the clothes could have been issued some years before. The dead woman was unremembered and unmemorable and no clues were offered by the rest of her apparel. It was a pitiful collection. Only the black straw bonnet was new and feminine; by contrast her boots were men's wear, steel-tipped, battered and cut on the uppers.

The police made the rounds of lodging-house keepers and read them their description: 'Age about 45; length 5ft 2 or 3; complexion dark; hair brown turning grey; eyes brown . . . one tooth deficient front of upper jaw, two on left of lower. Found wearing black ribbed woollen stockings, brown linsey frock, men's spring-sided boots and a brown ulster with 7 large embossed brass buttons. The buttons showed a woman on a horse with a groom at her side . . .' Before long these details brought an identification. She was 'Polly', a dosser at the common lodging house at 18 Thrawl Street, Spitalfields.

Within days a more complete identification was made. Mary Ann Nichols was mother of five and wife to William Nichols of Coburg Street, Old Kent Road. William had broken with her, at first because of her habitual drunkenness. They had had no contact for some three years, after he'd discovered she had turned to prostitution.

Polly's movements on the night of her death were fairly easy to trace. At about 1.40 a.m. she was in the kitchen of 18 Thrawl Street. At that time she had no money for a bed, but she left confident of earning some. She was next seen at 2.30 a.m. on the corner of Osborn Street and Whitechapel Road by Ellen Holland, who tried to persuade her to come back to Thrawl Street: she was sorry for Polly, who was by then hopelessly drunk. But persuasion failed and Polly reeled off down the Whitechapel Road to her death. That was the last sight and sound of her. At her death place no one, not even night watchman William Louis, heard anything that could have alerted them to the tragedy.

When the newspapers took up the story, the first lines in Jack's history were written, only at that time he was still faceless and nameless. The *Penny Illustrated Paper* for 8 September 1888 shows how the initial reasoning went. Of Nichols' death it said: 'This crime has so many points of similarity with the murders of the two other women in the same neighbourhood – one, Martha Turner, as recently as August 7th and the other less than twelve months previously – that the police admit their belief that the three crimes are the work of one individual. All three women were of the same class, and each of them was so poor that robbery could have formed no motive for the crime. The three murders were committed within a distance of 200 yards of each other.'

A lapse of memory seems to be involved here, for the murder of Emma Smith just five months earlier had been overlooked, and if the paper was seeking crime patterns, she needed to be taken into the reckoning: she, too, had been a prostitute living not far from Buck's Row, in George Street. Others, however, did take Emma into account and until the first editions of 8 September, the killer was thought to have claimed four known victims.

The number jumped to five on the morning of the 8th – when at 6 a.m. Spitalfields market porter John Davis went into the back yard of the house where he lived. Lying near the wall was the body of a woman, mutilated and with her throat cut.

He ran terrified to the Commercial Street police station, blurted out his story, then returned to 29 Hanbury Street with Inspector Chandler. Chandler's report reads: 'I . . . found a woman lying on her back dead, left hand resting on left breast, legs drawn up . . . small intestines and flap of the abdomen lying on right side above right shoulder, attached by a cord with the rest of the intestines inside the body. Two flaps of skin from the lower part of the abdomen lying in a large quantity of blood above the left shoulder; throat cut deeply from left and back in a jagged manner right around the throat.' The divisional surgeon, Dr Bagster Phillips, was summoned and on arrival he judged that the woman had been dead for at least two hours. A police ambulance then took the body to the Whitechapel Mortuary.

The woman's identity was easily established. She was 45-year-old Annie Chapman, also known as Annie Siffey and nicknamed 'Dark Annie', a widow who had turned to prostitution. On the morning of her death she had last been seen in Crossingham's lodging house at 35 Dorset Street, Spitalfields. This was at 1.45 a.m. – at that time she was sozzled and unable to pay for her bed. Like Nichols, she went out into her dark night simply to raise enough cash for a few hours' passable sleep.

The inquest brought out the full horror of her death. Bruising seemed to show that the woman had been grasped by the throat and semi-throttled – perhaps a measure aimed at stifling cries. The killer then had slashed the neck deeply, almost to the point where the head was severed. After that, he'd coolly tied a handkerchief around the neck as if to hold the head in position. Then he'd sliced out the uterus and taken it away as a grisly trophy.

The inquest report, coupled with various newspaper accounts, set in circulation a number of myths. The Coroner, Mr Wynne E. Baxter, mentioned that some brass rings had been wrenched from Annie's middle finger and were missing. A reporter from the *Pall Mall*, on the other hand, filed a story which alleged that he had seen the rings, together with some trumpery articles '. . . placed carefully at the victim's feet'. This flashy touch was picked up by writer after writer and enlarged into something of symbolic significance. Extra bits were thrown in over the years. In 1929, it was two or three coppers at the feet. By 1959, it was a few pennies and two farthings. By 1965, it was two new farthings! But the police inspection report of the time makes no mention of these things. In the yard they had found two pills and a portion of a torn envelope bearing a postmarked date of 20 August and the crest of the Sussex Regiment. But it was a stray fragment that meant nothing and led nowhere. The rings and coins, on the other hand, led to some remarkably weird theories which in due time we'll meet.

The contemporary reports of the murder show a ghoulish interest by the public in Hanbury Street. Now that it was certain a fiend was at large, the death site became a show piece, throngs milling outside the place. The *Penny Illustrated Paper* says: 'During the whole of last Saturday and Sunday a large crowd congregated . . . in front of the house . . . and the neighbours on either side did much business by making a small charge to persons who were willing to pay to view from windows the yard in which the murder was committed.'

This near-hysterical interest led to waves of groundless rumours. One had it that the killer had been arrested in Spitalfields market, but this turned out to be a blind man involved in a fracas. More persistent was the charge that a character nicknamed 'Leather Apron' was the culprit.

He was portrayed as a monster who crept around the Whitechapel area at night looking for lone whores. The *Star* said of him: 'He exercises over the unfortunates . . . a sway that is based on universal terror. He has kicked, injured, bruised and terrified a hundred of them who are ready to testify to the outrages. He has made a certain threat, his favourite threat, to any number of them, and each of the three [*sic*] dead bodies represents the threat carried out. He carries a razor-like knife, and two weeks ago drew it on a woman called "Widow Annie" as she was crossing the square near London Hospital, threatening at the same time, with his ugly grin and his malignant eyes, to "rip" her up.'

Other papers helped whip up the feeling against the unnamed be-aproned fiend. One man was so terrified of a lynch mob that he went into hiding and trembled away at his stepmother's home in Mulberry Street. He was a Polish Jew named John Pizer: as a boot-finisher, he wore a leather apron, and naturally, the tools of his trade included razor-sharp, long-bladed knives.

Pizer was arrested on 10 September by Detective-Sergeant Thicke. 'Just the man I want,' said the detective, then he charged Pizer with being concerned in the murder of Annie Chapman. All the long-bladed knives were gathered up as evidence and the protesting Pole was hauled off to the station cells. Yet the police description of the man they *really* wanted was very different. He'd been seen talking to the dead woman at the entrance to the passageway leading to the Hanbury Street back yard: 'Age 37; height, 5 feet, 7 inches; rather dark beard and moustache. Dress – shirt, dark jacket, dark vest and trousers, black scarf, and black felt hat. Spoke with a foreign accent.'

Pizer's family vouched for his movements. A good alibi was also produced for the night of Nichols's killing and on top of that none of the women who confronted him recognized Pizer as the 'Leather Apron' they had talked about. So he was released, and the search for the Gothic villain continued.

Many other 'Leather Aprons' were nominated but few were chosen. One who was pulled in was a wanderer named William Henry Pigott, discovered unkempt and bloodstained. A woman had bitten him, he said, then he told a rambling story of the events leading up to the bite. Again, no one identified him as the suspect, and the poor wretch ended up in a mental asylum.

There were many other suspects, apart from the apron clan. A sad procession of down-and-outs and the feeble-minded slouched through the entrances of police stations and out of the exits. It was all futile groping in the dark. Nothing of value came to hand, and on 30 September the killer struck again. Not once, but twice.

Berner Street was the scene of the first murder. The exact site of the killing was an uninviting place. As *The Times* put it: '. . . a narrow court, at the entrance . . . are a pair of large wooden gates, in one of them of which [*sic*] is a small wicket for use when the gates are closed . . . When the murderer accomplished his purpose these gates were open. For a distance of eighteen or twenty feet from the street there is a dead wall on each side of the court, the effect of which is to enshroud the intervening space in absolute darkness after sunset.'

Usually the only light illuminating this stark backwater came from a scatter of cottages on one side and from the windows of the International Working Men's Educational Club on the other. On the night of the murder, though, the cottage windows were dark and only the club windows threw out a few beams. Inside its rooms some members sang and relaxed after a heated discussion about the appeals of socialism for the Jewish people.

The club's steward was Louis Diemschutz, a man with two jobs. Most of the time he left the club in the hands of his wife while he went around peddling cheap costume jewellery, and on the murder night, after much peddling and haggling, he returned home late, at about 1 a.m. As he drove his pony and cart into the court he felt the pony shy and pull hard to one side. Peering around to spot the cause, Diemschutz saw a shapeless heap on the ground. He jumped from his cart, struck a match and in an instant saw that the heap was a woman – either drunk or dead.

He rushed into the club, calling on members to help, then rushed back out with a candle. The members with him helped lift the woman's head, but her gashed throat told them they were wasting their time. Only the police could help now.

The first constable located, quickly whistled up aid and the police then sealed off the court and began a thorough search of the cottages and any place where the killer could be hiding. As a matter of course everyone in the court had to submit to an examination for bloodstains, but not one useful find was made. While the Metropolitan Police were still searching, news came in that a second murder had taken place, this time on territory controlled by the City of London Police.

Mitre Square was just on the edge of the historic square mile forming the City. Two sides of it were taken up with warehouses patrolled by a night watchman while the square itself was patrolled every fifteen minutes by a City constable. On his passage through the place at 1.30 a.m. PC Watkins found the square quite empty. On his return at 1.45 a.m. he discovered another victim. Her face was mutilated almost beyond recognition. There were slashes to the cheeks, the lobe of the right ear was nearly severed and part of the nose was cut off. The throat was cut through and like Chapman she had been disembowelled.

The killing at Mitre Square was many times more audacious than that at Berner Street. The square was not only visited throughout the night but had three entrances to keep an eye on. And the audacity didn't stop there. Police combing the area came upon two mocking clues at Goulston Street, about a third of a mile east of Mitre Square and in territory under Metropolitan Police jurisdiction.

The finds were made in the passageway leading into Nos 108 to 119 Wentworth Buildings. On the ground was a piece of blood-stained apron, later identified as cut from that worn by the Mitre Square victim. Above the bloody rag, on the black brick wall, was chalked the enigmatic message: 'The Juwes are The men That will not be Blamed for nothing.'

Although these finds were on Metropolitan grounds, Daniel Halse, a City detective, stayed at the spot and sent word of the event to the City's CID who wisely wanted to photograph the wall-writing as soon as it was light enough. The Met, by contrast, were in favour of wiping the wall clean before any of the public could read the taunt.

The Met's reasoning was somewhat confused. There had recently been a noticeable wave of anti-Jewish feeling: dark hints of ritual murder had been dropped here and there. It was safer then, to expunge the writing before the ignorant and the malicious saw it and made capital out of it. Perhaps so, but why not photograph it first?

The Met officers guarding the wall played safe by waiting until a higher authority gave a 'wipe-clean' order. And just after 5 a.m. the highest authority of all came in person and spoke the magic words: Sir Charles Warren not only gave the order, but impetuously picked up a sponge and wiped the words out with his own firm hands. Only a hand-written copy remained in a police notebook. This mysterious writing on the wall led later investigators to some grotesque theories, but at the time it simply promoted ill will between the two police forces. Still, there were bigger mysteries to unravel just then. There were two new victims. Who were they?

The woman at Mitre Square was in some ways the most tragic victim of all. She was Catherine Eddowes, aged 43, but so life-battered that she looked 20 years older. And she had met her death because of the very humanity of the local police. All the local bobbies knew her well: many a time they'd found her blind drunk in some doorway or alley. At 8 p.m. on the 29th, she had been taken incapably drunk to Bishopsgate police station. The officers there gave her a chance to sleep and recover then, at 1 a.m. on Sunday morning, they'd roused her and told her she was free to leave. She'd gone in a teasing, happy mood to enjoy her life for just half an hour more.

The Berner Street victim was more of a problem. Her face was intact and her mutilations were confined to a slashed throat, so identification should have been easy. At the inquest hearing on 4 October she was identified as Elizabeth Watts. This identification was made by Mrs Mary Malcolm, who stated that she had viewed the body in the mortuary and was certain it was her sister Elizabeth. She swept aside earlier claims that the body was that of Elizabeth Stride – 'Long Lizzie' of Flower and Dean Street.

Coroner Wynne Baxter questioned her searchingly, but Mrs Malcolm stuck to her certainty and went further. She declared she had had a presentiment of her sister's death on that fatal Sunday morning. At about 1.20 a.m. she had felt a pressure on her body and heard the sound of someone kissing her three times. That in itself warned her that something had happened to her sister. This psychic contact led her to visit the mortuary. Mrs Malcolm's testimony looked good for a brief while but it was soon negated when her sister turned up alive and well and full of indignation. With the air cleared, the original identification of Swedish prostitute Lizzie Stride was then shown to be correct.

This double murder raised the general feeling of terror to new heights. The killer not only had an iron nerve but outstanding cunning. The whole nation began to wonder about the identity of Jack the Ripper – for by now the anonymous knife-man had been named. Two missives gave the public the unforgettable sobriquet.

The first was a letter addressed to 'The Boss, Central News Office, London City.' It was dated 25 September 1888 but postmarked the 27th and read:

> Dear Boss, I keep on hearing the police have caught me, but they won't fix me just yet. I have laughed when they look so clever and talk about being on the right track. That joke about Leather Apron gave me real fits. I am down on whores and shant quit ripping them till I do get buckled. Grand work the last job was. I gave the lady no time to squeal. How can they catch me now. I love my work and want to start again. You will soon hear of me with my funny little games. I saved some of the proper *red* stuff in a ginger beer bottle over the last job to write with but it went thick like glue and I can't use it. Red ink is fit enough I hope *ha ha*. The next job I do I shall clip the ladys ears off and send to the police officers just for jolly wouldnt you. Keep this letter back till I do a bit more work, then give it out straight. My knife's nice and sharp I want to get to work right away if I get a chance. Good luck.
>
>   yours truly,
>   Jack the Ripper
>
> Don't mind me giving the trade name.
> wasnt good enough to post this before I got all the red ink off my hands curse it. No luck yet. They say I'm a doctor now *ha ha*.

Opposite: Benign in mufti – bristling in uniform. Did Sir Charles Warren engineer a cover up?
Overleaf: 9 November 1888, the Lord Mayor's Procession – soon to be marred by paperboys shrieking news of Kelly's murder.

The second was a postcard also sent to the Central News Office and it read:

> I wasnt codding dear old Boss when I gave you the tip. You'll hear about saucy Jackys work tomorrow double event this time number one squealed a bit couldn't finish straight off. had no time to get ears for police thanks for keeping last letter back till I got to work again, Jack the Ripper.

Were these actually written by the killer? Over the years many writers have treated them as authentic, arguing that the postcard with its talk of a double event is certain proof: after all, it *was* posted before the killings were public knowledge. According to these people, the card was posted on 30 September. Cullen, Farson, McCormick, O'Dell, and even the usually precise Donald Rumbelow have all made this blunder, yet it has been public knowledge since 3 October 1888 that the postcard was, in fact, postmarked 1 October: facsimiles of both the letter and the postcard were issued by the Metropolitan Police on a large poster which made the following plea: 'Any person recognising the handwriting is requested to communicate with the nearest Police Station.'

Once the correct posting date is established the evidential value of the postcard vanishes: by 1 October the news of the double event was surging through London. Even the mention in the letter of 25 September to clipping the lady's ears off has no real touch-point with either killing: the cutting into the ear lobe at Mitre Square could easily have resulted from the follow-through motion of throat slashing.

Nothing about these letters stamps them as genuine. Macnaghten, the police chief, held that they were the work of a seamy journalist and he was more than likely correct – the choice of a news agency as the target, the internal evidence that the writer, despite the crude errors, knew how to write – all these things point to the newspaper world. The writings may not have been for specific gain but simply to keep the pot boiling and give journalists a label to pin onto Mr Anonymous. The aim succeeded beyond the writer's wildest hopes. The whole world grasped at the name – it gained immortality overnight. Once the public knew of it, cranks everywhere began composing their own Ripper epistles. They flooded in to the press, the police and to any public figures who spoke out about the murders.

The vilest letter of all was received by George Lusk of the Whitechapel

---

Opposite: Could the Ripper hunt have climaxed on
St Paul's broad steps?

Vigilance Committee in a small parcel which contained part of an unsavoury human kidney. The letter read:

> From Hell, Mr Lusk Sir I send you half the Kidney I took from one women prasarved it for you tother piece I fried and ate it was very nise. I may send you the bloody knif that took it out if you only wate a whil longer
> signed Catch me when you can Mishter Lusk

Now a kidney had been removed from Eddowes's body by the killer, but was this part of it? Dr Thomas Openshaw of the London Hospital examined the piece and apparently concluded that it was. One inch of renal artery still clung to the specimen, and it's usually claimed that Openshaw matched this severed artery with a section still remaining in the corpse. Then he worked out that the kidney came from a woman of Eddowes's age suffering from Bright's disease.

Richard Whittington Egan has most amusingly drawn together all the fanciful versions of Openshaw's exploits to show that the whole episode is tainted by fictional flourishes. Bright's disease is not something specific but a class of diseases. Age could not have been calculated from the portion of kidney examined and in 1888 there was no way in which Openshaw could have determined sex from the kidney. Finally, no comparison with Eddowes's body was possible since she had been buried eleven days before the kidney section arrived, and no exhumation took place.

My own independent checks with forensic experts, including Professor D.J. Gee of Leeds University, confirm Egan's findings. So 'the kidney from hell' has about it all the odour of a stupid, morbid hoax.

After the double event of 30 September each day brought with it the special fear that attends anticipation. The police seemed to be playing blind man's buff as they groped their way from one false lead to another. The public cried out for some determined action and the critics of the police grew even more vitriolic. Warren, in particular, came under repeated attack, and the *Pall Mall Budget* lampooned him in stinging cartoons. In their view he was wading in a morass of muddle.

Six weeks went by without sight or sound of Jack. Then, on 9 November, as the Lord Mayor's procession wound its way down Ludgate Hill, the newsboys rushed into the streets with cries of 'Horrible Murder!' Jack had made his bloodiest strike, this time indoors and at leisure.

Unlike his previous victims, Mary Kelly had been young, spirited and attractive. When Jack had finished with her she was a scarcely recognizable heap of flesh draped on a blood-saturated bed. Her face had been slashed repeatedly. Her ears and nose had been cut off, so had her breasts. These severed parts had been laid out on a table by the bedside.

Her stomach and abdomen had been ripped open. Her heart, kidneys, liver and uterus had been excised. Bits of her flesh hung from the picture rail round the walls.

This miniature slaughterhouse was a downstairs room at No 13 Miller's Court, off Dorset Street, and the killing only came to light when John Bowyer called to collect arrears of rent. His knock wasn't answered, so he went to a side window, putting his hand through a broken pane to pull back the curtain. Perhaps Mary was sleeping hard? He gagged at the sight that met his eyes.

When the police arrived, even the tough veterans found the slaughter hard to take. Constable Dew later said: 'It remains with me – and always will remain – as the most gruesome memory of the whole of my police career.' And Dew had only peeped through the broken pane while waiting for certain orders to be carried out: the police had been issued with instructions to do nothing about any suspected Ripper murders until specially hired bloodhounds arrived.

The order about the bloodhounds arose out of trials with a frisky pair called Burgho and Barnaby: their tracking skills, it was imagined, would prove invaluable. So a message was sent that morning of 9 November to Sir Charles Warren, asking for the hounds to be dispatched post-haste. None of the waiting officers at Miller's Court knew that Warren had already resigned after clashing with the Home Secretary.

After a long frustrating wait, police patience ran out. At 1.30 p.m. Superintendent Arnold had one of the windows taken out to gain entry. The police photographer recorded the shambles. Notes were made, then the locked door was broken open with a pickaxe.

The inquest on Kelly was a strange, mishandled affair. Ex-police surgeon Dr McDonald took charge, not the coroner, Wynne Baxter. Perhaps the police felt that Baxter was too harsh on them; perhaps they wanted the latest horror handled with sympathy and speed. And speed certainly marked the hearing.

It was all over within days, even though Dr Bagster Phillips did no more than state that the cause of death lay in the severing of the carotid artery, withholding all other details. Amazingly, the jury took guidance from McDonald and decided that they could return a verdict without hearing any more evidence: it was wilful murder.

At this hearing, witnesses clashed with each other. Sara Lewis attested that she had heard the cry of murder at about 4 a.m. Mrs Prater agreed with her. This matched the established time of death at between 3.30 and 4 a.m. Yet Mrs Maxwell stated that she had actually spoken to Mary at 8 a.m. on the morning of her death. Even when cautioned by McDonald, she clung to her story, adding that she had seen Kelly once more at 8.30. Soon the story developed into the idea that Mrs Maxwell had seen the Ripper in drag, but the account of her talk with Kelly ruled that out: it was one woman to another – two people who knew each other.

One person not heard at all at the inquest was George Hutchinson, an unemployed labourer who knew Kelly well. On the Friday of her death he had seen her near Thrawl Street at about 2 a.m. With her had been a man so well-dressed that Hutchinson immediately took notice. *The Times* for 14 November carried his description: 'The man was about five feet six inches in height, and thirty-four or thirty-five years of age, with dark complexion and dark moustache turned up at the ends. He was wearing a long dark coat trimmed with astrachan [*sic*], a white collar with black necktie, in which was affixed a horseshoe pin. He looked like a foreigner . . . I could swear to the man anywhere. The man I saw carried a small parcel about eight inches long and it had a strap around it . . . It looked as though it was covered with dark American cloth. He carried in his right hand, which he laid upon the woman's shoulder, a pair of brown kid gloves. He walked very softly. I believe that he lives in the neighbourhood, and I fancied that I saw him in Petticoat Lane on Sunday morning but I was not certain.'

Hutchinson's description was of importance for the growing Ripper legend, for in time it was pinned on to more than one candidate. What's more, when it was first published the *Police News* artist used it to create a full-length portrait of the Ripper which fixed the way the public came to see him.

Kelly's murder jogged people's memories. They recalled that Catherine Eddowes had once used the name Kelly, borrowing it from a man she'd lived with. So could it be that Jack was, all along, simply hunting for a Kelly for some reason? Did Eddowes die because of an error? If she did, that implied that Jack had only a name, an area and an occupation to guide him to his victim: there would have been no possible way of confusing Mary Kelly and 'Kate Kelly' *if* the Ripper had known more about them. Here was something fresh for the theoreticians to ponder on.

Was Kelly's the last Ripper murder? In the Scotland Yard files is a statement by Macnaghten which says: 'The Whitechapel murderer had 5 victims – & 5 victims only.' He places Nichols on 31 August as the first and Kelly on 9 November as the last. But that's a police chief looking back. At the time, few people believed that the Ripper had given up. He may have gone to earth for a spell, but he was only resting and gloating before taking up the knife once more, a belief well illustrated by the welter of cases that were, at first, thought to be Jack's work. For a while, all attacks on women brought the dreaded name into prominence. Even some attacks on youths had the same effect. Nothing, however, really resembled the Ripper's style until a body was found in Whitechapel's Castle Alley, on 17 July 1889.

Castle Alley was long, dark and narrow, an ideal place for thieves and muggers; even the prostitutes found it off-putting. But one of them overcame her fears and led a client into its gloom. She was found with her throat cut and her abdomen seemingly gashed. Identification followed very swiftly after the police found a clay pipe under the body. She was 'Clay-pipe Alice', real name Alice McKenzie, of Gun Street, Spitalfields. But was she a genuine Ripper sacrifice? Expert Dr Bagster Phillips had his doubts. He found that the injuries 'were not similar to those in other East End murder cases'. A short-bladed knife had been used, not the long blade favoured by Jack. All the abdominal wounds were superficial, nothing like the extensive slashes in the earlier cases.

Yet the doctor's doubts were lost on most people. They went along with the popular papers, like the London edition of the *New York Herald*: 'Jack the Ripper has returned to the centre of his field of operations, around which it is apparent he has been hovering all the time when in his murderous moods. He has been bent all along on killing his victims in that limited district of four or five blocks . . . He lives now, or has lived, in this crime centre, or at all events has been a frequenter of it. This conclusion is warranted not only by the fact stated, that he seems to gravitate toward it constantly, but also by the intimate acquaintance with its many dark and tortuous passages and bye-ways which the murders show him to have.'

Two months after the Castle Alley murder the papers were clamorous once more. Jack's most grotesque outdoor killing had been staged in a railway arch off Backchurch Lane.

The lane was well south of Spitalfields, but quite near Berner Street, so still in the Ripper's realm. At 5.30 on the morning of 10 September, PC Pennett flashed his lantern into the pitch-black cavern of the arch. A shapeless something lay on the ground, yet thirty minutes earlier the ground had been bare; so he entered the arch to take a closer look. The shapeless mass resolved itself into the headless and legless torso of a naked woman. Had the Ripper altered tack?

A doctor's examination soon showed that this corpse had nothing in common with the Ripper's victims. The woman had been dead for some days and all the cuts had been made cleanly and with decision. There was not a hint of frenzy. It could well have been the work of some leisurely medical student.

One more factor distanced this body from the Ripper. On the Sunday three days before the discovery, a young man had called at the London offices of the *New York Herald* just after one in the morning and had spoken to the night editor. He gave his name as John Cleary, living at 21 White Horse Yard, Drury Lane, and informed the editor that Jack the Ripper had struck once more: the mutilated body still lay in Backchurch Lane. The editor cross-questioned him. How did Cleary come to know this? There was nothing like it in from the wire service, and nothing in from their men in touch with the police; and that was very strange. Cleary was by no means thrown by the questions. A friendly police inspector had told him: the news had been out since half past eleven – just after the corpse had been found. After getting the tip he'd rushed over to the *Herald* building in the Strand, since he knew of their interest. And, of course, he hoped to be rewarded. The editor decided to take a chance. A cab was called and two reporters set out. They tried to persuade Cleary to come with them, but he refused: too far from home was the excuse.

On reaching Backchurch Lane the reporters made a thorough search. They even included the archway but found nothing. Two policemen they met couldn't help: they knew nothing of any murder. So the newsmen returned to the offices, cursing Cleary as a hoaxer.

On 10 September they reversed their opinion. Cleary was obviously a man with advance knowledge: that made him an accomplice to murder, and a man worth laying hands on. But Cleary's address turned out to be false, and days of searching led nowhere. Not even the CID were able to find anyone who could identify Cleary beyond question, so the trail petered out.

There were unexpected repercussions, though. As Cleary's description circulated, other newsmen began to recall a parallel incident from the previous year. In October 1888 a youngish man had called at the offices of one of the leading daily papers trying to sell a story involving the dismembered corpse of a woman. He swore the remains were on a building site on the Thames Embankment, the very place where a new police headquarters was being built. Despite their doubts, the paper sent a reporter to check the site. Once there, together with a policeman, he made an exhaustive search, but not a trace of anything unpleasant was found except a dead rat or two. By the time the peeved reporter returned, the young man had slipped out of the newspaper offices. So the story was spiked.

Yet remarkably, a few days later a woman's remains were found just where predicted. The torso had had the head, arms, and legs cut and sawn off. And, as in the later murder, the woman had been dead some time before being dumped. So the strange informant had had prior knowledge, and now it seemed that he also matched in all essential particulars the description given of the 'hoaxer' Cleary.

This was a sensational diversion that seemed to show Jack in a new light. Had he an accomplice? More than one perhaps? In fact, the dismembered corpses had nothing in common with Jack's victims; these gruesome discoveries were more in the nature of an inhumane side-show. But they did serve to keep the Ripper's name constantly in mind.

Yet only the name was in evidence – Jack refused to act. And the New Year came and went without a single genuine Ripper murder. Throughout 1890 there were repeated false alarms but nothing resembling Jack's handiwork. Then in 1891, on 13 February, it was 'Shocking Murder in Whitechapel' once more. Prostitute Frances Coles was found slashed and ripped under a railway arch off Royal Mint Street. There was still a spark of life left when she was found, so the killer must have sped off just seconds before the police arrived. Urgent search parties of police and civilians were organized, the area was sealed off, every house was entered. This was a first-class chance to trap the Ripper before he could get far.

The search itself failed to find the knife-man, but a lead came from Coles' lodgings. A man had called there asking for her, a man with a bleeding hand. He explained the injury away by saying that some ruffians had attacked and robbed him, but when the same man returned at three in the morning, his story became unbelievable. He now said he had been attacked a second time. He had no money but the shipping company owed him £4.15s. On the strength of that, could he have a bed for the night – on tick? The lodging-house keeper had heard such tales before, so he threw him out. And the blood-stained man went off in search of a hospital. It wasn't long before he was traced and arrested. He was James Saddler, a ship's fireman. Yes, he knew Frances Coles, he had even bought her a hat; but he'd left her at her lodgings and not seen her since. He was arrested and charged with her murder.

Had the Ripper been traced and trapped at last? The public thought so and the press played its part in pandering to the idea. In fact the papers were so vociferous that Saddler's case was brought up in questions at the House of Commons: even the Home Secretary was alarmed at the irresponsible press coverage. The open hostility put Saddler in the deepest despair, shown in a letter he sent to his union: 'What a godsend my case will be to the police if they can only conduct me, innocent as I am, to the bitter end – to the scaffold.'

31

But there was no march to the scaffold. The Stokers' Union acted and brought in Harry Wilson to defend Saddler. Bit by bit Wilson demolished the prosecution's case and finally the Attorney General decided that in the interests of justice, the case had to be dropped. Saddler was released and left for South America. With his release, the press and public had lost their one and only chance of seeing the 'Ripper' hanged.

After that, it was anticlimax after anticlimax. And gradually it dawned on everyone that the real Ripper had gone out of business. Was he dead? In an asylum? Safe overseas? Or just too spent to bother any more? The armchair theorists began to look at all angles. Anyone and everyone who could be remotely connected with woman-hating, religious mania, sadistic impulses, secret vices, and even with plain furtiveness was duly considered as a potential candidate.

Apathy, hostility and ignorance: the police faced all three as they groped for clues

3

Suspects Galore

Whoever or whatever he was, what made Jack so elusive? The *New York Herald* had its own trenchant answer: 'The reason why Jack the Ripper has not been caught . . . is a distinctively London reason. In all cases of mysterious murder, in all countries, the murderer has not been caught at or near the scene of the crime, or the case would not be mysterious. His detection has always been due to suspicions excited in everybody's mind either by him or some relic of the murder belonging to him. The police are informed of the suspicion and work up the clues. This would be the result in the present instance in any other part of the civilized world except Whitechapel. The sodden stupidity of a large part of the population is inconceivable. A large number of them cannot read, and a still larger number have not the ha'penny to squander on a newspaper . . . The pressure of life is so hard; the obtaining of a few pence necessary for dinner and bed and breakfast is so precarious and so doubtful that any such flight of the imagination as is described by the word suspicion is entirely out of keeping with their habits. More than this, there's a strong feeling in the worst parts of Whitechapel . . . against helping the police or giving information of any kind.'

But the *Herald's* view only provided part of the answer. Jack himself must have possessed some remarkable talents to stay loose for so long. Think of the narrow escape at Berner Street. The operations there were obviously cut short, if you'll forgive the expression, but within minutes he was away stalking yet another drab. Then away again, dropping his bloody rag for the police to find, writing his strange 'clue' on a passage wall.

So little was really known of him. He was said to be left-handed – the throat-cutting provided that clue, or seemed to. Then again, he was said to have medical knowledge – after all, he knew where and how to locate a human kidney in the dark. But what can we say of him as a man? No man, opined some, the murders were done by a baboon or a trained ape. Such folk had obviously drawn inspiration from Poe's *Murders in the Rue*

Morgue. No man, opined yet others, but a lady. This was a view voiced by Sir Arthur Conan Doyle, and resurrected years later by William Stewart. There was even a tale that named the lady: she was Olga Tchkersoff, who had set out to avenge her sister's death. Sister Vera had taken to the streets, become pregnant and died following an abortion. At this, Olga's reason had snapped. Vengeance must be sought by wiping out the whores who'd encouraged Vera. So an avenging angel swept into the East End streets, an angel in men's clothes, an angel who fled to the United States once honour was satisfied.

Quite a different theory involved the idea of a Jewish butcher with a secret hate of Christians. Why he had chosen only Christian whores was never made clear, but the published theory argued that '. . . the clean cuts inflicted on the victims are peculiar to the Jews' mode of killing cattle.' Seventy-six years later, this idea was taken up by Robin O'Dell as the basis of his ritual slaughterman, or shochet theory.

Others at the time, of course, knew that this was all nonsense. One camp opted for a Norwegian sailor named Fogelma; after killing the women he too had fled to New York. His mind broke and in delirium he had raved about his role as the Ripper. Placed in Morris Plains Lunatic Asylum, Fogelma eventually died in 1902. His sister swore that everything he'd said was true – and more. In his trunk they had found press-cuttings on the murders, each one carrying sarcastic comments written by her brother. They were cuttings that he'd brooded over for hours on end. Wasn't that proof?

Elizabeth Ross of Brooklyn would have certainly have said no. She knew the killer – he was a South American, Alonzo Maduro. She was certain of this because her father had found out and had helped the Latin leave London. Alonzo had been in a tearing hurry; her father had helped him to pack and discovered that the trunk he was filling had a false bottom. Inside the secret compartment was an ankle-length black cape, a black slouch hat and an oilskin package containing glittering surgical instruments. All this took place in November 1888 – so it had to be him.

Such slender evidence was used to 'convict' – on paper that is – a host of suspects. Even Dr Barnado was taken for the Ripper at one point. The famous reformer was inevitably around the Whitechapel area, and four days before Stride was killed in September 1888, he had actually been talking with her in the kitchen of her lodging house at Flower and Dean Street. So tongues wagged and Barnado was named.

In Vienna, however, they came up with a mad sausage-maker. Alois Szemeredy was an army deserter who escaped to Buenos Aires and while there committed murders, or so it is said. He later spent a while in a lunatic asylum and in 1892 committed suicide back in Vienna after being arrested on robbery and murder charges. But was he ever in London? To this the Austrian police president in Vienna gave a most strange, eccentric answer. He produced two police forms filled up by Szemeredy, and said: 'In both forms he calls himself an "Amerikanischer Wundarzt" [an American surgeon]. His age is given as forty-nine, his confession Catholic, his condition single, and on the last form he says as to his destination, "Going to America". Whether he went to England instead, to commit the crime detected in Whitechapel on September 12th [sic], I cannot say, but it is curious that on his later visit to Vienna, in 1892 he described himself as "a sausage maker".'

Buenos Aires was involved in yet another Ripper theory, a world-famous one, floated in 1929 by journalist Leonard Matters. It involved a vengeful Dr Stanley: his brilliant son had been infected by a prostitute, syphilis took hold remorselessly and destroyed the lad. So Stanley went hunting for the whore Kelly to make her pay the supreme price. To find her he had to question other whores, and each one questioned had to die in case they reached Kelly and alerted her. His mission over, the doctor retired to South America and confessed all when on the point of death. At the time, Matters alleged, the story had appeared in a Buenos Aires newspaper, but he never gave its name or a date of publication. Searches over nearly sixty years have failed to locate the article, so regrettably, the verdict has to be: deliberate fiction.

Nastiest and oddest of the minor candidates was Frederick Deeming. In December 1891, he killed his wife Emily at their rented home in Windsor, Australia. He then placed her body in a cavity under the dining-room hearth and cemented it up. But his workmanship was so defective that after Deeming left the landlord had the floor taken up, and the corpse came to light. After his arrest, the British police were alerted to search for Deeming's previous wife, an Australian, and their four children. They visited a villa in Rainhill, Liverpool and there found the missing relatives. They, too, had been murdered and cemented under a floor, covered over with floorboards.

Deeming was proclaimed Jack the Ripper with some certainty after his picture appeared in the British press in April 1892. A young dressmaker from the East End identified the portrait as that of a man she'd known by the name of Lawson, back in 1888. This Lawson had shown an inordinate interest in the Ripper murders: following the double event in September that year she noticed that Lawson became greatly agitated and then broke off contact with her. The *Illustrated Police News* quickly seized on her statement and had their artist reproduce the full-length sketch they

A dressmaker 'recognized' Deeming as the Ripper
and the wild notion won overnight acceptance.

had run in 1888, a portrait of the Ripper based on Hutchinson's description. Alongside this they reproduced one of Deeming based on the recent photograph. It showed a man dressed very much like the hypothetical murderer of 1888. Everything was there – astrakhan coat, sardonic features, black moustache and all.

When people saw the two portraits side by side they could be forgiven for thinking that Jack had at last been caught. Unfortunately, there is the awkward question of dates. In 1888, Deeming was an inmate of one of Her Majesty's prisons. Against such facts there is no argument.

In all, the minor candidates never added up to much. It's a wonder that any of them were considered in the first place. With the major candidates, though, it's somewhat different. In each case there's the semblance of something worth looking into, but apart from that, there's a fascination in each of them, fascination not so much with what they did, but with what they were supposed to have done. Which implies that at times the investigator was much more active than the investigated had ever been.

4
The Madman Who Loved St Paul's

'It was I and not the detectives of Scotland Yard who reasoned out an accurate scientific mental picture of the Whitechapel murderer.' With such due modesty Dr Lyttleton Forbes Winslow staked his claim to fame. He was one of the well-known flamboyant characters of the period, renowned also as an authority on criminal lunacy and lunacy in general. Hardly surprising, that, since he'd been reared in a private asylum; not as an inmate, though, but as the son of the proprietor. For many years Winslow gave expert testimony in criminal cases, so when the Ripper terror began he naturally decided to put his experience and judgement to work.

Winslow became convinced that an insane monster was at large. In general he visualized him as shrewd, cautious and intelligent – by no means a wild-eyed maniac but a man ever alert to the dangers of being caught and 'cunning as all lunatics are'. Winslow hunted for clues to this lunatic and became, in his own words, 'a practical detective'.

The doctor took his quest with urgent, deadly seriousness. He wrote later: 'Day after day and night after night I spent in the Whitechapel slums. The detectives knew me, the lodging house keepers knew me, and at last the poor creatures of the streets came to know me. In terror they rushed to me with every scrap of information which might to my mind be of value. To me the frightened women looked for hope. In my presence they felt reassured and welcomed me to their dens and obeyed my commands eagerly, and found bits of information I wanted.'

In his view the Ripper killed nine times, beginning in 1887 and ending in July 1889 with the murder of Alice McKenzie. And why did the killings stop? Because, Winslow insisted, his detective work unmasked the killer who swiftly went to earth.

Winslow had first deduced that the Ripper's madness was due to a type of masked epilepsy: during seizures he would lose touch with reality and perform '. . . the most extraordinary and most diabolical actions'. On returning to consciousness he would be in a state of complete ignorance of his crimes and would carry on a normal, unspectacular life. To back up this fantastic diagnosis Winslow fell back on two cases he had dealt with in 1877. Both had involved murder and in both cases a death sentence had been passed, yet both murderers were later reprieved 'in consequence of the liability to epileptic seizures'.

In the first case, that of the murderer Drant, it was shown that when he murdered he was in a condition 'of maniacal excitement and violence, whilst under an actual epileptic paroxysm'. In the second case, Edward Treadaway shot John Collins in the course of a banal conversation. Treadaway was armed only because he had planned to kill himself – hereditary epilepsy and severe depressions had made his life seem pointless. But an epileptic bout led to a murder which was only remembered by him on the following day.

It is easy to understand that such cases would seem to have a bearing on the Whitechapel killer, and for a time Winslow was reinforced in his beliefs by the knowledge that '. . . epileptic seizures of this description are frequently accompanied by a form of erotic frenzy'. This frenzy 'would account for the particular class of women which the murderer selected for his victims'. Even so, Winslow jettisoned this theory after the third murder and announced that a dangerous homicidal lunatic was at large, not someone from the lower classes, but 'in all probability a man of good position and perhaps living in the West End of London'.

One of Dr Winslow's bright ideas at the time was to withdraw the police from the case and replace them with '. . . attendants experienced in dealing with lunatics placed about Whitechapel'. These experts would be able to note whether anyone was of unsound mind or not. The idea was passed on to Sir Charles Warren, who understandably ignored it and left Winslow fuming over gross police incompetence.

More murders led to yet another change of mind. Winslow now surmised that the 'perpetrator was . . . goaded on to his dreadful work by a sense of duty.' The homicidal instincts must be closely allied to a religious monomania 'because his efforts were solely directed against fallen women, whose extermination he probably considered his mission'. He concluded: 'Jack the Ripper possibly imagined that he received his commands from God.'

Fired by his latest and most gratifying theory, Forbes Winslow put forward a masterly plan to Scotland Yard, explaining that lunatics could frequently be caught by humouring their ideas. He proposed that an advertisement should be placed in all the papers along these lines: 'A gentleman who is strongly opposed to the presence of fallen women in the streets of London would like to cooperate with someone with a view to their suppression.' That was the first part of his plan. The second part involved a place of appointment which everyone falling for the suggestion would be asked to visit. Six detectives would be concealed at the place with instructions to seize and interrogate anyone who turned up. It was a brilliant scheme – so he thought. But Scotland Yard thought otherwise. So the doctor-detective called off the operation saying ' . . . it was quite impossible for me, as a private citizen, to seize and detain possibly innocent persons . . .'

He was bitter about the rejection, declaring: '. . . a simple expedient like this would be more likely to entrap the murderer than anything else, for the diabolical cunning of the homicidal lunatic, who conceives he has a mission, renders his capture red-handed extremely problematical. I claimed that a man of this nature would be sure to read the newspapers carefully and gloat over the results of his crime. The savage hacking and cutting of some of his victims showed that he was under the influence of a religious frenzy, and every horrible detail he probably considered redounded to his credit and proved that he was performing his mission faithfully.' It was small wonder, Winslow felt, that there were '. . . loud complaints about the inefficiency of the London police'.

Winslow's hunt evidently became known to Jack himself, or so the doctor would have us believe. He claimed that as early as 4 October 1888 he had received a letter signed by Jack. Remarkably, this letter '. . . was in the same handwriting as the writing found under the archway'. The reference to the archway involves a puzzling claim by Winslow. He records that 'During the month of August 1888 a man was seen whose description . . . corresponded with the man who was found writing on a wall under an archway. The inscription read: "Jack the Ripper will never commit another murder".' As stated, this seems to imply that the Ripper name was in use some time in August 1888 yet this nickname was only made public in *The Times* on 2 October that year and on posters next day. There's something very strange about the whole of the correspondence from Jack to Winslow: 'three letters' were received and one of them, delivered 'on the 19th October 1888', gave an accurate forecast of the murder of Kelly on 9 November. This letter is reproduced in facsimile in Forbes Winslow's autobiography of 1910, and sure enough it *does* state that another killing could be expected about the 8th or 9th of November 1888. Yet all is not what it seems to be.

The long hunt continued into the second half of 1889. There were many false leads and false hopes, then a breakthrough, following the death of Alice M'kenzie on 17 July. A streetwoman known to the doctor came to him on 30 August to inform him that a suspicious man had tried to lure her into a court off Worship Street in Finsbury. She'd rejected his offer of a sovereign and even stayed firm when he'd doubled the price. The man made off but was stealthily tracked by the woman and some of her cronies: they watched him enter a house in Finsbury. Then, on the morning after the M'kenzie murder, she had again seen this man, in the yard of the Finsbury house openly washing blood off his hands. 'She noted a peculiar look on his face.'

An alarm was raised, the Finsbury house was searched but the suspect had flown. Still, as his description circulated, others came to recognize the man. Within days a lodging-house keeper, Mr E. Callaghan, called on Winslow with important clues. In 1888 Callaghan had let rooms in his

Forbes Winslow – devious 'Doctor-Detective'.

house at 27 Sun Street, Finsbury Square. In April that year Mr G. Wentworth Bell Smith had rented one of his large bed-sitting-rooms. It was an arrangement that would last for months, perhaps a whole year, said Mr Bell Smith; his business schedules were quite flexible, for he was in England raising funds for the Toronto Trust Society of Canada.

It soon became obvious that Mr Bell Smith had an obsession with fallen women. He would fulminate at length about their brazen conduct and their freedom to fan the flames of immorality. They were even invading the aisles of his beloved cathedral, St Paul's. At times he would fill up sheet after sheet of foolscap with his religious ravings about licentious conduct. On developing writer's cramp he'd then read the pieces out loud to his landlord. They were '. . . very violent in tone and expressed bitter hatred of dissolute women', testified Mr Callaghan.

Winslow was delighted with everything Callaghan told him. Now it was possible to draw a detailed profile of the Ripper, for this man conformed to the sketchy picture already fixed in Winslow's mind. Bell Smith and Jack were one and the same person: it had to be so. The doctor then drafted his final conclusion, with eight main points elaborating his case against Bell Smith.

He started from the premise that the murders were the work of one unaided man in the grip of religious monomania. He then showed that his suspect had 'changed his lodgings after each respective murder'. Next, he claimed that at each new lodgings bloodstains were found in his rooms and so were pieces of ribbons and feathers, presumably taken from the victims. These finds were all said to have been made on the morning following each murder. Continuing his case the doctor made the following further points: 'Fourth, in some of these lodgings he left behind him written scrawls bearing directly on the subject of his proposed mission. Fifth, I was in communication with those persons who possessed these writings. Sixth, I interviewed the woman at whose house he lodged on the night of one of the murders, when he was seen to come home at 4 a.m. and wash his hands in the yard. Seventh, I made myself thoroughly conversant with his habits in every way. I also knew his haunts, how he spent his Sundays. Eighth, I knew that every Sunday at 11 a.m. he went to St Paul's Cathedral.'

Having pondered over these points Dr Forbes Winslow then approached the police once more and outlined yet another foolproof plan for capturing the Ripper. He would intercept the madman one Sunday on the broad steps of St Paul's, would hold him in close conversation until the concealed policemen could emerge, move in and make the arrest. To his great surprise the police again refused to cooperate.

The doctor-detective grew enraged, warning the police that unless they changed their minds he would publish his clues for the whole world to inspect. Once more the police declined his offer, so Winslow talked to the London office of the New York Herald. The initial report ran in its issue of 19 September 1889. Two days later the Herald reported that the story had '... created a profound sensation throughout the country. It has been quoted in some fifty or sixty London and provincial dailies. The town rang with the story all Thursday. It was quoted in the train, on the omnibus, on the penny steamboat, and on the pavement, and generally it was regarded as the most important contribution to the "Jack the Ripper" discussion yet made.'

The *Herald* also pointed to some curious phenomena – in a way, a warning to every Ripper investigator and with some bearing on this

particular one. Following the appearance of the article Forbes Winslow had been inundated with letters and callers: 'It would seem that hundreds of men and women have clues which they are morally certain would lead to the speedy capture of the most notorious criminal in the world, while thousands of theories are floating aimlessly in the air.'

No more theories were needed though, according to Winslow. His profound insights had caused the Ripper to take flight and the killings ceased. Everyone in England, except for the police, recognized that. To the police he directed this question: 'If I did not arrest the murderous hand of Jack the Ripper, who did, and what part did they play in the transaction?'

Yet if the Ripper truly took flight, where did he relocate himself? Forbes Winslow had an answer for that question too, though it only came to him twenty years after the *Herald* piece appeared. It came in the form of a letter from a lady in Melbourne, Australia dated 10 June 1910, and read:

> Your challenge is more than justified re 'Jack the Ripper'. You indeed frightened him away, for he sailed away in a ship called the *Munambidgee*, working his passage to Melbourne, arriving here in the latter part of 1889. He is a native of Melbourne, Victoria, but before his return had been in South Africa for several years. He was educated at the Scotch College here; the late Dr Blair was a great friend of his family, and it was from him he gained his surgical knowledge, the doctor taking him with him to

post-mortems. When he arrived in Melbourne he married a Miss ——, who lived only a little over a year, but died from natural causes; she was only dead a short time when I met him. He told me he had a hard time in London, and he was always buying sensational newspapers.

I said to him, 'Why do you buy those horrid papers? They are only full of police reports of terrible crimes.' He said, 'I want to see how things are in London.' Then he commenced reading the trial of a man named James Canham Reade. This man married and deserted several women, and finally killed one, for which he was hanged. When he had finished reading, I said, 'What a fearful fellow!' He said, 'Strange those crimes ceased once I left England.' I was astounded at his remark, and said, 'My God! Jack, I believe you did those crimes,' he having told me about living in that part of London previously. I tried to banish the thought from my mind, as I loved him; but I referred to it many times after, and finally he told me he did do them. I said, 'Why did you do those crimes?' He first said, 'Revenge,' then said, 'Research.' I said, 'But you never made use of the portions you removed from those women; what did you do with them?' He said, 'Oh, there are plenty of hungry dogs in London.' I wrote to Scotland Yard telling them all. Sir Robert Anderson answered my letter; but as I told him all I had to say, I did not write again till last year, but have heard nothing from them. It is my opinion they all bungled this matter up and do not like owning up to it. I even gave him up in Melbourne in 1894. The police examined him; he told them he was in Melbourne in 1890, so they found this was true, and without asking him where he was in 1889 they let him go. He laughed, and said, 'See what fools they are. I am the real man they are searching the earth for, but they take me in one door and let me go out the other.' I even gave one detective a letter of his, but he only laughed at me. I asked him to have the writing compared with that at home signed 'Jack the Ripper', but he said nothing. Now I have burnt his letters long since, but the monster's name is ——, called Jack by relatives and friends. His brother told me he is in Durban, South Africa, employed by the South African Railway Co. He left here for South Africa about six years ago. Your plan is to get a sample of his writing and compare with yours. If you cannot find him there, cause an advertisement to be put in the papers purporting to come from his brother – who has been lost sight of for many years and has never claimed money left by his father to him. Advertise, and Jack will soon answer this, but to some address in London or South Africa. However, get his writing. He was a very good writer. He often used to attend St Paul's here, and I would tell him what a hypocrite he was. I only wish I could see you . . . Go very careful about all inquiries, as he always told me he would never be taken alive, but would kill himself on the first inkling of being captured. . . .

After studying that letter Forbes Winslow declared: 'It seems in every way to corroborate my views on the matter . . . That Jack the Ripper is the man in South Africa, who left London after I drove him away by publishing my clue in 1889, I believe; and to complete this weird account of him, I have every reason to hope I shall be the means of bringing his capture about.'

He wrote that in 1910, but no dramatic arrest was ever made; the emphatic doctor found it more comforting to sit back and bask in self-satisfaction. He had stopped the killings – what more could any humanitarian want?

Could he have been right? Was he, alone of all the trackers, on the right scent? Hardly, I'd say. There are serious defects in his published statements. They clash with each other.

In his autobiography *Recollections of Forty Years* (1910), Winslow mentions the man found writing on a wall under an archway. The inscription read: 'Jack the Ripper will never commit another murder.' The man's description was said to have been given to him in August 1888. The doctor told a similar story in the *New York Herald* piece of 19 September 1889, only in that version the man was first described to him shortly before that interview. This 'fresh' story, spelled out a year later, ran: 'This same man was seen to write on the wall: "I will commit another murder soon." '

Somewhere, somehow, the tale has become transformed. What's more, if the doctor knew Jack's description as early as August 1888, why did he withhold it from the police, and why didn't he tell them about the remarkable letter, delivered 'on the 19th October 1888', which seemingly foretold the murder of Kelly?

Consider as well his claim that his particular Ripper letters of 1888 were in the same handwriting as the letters left behind by the shifty lodger, G. Wentworth Bell Smith. In 1889 Winslow actually wrote: 'His writing in minute particulars resembled that of the letters sent to the police purporting to come from "Jack the Ripper".' In minute particulars? If this was true, why didn't he prove his point by publishing facsimiles of those discarded writings alongside the published facsimiles of 'his' Ripper letters? Later on he took the trouble to have two of his Ripper letters photographed and reproduced in his book. Why did he stop there? Why not make the triumphant comparison?

I suggest there were very good reasons for this omission. I suggest that the doctor was overwhelmed by his driving dedication, that he became the victim of his own theories. He so wanted them to be true that he bent the facts to fit.

When Winslow laid hold of some rubber shoes left behind by 'the lodger', he insisted they were covered in dried blood. Yet when Chief Inspector Swanson of Scotland Yard examined the same shoes he dismissed the idea that they were gory: there was plenty of dirt but no trace of bloodstains. Then there were the other objects found in 'the lodger's' rooms: three pairs of women's shoes and a quantity of bows, feathers and flowers, 'such as are usually worn by women of the lower class'. Once again some of these things were said to be bloodstained. But were they? Even if they were, what possible connection did they have with the Whitechapel murders? None of these items was stolen from the Whitechapel victims.

If anything, they point to someone who was at worst a fetishist, not a killer. Bell Smith's written and verbal onslaughts on fallen women may have concealed a deep self-loathing: at times his thwarted and little-understood sexual impulses may have led him to lust after objects symbolic of femininity and after yielding to these lusts his shame may have been too great to cope with for a while. A move of lodgings would help recovery. Without doubt the wandering lodger was a shifty and unwholesome person, but there were many of those around, as police files of the period show. Forbes Winslow's certainty was nothing more than his own brand of dogmatism given free rein. His self-deception even became translated into public deception, for he tampered with his 'evidence' to make it more compelling.

One of the two epistles that gave the killer his immortal name and (right) Forbes Winslow's famous 'Ripper letter'. The date has been altered.

Let us begin by taking his famous letter from the Ripper of 19 October 1888. Part of it reads: 'I defy you to find out who has done the Whitechapel murder in the Summer not the last one'. As a reference to 1888, that doesn't make sense, since there were two murders in August and three in September. It *does* make sense, though, if the letter refers to 1889: the summer 'Ripper murder' would then be that of Alice M'kenzie in July, while 'the last one' would be the Backchurch Lane murder of 10 September. But how could a letter written and received in 1888 comment on murders that were yet to come? It couldn't and it didn't. That letter was, in fact, written and sent to Forbes Winslow in 1889. If the date on the facsimile letter is examined, it can be seen that the year has been altered from 89 to 88, a crude alteration made with a thicker nib, with part of the original date easily seen in the top loop of the first 8. The only person in a position and with the motive to forge this date was Forbes Winslow himself.

The letter from Melbourne is different. This is authentic but of no value to Winslow or anyone else. The lady's case rested on nothing save some boastful remarks a man is said to have made, plus the fact that he read 'horrid papers'.

What is certain is that Forbes Winslow's lodger theory was highly influential. Within weeks of its first appearance in 1889, all lodgers were looked at with fresh eyes. Any lodger who had too private a life, too quiet a disposition, or even an unexplained hangover, became an object of grave suspicion. A bevy of lodger anecdotes began to circulate and some of them became incorporated in later Ripper theories, like the ones involving Sickert and Druitt examined in later chapters.

On another plane, one such story inspired Marie Belloc Lowndes to write first a short story, then a novel on the Ripper theme. Her best-selling *The Lodger* in turn inspired the young Alfred Hitchcock to adapt it for the silent screen. Then Hollywood stepped in and made a number of lodger films under various titles, *The Man in the Attic* for one. Even composers were seduced by the theme, Phyllis Tate so much so that she wrote a two-act opera based on the Lowndes text.

So, in the end, Forbes Winslow certainly left his mark behind, though not in the way he dreamed of. And the Ripper, in turn, left his mark on Winslow, for he was the first of the leading Ripper-hunters to become corrupted by the excitement of the chase. Indeed, no other single unsolved case has so warped the judgement of the investigators who have tangled with it. Thus any study of the Ripper becomes, inevitably, a study in investigator duplicity and gullibility. And that, of course, doubles the fascination.

5

Chapman and Cream
– A Poisonous Pair

They both had medical training. They were multiple murderers; their victims were women; they were unmasked, tried and paid the supreme penalty. Yet for all that, their hands were 'unbloodied' – all their proven killings had been accomplished with poisons. Why then, was each man in turn nominated as the Ripper?

The first of them to hang was Thomas Neill Cream. He was born in 1850 in Glasgow but brought up in Quebec, Canada. In 1876 he graduated from McGill College as a doctor of medicine and seven months later arrived in England to expand his qualifications. Further studies at St Thomas's Hospital, London and at Edinburgh earned him a double first as a physician and a surgeon. Covered in paper glory he then headed back home and set up practice in London, Ontario.

Scandal hit soon. A chambermaid was found dead behind Cream's surgery; a bottle of chloroform lay beside her and at first glance it looked like suicide. But the inquest jury heard medical testimony which insisted that the girl could not have killed herself. They also learned that she had visited Cream intent on having an abortion. Cream vehemently denied any involvement, agreeing that the girl had pressed him to abort her baby, but maintaining that his ethics had led him to refuse, he was blameless, and her death was no more than her chosen way out of an unbearably shameful plight. The inquest verdict dismissed the suicide angle and opted for 'Death from chloroform administered by an unknown person'. Superficially this cleared Cream, but he felt so uneasy that he bolted for a safe haven in the USA.

In Chicago he soon became known as an abortionist. And there, in August 1880, he was held in prison on suspicion of murder. Julia Faulkner had died after an abortion and Cream seemed implicated. No conviction followed, however: the evidence then was deemed far too slender. But less than a year later, fresh charges led to the trial, conviction and the passing of a life sentence on Cream. This time it was murder by poisoning: his victim had been David Stoll, a man of 63 suffering from epilepsy. There was still a woman in the case, though, for Stoll's pretty young wife Julia was Cream's mistress. Julia Stoll first visited Cream to buy supplies of his patent cure for epilepsy. Cream sensed her frustrations, seduced her and, when her husband grew tetchy, laced his medicine with arsenic.

The life sentence was later reviewed, cut down to seventeen years and then further reduced to ten years 'on account of good behaviour'. Cream was released on 31 July 1891 and in October of that year arrived in England, headed for London and set himself up as a serial murderer under the name Dr T. Neil: this misguided 'compassionate release' had condemned at least four more women to death.

Less than two weeks after Cream's arrival, Ellen Donworth of Lambeth died in agony. The young prostitute had been given a strychnine-laced tonic to drink. The man who gave it to her was 'a tall gentleman with cross eyes, a silk hat and bushy whiskers' – a neat description of Cream. Seven days later on 20 October, another prostitute, Matilda Clover, writhed in pain for the greater part of the night. By eight o'clock she was mercifully dead and the doctor who signed her death certificate simply diagnosed the cause as 'Delirium tremens followed by syncope [respiratory arrest]'. Once again, though, Cream's strychnine was responsible.

Since Matilda's death was officially above suspicion she was buried without fuss and no one started hunting for the strange, cross-eyed man she had entertained just hours before her terrible spasms. Then, on 30 November 1891, the police were shown an odd letter received by Dr W.H. Broadbent, a society physician of Portman Square. The letter accused him of having poisoned Matilda Clover with strychnine. The writer claimed to have incriminating evidence which he would sell for £2,500, but he could only be reached through the personal column in the *Daily Chronicle*. It was a baffling turn of affairs, but the police urged Dr Broadbent to go along with the request and place an advertisement. Then they kept watch on the doctor's residence to see if anyone responded.

Weeks passed, no one answered the ad and the surveillance was called off. In the meantime, the police had linked this letter with other crackpot missives received by people as unconnected as Lady Russell, the Member of Parliament, W. F. Smith, and the Lambeth Coroner, George Wyatt. Lady Russell's letter had accused Lord Russell of being Matilda Clover's murderer, while the letter to Smith had accused him of the murder of Ellen Donworth. It now looked possible that the letters' writer might have more than just a ghoulish interest in the women's deaths. But who could have written them?

While the police pondered and waited, Cream set out to kill his third whore. This time he chose one of the higher class of trollops – a Miss Lou Harvey, living in genteel St John's Wood and working in the plush cocoon surrounding West End theatreland. Having enjoyed her expensive delights Cream sought a perverted pleasure in planning her death, but when he gave her his poison capsules the girl astutely tossed them into the Thames and pretended that she'd swallowed them. Well for her, since

A 'humane release' from jail led to five more graves.

Cream had timed the dose to take effect just when she was due to be comfortably seated in the Oxford Music Hall. Her death agonies were meant to be as public as possible.

Imagine Cream's frustration as he scanned the newspapers. No dramatic death reports. No sensational scenes in the theatre stalls. For once, his plans had misfired. Even so, he still chose to believe that the girl was dead. Perhaps the body lay in an alley or ditch somewhere, perhaps it was unidentified, perhaps natural causes had once more been seen as the cause of death. In that thoughtful state Cream decided to ease off for a while and concentrate on wooing his fiancée, a Miss Laura Sabatini – for Cream indulged in a separate, respectable existence as well as the sordid one. In January 1892, he left England for a short visit to Canada: apparently, he needed more funds from his father's estate. By 9 April he was back again in his Lambeth Palace Road rooms, and two days later he poisoned Alice Marsh and Emma Shrivall. This time his mad streak led to his eventual capture. In a crazy fashion, Cream named Dr W. J. Harper as the killer of the two women. Harper actually lodged in the same house as Cream and by involving him Cream brought about his own downfall. For when the police visited Harper's father they were shown a blackmail letter which also accused the young doctor of murder. The letter was in Cream's handwriting, thus allowing the police to arrest and hold him on an attempted blackmail charge. Next, they exhumed the body of Matilda Clover and found strychnine in the organs, just as the first blackmailing letter to Broadbent had claimed.

The full, fascinating details of Cream's trial for murder need not concern us. Yet three features of the trial led to the incredible surmise that Cream had earlier been the Whitechapel killer. In an insipid form, this idea had floated around soon after Cream's conviction, but it was never taken seriously. Then, in 1974, a Canadian journalist, Donald Bell, claimed that new clues had turned up which suggested that Cream was the Ripper after all.

Bell's 20-page article in the *Criminologist* lays out his case in full. It's an amazingly weak indictment which presents no evidence of value but plenty of conjecture. Take the chronology for a start. Cream was in Joliet

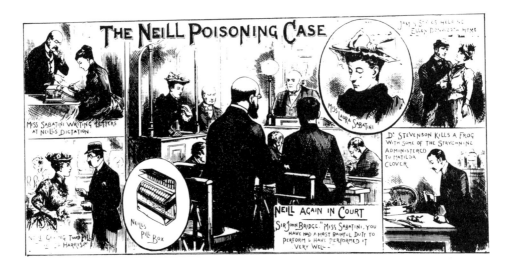

Prison at the time of the Ripper murders. His release order came only in June 1891. A death blow to Bell's theory? Not a bit of it. He simply argues that corruption was rife in Chicago '. . . graft and skullduggery extended from the lowest bureaucrats to the highest officials in the land. Prisoners sometimes bought their way out – or made deals.' Having said that, Bell fails to name one convicted murderer who was released as a result of such a deal. As for Cream, he first suggests that Cream's father might have paid for his son's release, then that Cream himself may have bribed his way out. This is the notion Bell favours but he covers all his options by further arguing that 'It is also possible that Cream simply escaped, and officials, for political reasons, were loath to admit it.'

At this juncture the fanciful needs to be matched with the factual. On the factual side we have telling affidavits from Cream's sister Jessie and the elder Cream's executor, Thomas Davidson. The sister affirms that Neill Cream left Joliet Prison in July 1891 and lived with the family until he left for England in September of that year. Davidson states that he became convinced of Cream's innocence and '. . . exerted every legitimate influence I could command to secure his liberation and succeeded eventually in getting him released in the early part of the summer of 1891.' Davidson then states that '. . . he came immediately to me in Quebec on being liberated, and . . . at my first interview with him I concluded that he was unmistakably insane, and stated my conviction to his brother, Daniel Cream, in whose house he was stopping.'

There are other facts to contend with. A report in the *Joliet Daily News* on 13 June 1891 notes that Cream was pardoned the day before, while the Pinkerton National Detective Agency received a letter from Joliet Prison written by Cream in December 1890.

Bearing all this in mind, the Cream Ripper theory seems cranky, to put it mildly. Yet Donald Bell does his best and some of his points are colourful, even if they are irrelevant. For instance, he tells us that a letter in the McGill archives refers pointedly to the photographic record of the 1876 class of graduates. The letter says: 'Jack the Ripper's picture is in that book.' 1876 was of course Cream's year, so the connection is plain; but the words quoted are nothing but the recollections of a medical man remembering the words of the widow of one of Cream's classmates. As such the letter is hardly evidence and, as we'll see, its view was easily derived from rumours generated at Cream's London trial.

These trial rumours are responsible, too, for Bell's second anecdote, one involving humorist Stephen Leacock. Leacock had been Professor of Economics at McGill and in a letter to the Dean of Medicine dated 15 May 1935, he refers to an after-dinner speech he had made. In it he had joked that McGill had a long honour roll of names of distinction, including one graduate who 'achieved a sudden reputation . . . under his professional name of Jack the Ripper'. Leacock's speech gave no specific name, but his letter says: 'I suppose you know that it is practically certain that Jack the Ripper was on our rolls as Dr Neill Cream.'

These strange beliefs stem from nothing stronger than a hoax letter received by Coroner Braxton Hicks. It read: 'The man that you have in your power, Dr Neill, is as innocent as you are. Knowing him by sight, I disguised myself like him, and made the acquaintance of the girls that had been poisoned. I gave them the pills to cure them of all their earthly miseries, and they died . . . If I were you I would release Dr T. Neill, or you might get into trouble . . . Beware all, I warn but once . . . Yours respectfully, Juan Pollen, alias Jack the Ripper.'

Once the Ripper had been tied in with Cream, however loosely, people started to look for extra points of resemblance. It was noted that both killers slew prostitutes and the killings were for pleasure, not gain. What's more, both Jack and Neill apparently had the urge to write grotesque letters about their killings. Such things seemed to point to one man. Backed by faulty facts, this faulty reasoning was toyed with and believed by some of the gullible, including some associated with McGill.

As for solid evidence, Bell offers only a photograph of Cream wearing a horseshoe tiepin. Its significance? Well, this lies in the description of a suspect furnished by George Hutchinson, of a man who wore a 'black necktie, in which was fastened a horseshoe pin'. For Donald Bell, that is a clue of utmost importance: Hutchinson was of course talking about Cream. The many thousands of other men at that time who also sported horseshoe tiepins are ignored and, animated by this false lead, Bell ploughs on, eagerly grasping at other useless supports like the *Times* report he seizes on dated 12 November 1888.

This deals with a man who proclaimed himself Jack the Ripper and '. . . was almost lynched by an East End crowd'. This is the quote as offered by Bell: 'He refused to give any name but asserted that he was a doctor at St Thomas's Hospital. He is about 35 years of age, 5 feet 7 inches in height, of dark complexion, with dark moustache, and was wearing spectacles.' For Bell this is 'close to a perfect description of Cream. Police rescued the gentleman from the infuriated crowd.'

A perfect description? A glance at *The Times* in question shows that Bell's quotation is not only mutilated but doctored as well. This *Times* story deals with a character well-known in Ripper-lore: the famous man 'with cork-blackened face who stood on the corner of Wentworth Street terrifying passing women' with his shouts that he was the killer. As for the hospital the man pretended to work at, that was St George's. This is specifically stated in all the newspaper reports, including that of *The Times*, but Bell makes it read 'St Thomas's', Cream's one-time place of study. Perhaps Donald Bell was badly served, perhaps he was supplied with his rigged extract. Maybe; but it still makes his research look trivial and misplaced.

There are further damning howlers along these lines. As a key item, Bell introduces the tale of an eight-year-old boy found stabbed to death 'in Portsmouth' in November 1888. The blunt knife that killed him was near the body. The only link with Whitechapel lies in the fact that the boy apparently used to like playing at being Jack the Ripper, yet Bell visualizes this as yet another of Cream's killings. Five days before, he reminds us, on 21 November 1888, the Thames Police Court Magistrate received a Ripper letter with a Portsmouth postmark. Cream, he argues, had gone to Portsmouth to pick up a ship at nearby Southampton. By an incredible coincidence he must have met the boy, Percy Searle, and '. . . the boy's "Jack the Ripper" behaviour may have annoyed Cream – and the blunt knife was all that he had available.'

This 'significant' killing and the letter that preceded it then led Bell to search the passenger lists of ocean-going ships leaving Southampton '. . . and arriving in New York during December 1888 and January 1889 . . . in other words – *after* Percy Searle was murdered on 26 November 1888. He found two physicians only, a Dr Waite and a Dr Grant, but undeterred he concluded: 'So Cream used a fake name . . . Was one of these doctors Thomas Neill Cream?'

To begin with, it's all too much to be logically acceptable. At one moment Bell pictures Cream in the hands of the East End police after nearly being lynched and days later places him in Portsmouth busy posting yet another silly letter. How on earth does Bell reconcile the two events? Does he imagine that anyone causing such a serious breach of the peace could conceal his identity, escape charges and be free in such a short time?

The logically unacceptable also turns out to be factually absurd. Young Percy Searle's death had no possible connection with Cream or the Ripper. The boy wasn't killed in Portsmouth but in the tiny market town of Havant. What is more, the murderer was arrested two days after Searle's death. The killer was an eleven-year-old boy called Husband and the knife used belonged to his brother. So ends the saga of Cream's provincial exploits.

As can be judged, the whole Cream Ripper candidature is preposterous in the extreme but amazingly it received the independent backing of Mr

Derek Davis, a specialist in the examination of handwriting. Mr Davis has been called in on a number of forensic disputes and this experience led him to look at two 'Ripper letters', the 'From Hell' letter to Mr Lusk and one to Dr Openshaw, comparing them to a holographic copy of a Cream letter. Mr Davis made many calculations and reached the conclusion that Cream wrote the two 'Ripper letters' after heavily disguising his writing. But a Miss C.M. MacLeod, a Canadian handwriting expert, analysed the same letters and concluded that only the one to Lusk was likely to be legitimate. She added: 'I would have looked for this killer among such men as cabdrivers who have a legitimate excuse to be anywhere at any time.'

Let us agree that handwriting experts have their occasional uses – in cases of forged or traced signatures, for example – but they tend to have an inflated idea of their powers and importance. So we can cheerfully allow them to fight their own duels on grounds of their own choosing. For in Cream's case as a Ripper suspect, they are superfluous and have nothing useful to reveal. The truth is that in 1888 poisoner Cream was still prisoner Cream and all the rest is moonshine.

By contrast, George Chapman (the name was assumed) was most definitely in and around Whitechapel in 1888. His background differed greatly from Cream's. He was a Pole, born in 1865, christened Severin Antoniovich Klosowski, and unlike Cream he was only able to study medicine through being apprenticed to a practising surgeon. After six or more years he still remained an assistant only, earning his living as a *Feldscher* or 'barber-surgeon'. At best that implies that he removed warts, small wens and other minor blemishes.

On arriving in England Klosowski headed straight for Whitechapel – nothing strange in that; almost every Pole and Russian did the same. It proved easy for him to find employment and at the time of the first murders, his place of work was in the Whitechapel High Street, in a hairdresser's shop under the White Hart pub. But does that in itself make him a candidate? Not quite, the Chapmanite argument runs, but when coupled with later events, it certainly does.

The primary case against Klosowski/Chapman rests on his medical knowledge, his callous nature, the time-table of the murders and the description of the man seen with Mary Kelly. This is once more the somewhat shop-worn description by Hutchinson: 'five feet six inches in height, and thirty-four or thirty-five years of age, with dark complexion and dark moustache turned up at the ends.' For Bell's investigations this had to be Cream. For Chapmanites, it points to the Polish *Feldscher*.

Then there is 'the remarkable fact' that the Whitechapel murders ended when Chapman left for America in May 1890 and recommenced in Jersey City, where he had opened a barber's shop. This new batch of American Ripper murders suddenly ended at the beginning of 1892 – just at the time when Chapman returned to London. That is how the tale runs. If it is true it certainly adds a new dimension to the search.

Yet Chapman was never charged with any murder involving knives or brutality of any sort. His first known victim, Isobella Spink, lived with him as his wife for two years before dying from antimony poisoning. By

Klosowski had the look of a wild beast.

that time, December 1897, Chapman had taken up the tavern-keeping trade. His second victim was yet another common-law wife, Bessie Taylor. Together they ran the Grapes public house in Bishop's Stortford, followed by the Monument Tavern in Union Street, Southwark, where, on 13 February 1901, Bessie died. Once more the death was certified as due to natural causes. After waiting a mere six months, Chapman engaged Maude Marsh as a barmaid, went through another of his fictional weddings and proclaimed her his wife. She lasted until 22 October 1902, then died after two weeks of agony. This time the physician refused to issue a death certificate without a post mortem, which showed the presence of arsenic. The police were called in, Chapman was arrested and the exhumations began.

Chapman's identification as the Ripper stems directly from his arrest and trial. On hearing of his arrest by Inspector Godley, Inspector Abberline said, 'You've got Jack the Ripper at last.' Abberline was one of those who felt that the Whitechapel crimes were un-English and as such could well be the work of one of the uncouth aliens who flocked into the East End. There had earlier been talk of Russian surgeons and other such villains, and Klosowski seemed to fit this criminal profile perfectly. Abberline's view was included in Hargrave Adam's full account of Chapman's trial and given wide circulation. Adam also referred to the startling correspondence between the New Jersey killings and those in Whitechapel, something that was repeated as gospel by other commentators – and yet it's a fabrication. Thorough research refutes it easily: there were no Ripper-style murders in New Jersey during Chapman's stay there or at any other time.

It is true that on 25 April 1891 the New York papers ran headlines shrieking 'HAS JACK THE RIPPER ARRIVED?', but that was just a circulation-booting ploy. The sensation involved the killing of a wretched, drink-sodden woman in Manhattan, an ex-actress known by the quaint nickname 'Old Shakespeare'. An arrest and trial took place and an Algerian, Ameer Ben Ali, was sentenced to life imprisonment. Later findings pointed the finger at a very different man and Ali was released. The other man was never caught, but he was described as a medium-sized, stocky, blond, seafaring man, which immediately rules out dark, slim, saturnine, landlubber Chapman.

Like Cream, Chapman has recently been pushed forward once more into the Ripper limelight, this time with a difference. Now he's presented as part of a cover-up operation which helped shield the real culprit. Yet neither role fits the poisonous *Feldscher*. Like Cream, he chose the cowardly, surreptitious mode of killing: the extended agonies, the remorseless suffering appealed to both men's twisted personalities. The knife was far too sudden, far too risky and far too bloody for their essentially timid natures. Rippers? Never!

6

Rasputin's Russian Ripper

In his time, William Le Queux (the name rhymes with cue) was the most prolific thriller writer around. His *Who's Who* entry describes him as 'Author of over 130 novels and many Kinema films.' In gossip, he was eternally spoken of in ornithological terms: a 'strutting game-cock'; 'as vain as a peacock'; 'a preening, self-regarding bird of feather'. Perhaps he over-compensated for his tiny stature. But for all that, Le Queux entertained and gripped thousands with his tales of espionage and double-dealing in high places.

Early in his career he combined a journalist's training with a vivid imagination and hit on a formula that both paid and corrupted: he took to writing fiction that was painstakingly dressed up as fact. His first success with this technique came with his 1905 best-seller *The Invasion*, a step-by-step account of the invasion of Britain by the Kaiser's army. It was applauded by Earl Roberts and other advocates of an expanded territorial army and later, when the Great War broke out, the book was eulogized and helped establish Le Queux as a man with inside knowledge of powerful intrigues.

It seemed only natural, then, that towards the end of the War, another Le Queux best-seller revealed the secrets behind Rasputin's pro-German plots. *Rasputin the Rascal Monk* was alleged to contain 'Official Documents revealed and recorded for the first time'. It said nothing about Jack the Ripper – but why on earth should it? Yet in 1923 the public learned for the first time that among those 'Official Documents' was one disclosing the name of the Ripper and the reasons for his actions. This unexpected bonus came in Le Queux's autobiographical *Things I Know About Kings, Celebrities and Crooks*.

According to Le Queux, Rasputin's actual words read:

London was horrified by the evil work of a mysterious criminal known as 'Jack the Ripper', who killed and mutilated a number of women of ill-repute in the East End of the capital. The repetition of the appalling crimes mystified the world. The true author of these atrocities was disclosed by a

Russian well-known in London, named Nideroest, a spy of our Secret Police, who was a member of the Jubilee Street Club, the Anarchist Centre in the East of London. One night in the club the identity of 'Jack the Ripper' was revealed to him by an old Russian Anarchist, Nicholas Zverieff. The mysterious assassin was Doctor Alexander Pedachenko, who had been on the staff of the Maternity Hospital at Tver, and lived on the second floor in the Millionnaya, but had gone to London, where he lived with his sister in Westmoreland Road, Walworth. From there he sallied forth at night, took an omnibus across London Bridge and walked to Whitechapel, where he committed his secret crimes.

Alexander Pedachenko, according to Zverieff – whose record appears in the reports of the Secret Police – was aided by a friend of his named Levitski, and a young tailoress, called Winberg. The latter would approach the victim and hold her in conversation and Levitski kept watch for the police patrols, while the crimes and mutilations took place. Levitski, who had been born in London, wrote the warning post-cards signed 'Jack the Ripper' to the Police and press. It was through Levitski that Zverieff knew the truth.

The report of Nideroest's discovery amused our Secret Police greatly, for, as a matter of fact, they knew the whole details at the time, and had themselves actively aided and encouraged the crimes, in order to exhibit to the world certain defects of the English police system, there having been some misunderstanding and rivalry between our own police and the British. It was, indeed, for that reason that Pedachenko, the greatest and boldest of all Russian criminal lunatics, was encouraged to go to London and commit that series of atrocious crimes, in which agents of our police aided him.

Eventually at the orders of the Ministry of the Interior the Secret Police smuggled the assassin out of London, and as Count Luiskovo he landed at Ostend, and was conducted by a secret service agent to Moscow. While there he was, a few months later, caught red-handed attempting to murder and mutilate a woman named Vogak and was eventually sent to an asylum, where he died in 1908.

After the return to Russia of Levitski and the woman Winberg the Secret Police deemed it wise to suppress them, and they were therefore exiled to Yakutsk. Such are the actual facts of the 'Jack the Ripper Mystery' which still puzzles the whole world.

What are we to make of these strange disclosures? Is there anything about them that impels belief? If there is it eludes me. In fact, Le Queux's record as a bogus historian makes the document worthless. In this specific case his earlier writings show the falsity of the revelations of 1923.

Le Queux's first book using the alleged Rasputin papers – *The Rascal Monk* – appeared in 1917; it used papers later said to have been supplied by the Kerensky Government. The second book denouncing Rasputin appeared in August 1918, but carried an introduction dated January 1918. This volume, entitled *The Minister of Evil – the Secret History of*

Rasputin's Betrayal of Russia, does not claim to be based on the original batch of papers used in Book 1. Instead, the introduction explains that 'After the issue to the public of the curious chronicle of *Rasputin the Rascal Monk*, based upon official documents, and its translation into a number of languages, I received from the same sources in Russia a bulky manuscript on very thin paper which contained certain confessions, revelations, and allegations made by its writer, Feodor Rajevksi, who acted as the mock-saint's secretary and body servant . . .'

At once we meet with absurdities. *The Rascal Monk* was not published until after November 1917, and the foreign language editions came some time after that. By that time, the Kerensky Government had ceased to exist and the Bolsheviks were in control, yet Le Queux insists that the 'same sources' – the Kerensky Government – were still able to send bulky packages out of Russia. At that late date what was the point of an exercise along those lines? Any ex-Kerensky supporters were too busy saving their hides to worry about yesterday's villains.

An alien, by God! It simply had to be . . .

A study of the two books shows that they owe nothing to real life but everything to romantic fiction. They even include standard Le Queux pet themes; for example, he loved dragging in tales of germ warfare, and these occur in both books, as well as in others of his on the Kaiser. But in *The Minister of Evil* we encounter the daftest tale of all. It centres around a diabolical German scheme to infect tins of corned beef and bottles of beef extract with a deadly virus. The virus is not named – that makes it much more mysterious – but it is described as newly discovered, closely allied to bubonic plague, highly infectious, and inevitably fatal. This plot was revealed to Rasputin when he made a secret war-time visit to the Kaiser in Berlin.

The doctoring of the bully-beef shows just how authentic Le Queux's tales could be: 'One of the assistants had carried up four small tins of beef . . . These he placed on the table, and as we stood around he took a small bradawl, and having punctured the tin at the large end close to the rim, he took from one of the incubators a test-tube full of a cloudy, brown liquid gelatine. Then filling a hypodermic syringe – upon which was an extra-long needle – he thrust it into the contents of the tin and injected the virus into the meat. Afterwards, with a small soldering iron he closed the puncture. "That tin, infected as it is, is sufficient to cause an epidemic which might result in thousands of deaths" – declared the Hun professor proudly.'

The syringe was a good idea but that tin, I'm afraid, would never have reached anyone's kitchen table: the 'Hun professor' had obviously forgotten everything he'd learned about micro-organisms. The crude puncturing of the tin would have admitted a throng of greedy bacteria bent on feasting on the moist meat. Decomposition would have produced enough gases to blow the sides of the tin. Any that were stupidly opened would have reached the dustbin double-quick. But this is simply Le Queux's sensational pen at play.

Believe it or not, though, Le Queux's 'informant' about the virus went on to claim that the fantastic, comic-book plot worked. A cargo of the infected tinned beef was shipped to Russia from Stockholm in 1916. It was distributed and sold in the towns of Vologda and Novgorod and many thousands died. The book records: 'Truly the result of that devilish plot was most awful. In the three months that followed – though not a word leaked out to the Allies, so careful were Protopopoff and the camarilla to suppress all the facts – more than half the population of the two cities died from a disease which to this day is a complete mystery, and its bacilli known only to German bacteriologists.'

It only remains to add that other equally fantastic secrets were 'leaked' to Le Queux by Count Ernst Von Heltzendorff, Lt.-Col. Otto Von Heynitz, Baroness Zeneide Tzankoff, and Colonel Vassili Grigorieff.

As can be seen, Le Queux was an undoubted poseur, basking in the glory bestowed on him by a string of imaginary high-placed confidants. His Rasputin Ripper revelations are likewise drawn from the archives of his imagination. As a contribution to the search for the Ripper they are just a time-wasting diversion, but unfortunately they can't just be dismissed out of hand for they were later revived and built into an enlarged and complex story authored by Donald McCormick.

William Le Queux: alone, he invented 'Rasputin's Ripper'.

In truth the substance of Le Queux's 1923 Ripper revelations was simply created from fragments of the past. At the time of the Whitechapel murders Le Queux, together with Charles Hands and Lincoln Springfield, had covered the Ripper case. All three now worked for rival papers and they took it in turns to debate the events. Le Queux testifies: 'One evening Springfield of the *Star* would publish a theory as to how the murders had been done . . . next night Charlie Hands would have a far better theory in the *Pall Mall*, and then I would weigh in with another theory in the *Globe*.' One of the theories he had to entertain involved a report from the Russian paper *Novosti*, laying the blame on a mad Russian. Later, in his *Minister of Evil*, Le Queux included a section dealing with a man from Tver who kills a young girl and escapes detection. In creating his 1923 piece, he fell back on this association, and killer Pedachenko became the man from Tver. Even the obscure Westmoreland Road is simply re-cycled, lifted straight from his novel *Who Giveth This Woman?* This tale of murder and Russian intrigues in London was written in 1915, two years *before* his alleged first sighting of the 'Rasputin Papers'.

How did this valueless intervention come to have a second life? According to Donald McCormick, there was independent proof of the Pedachenko theory, proof drawn not from one but from two unconnected sources.

The main proof is said to be derived from records kept by a Dr Thomas Dutton of Shepherd's Bush, London. As Donald McCormick tells it, this Dr Dutton compiled a three-volume hand-written diary called *Chronicles of Crime*. This was written over a period of some 60 years and included extraordinary claims relating to the Whitechapel mystery. It seems that Dr Dutton was not only immersed in the investigations, he was uniquely privileged: as a close friend of Chief Inspector Abberline, he was consulted about the crimes and was also permitted to make photographs of the Ripper letters.

At this point it must be emphasized that these photographs were not mere standard negatives and prints, but specialized forms called 'micro-photographs'. McCormick helps any unknowledgeable readers by explaining that Dutton 'had been a leading figure in the Chichester and West Sussex Microscopic Society and had specialized in micro-photography'. Mark this well.

Dutton himself claims: 'I made micro-photographs of 128 specimens of the alleged correspondence of Jack the Ripper to the police and other institutions and individuals. Of these at least thirty-four were definitely in the same handwriting . . . the authentic letter-writer was, to judge from the micro-photographs, deliberately disguising his true method of calligraphy, and in doing so, he not unnaturally fell into the error of frequently forming his C's, H's, R's and T's in a variety of ways.'

Dr Dutton writes at length about this correspondence and values it in a way that no one else anywhere ever has. No one else has ever dreamed of asserting that as many 34 letters were from the same hand that held the bloody knife. But Dutton is adamant: 'It was only by comparing a large number of letters and noting the frequency with which certain letters were formed differently and by examining the micro-photographs that one could detect positively minute similarities in writing . . .'

Dutton was aware of the many hoax letters, but insisted that 'The fact that there was more than one letter-writer does not detract from the importance of the thirty-four which were in the same handwriting. And thirty-four was the minimum number of letters which Jack wrote. Micro-photography in the 'eighties was still in its infancy, and I was only an amateur at it. But I dare say that modern methods would have shown many more to be the same man's work.'

Now these are powerful claims. Even more powerful is Dutton's revelation that he actually photographed the famous writing on the wall at Goulston Street: 'The Juwes are The men That will not be Blamed for nothing.' Until McCormick's book appeared, it was always accepted that this writing had been erased before anyone had had a chance to photograph it. But apparently not. The incredible Dr Dutton had got there with his incredible equipment and recorded it for history. These are said to be his very words: 'I was asked by the police to photograph the message on the wall before it was washed off, but Sir Charles Warren was so insistent that the message must not be preserved in any form that he ordered the police to destroy the prints I sent them. But the micro-photograph which I took definitely established that the writing was the same as that in some of the letters.' Yet another point to mark well.

This doctor certainly looks like a man to be reckoned with, so when he goes on to confirm that the Ripper *was* a Dr Pedachenko, we have to stay alert and attend to his every word. This, after all, is what Le Queux said, and now Abberline's 'consultant' says the same. But not, curiously, until Le Queux had published the name. According to McCormick, Dutton's diary for 1924 contained this passage: 'Another theory on the Ripper. This time by William Le Queux in *Things I Know*. It is a great pity that he did not follow up what is a useful clue. By failing to do so, and by taking the Rasputin MS at its face value, he has only made a fool of himself. Further examination might have shown that Pedachenko was Klosowski's double. The fact that Pedachenko was a doctor at a Russian hospital is neither here nor there. What Le Queux should have found out was that Pedachenko worked as a barber-surgeon for a hairdresser named Delhaye in Westmoreland Road, Walworth, in 1888.'

Klosowski/Chapman, as we've already seen, was at one time Abberline's nomination for Bloody Jack. By introducing the barber Delhaye and the idea of 'doubles', Dutton is able to reconcile Abberline's conflict, for he tells us that the Chief Inspector came to think of Klosowski and Pedachenko as one and the same man.

A witness is introduced by Dutton in the person of Levisohn, who had given evidence at Chapman Klosowski's trial. After the trial Levisohn told Abberline to look for a Russian who lived in Walworth; this Russian carried out some illicit doctoring and cut out warts and moles at barbers' shops. Nothing too offensive in that, so why should a Chief Inspector take notice? Because, Levisohn is said to have argued, this Russian was in Commercial Street, Whitechapel, on the night of the Berner Street murder.

That item of suggestive testimony is coupled by Dutton to another, attributed to a Russian named Lave. Lave was a member of the

International Workers' Club near Berner Street. On the night of Stride's murder he claimed to have seen a suspicious stranger in the club, a dark-moustached stranger calling himself a Pole – but Lave had his doubts about that. The man, aged between 30 and 35, also said he was a barber in business in a basement in George Yard.

According to Dutton, the police took notice: after all, George Yard was where 'the first' of the Ripper murders had taken place. They were startled, though, when they visited the basement barber's shop and did find a dark-moustached Pole in attendance; but he was younger, only 23 in fact, and Lave admitted he wasn't the man seen at the club. Even so, this Pole was also destined to be remembered as a murderer. He was hanged under the name of Chapman. He was, of course, Klosowski.

It needs to be emphasized both that these accounts are unconfirmed by police records, and equally that they are confirmed by no other known writer: they rest on Dutton's say-so entirely. And in Dutton's hands these curious scraps all lead to Pedachenko's two stamping-grounds, to his killing territory in Whitechapel, and to his plotting place in Westmoreland Road, Walworth.

Pedachenko not only lived at Westmoreland Road with his sister, as Le Queux said, but worked there at two different addresses. His innocent work involved removing moles and warts at William Delhaye's barber's shop. His sinister work was planned at the Infirmary attached to the Newington Workhouse at No 190 where he assisted one of the doctors on a part-time, unpaid basis. He used this post of trust to ingratiate himself with some of the women patients. One of these was Martha Turner; others were Annie Chapman, Mary Nichols and Mary Kelly. As they gossiped with him, he sized them up, discovered where they hung out and marked them down for future butchery – or so Dutton would have us believe.

If Pedachenko was the Ripper, why did he stop with Kelly? Dutton offers no explanation. He simply states that after Kelly's murder, Pedachenko stopped visiting the Infirmary and the doctor he'd assisted never saw him again. An 'official' Russian police bulletin is supposed to take up the story after 1888, yet even that document is mute about the murderer's movements. It reads:

KONOVALOV, Vassilly, alias PEDACHENKO, Alexey, alias LUISKOVO, Andrey, formerly of Tver, is now officially declared to be dead. Any files or information concerning him from district sections should be sent to the Moscow Central District of Ochrana. Such information, photographs, or identification details as may still exist might refer to KONOVALOV, PEDACHENKO or LUISKOVO either individually or collectively. If documents held by you do not contain these names, they should also be examined for any information concerning a man, answering to the description of the above, who was wanted for the murder of a woman in Paris in 1886, for the murder of five women in the East Quarter of London in 1888 and again for the murder of a woman in Petrograd in 1891. KONOVALOV's description is as follows: Born 1857 at Torshok, Tver. Height medium. Eyes dark blue. profession, junior surgeon. General description: Usually wore black moustache, curled and waxed at ends. Heavy, black eyebrows. Broad-shouldered, but slight build. Known to disguise himself as a woman on occasions and was arrested when in women's clothes in Petrograd before his detention in the asylum where he died.

That record of Pedachenko's deeds and end was said to be found in the January 1909 issue of a confidential Secret Police publication called the *Ochrana Gazette*. The Ochrana was the Czarist forerunner of the Cheka and OGPU etc. This was McCormick's other source of independent proof of the Pedachenko theory.

The *Gazette* was a fortnightly paper issued only to the heads of the Ochrana sections and meant to keep them up-to-date. Since it was a secret paper with restricted circulation, how was McCormick able to quote from it? According to him, the late Prince Serge Belloselski had a copy and supplied this translation. As a bonus, the Prince had added a personal touch, revealing that Myednikov, head of the Moscow Ochrana, had actually told him how they knew about Pedachenko's British exploits. A Latvian, named Peter Straume, who had once lived in London, had supplied the details. With such backing, 'Rasputin's Ripper' seems to take on substance.

I've simplified the Pedachenko story, since in McCormick's hands it becomes needlessly complex and confusing. But I have preserved all the essentials; nothing of importance has been omitted. We can now ask if the documentation is reliable and acceptable. Perhaps the prince should take precedence.

Belloselski's prize exhibit, the *Gazette*, looks authentic enough It's unsensational, mild in tone, bureaucratic in style, and tersely effective. Yet the prince's translation twice refers to the town of Petrograd. No authentic document of 1909 could use a name which only came into use after August 1914. In 1909, the town bore the time-honoured name of St Petersburg. That name and none other would have been in front of the prince's eyes. It was the name he'd grown up with, deeply engraved in his memory. No mistake would have been possible.

A murky cloud of suspicion now hovers over our prince. It grows even darker when we review his actions, or rather, lack of actions. We are told he was animated enough to write to Le Queux about Pedachenko. If so, it's strange that Le Queux never made use of this extra information. In

1923, his Russian Ripper was without backing of any sort and lack of backing meant that his claim was in fact ridiculed and rejected. If the prince had written and told him about the corroborative *Gazette*, then Le Queux would have leapt into print and triumphantly flayed his critics: his vanity would not have allowed him to do otherwise. Yet there's no trace of any public defence by Le Queux, no trace whatsoever of his knowing about the valuable support from the prince.

As for the prince himself, where are his public statements? He is supposed to have discussed this affair with both Le Queux and McCormick. He was certain that he had information of supreme interest, and yet at no time did he write to the press or invite a reporter to interview him. We have to picture him sitting back idly, while the papers dished out theory after theory about the Ripper. It just won't do. The story is too inconsistent to be acceptable.

There's a further problem attached to the prince's *Ochrana Gazette*. There is a conflict between its text as quoted in Richard Deacon's *History of the Russian Secret Service* and McCormick's Ripper book. This is not a question of two authors in conflict, for Richard Deacon and Donald McCormick are one and the same person! So the conflict is disquieting. Deacon's *History* says: 'The *Gazette* contained one specially illuminating item that throws a little more light on the Jack the Ripper murders. This was an official announcement, declaring as "officially dead" a man known under the names of Pedachenko, Luiskovo, Konovalov and Ostrog.' Compare this statement made in 1972 with the first appearance of the *Gazette* extract in 1959. Originally only *three* names were given – Konovalov, Pedachenko and Luiskovo. But now Deacon/McCormick adds a fourth – Ostrog – and identifies it as present on the *Gazette* page in 1909. Not so. Ostrog as a Ripper suspect only came into consideration after police chief Macnaghten's papers were openly discussed in November 1959. This addition is completely unacceptable behaviour. The moment an author doctors a quotation, even a fake one, for whatever purpose, he forfeits his right to be taken seriously .

For a while though, we will continue to take McCormick seriously. Indeed, his strongest ally, the formidable Dr Dutton, compels us to. And yet there's something unreal about the doctor too, as he appears in McCormick's book . None of the many reminiscences by former policemen and journalists ever mentions Dutton. There's no trace of him in the official Ripper files. This outstanding expert seemed to have hugged his secrets too close to his chest. Like the prince, he seemed willing to let the world remain in ignorance while he smirked away in the comfort of his private knowledge. Once more, this has a hollow ring to it, but we obviously need to find out more about the man. Perhaps his writings contain clues that have been overlooked until now?

To me, one feature of his writings leaps into prominence. Alone, out of all the Ripperphiles, he claims to have photographed a mass of Ripper letters and nailed some 34 as being authentic. Specifically he says: 'I made micro-photographs of 128 specimens . . .' Again and again he refers to his micro-photographs. He even tells us that 'Micro-photography in the 'eighties was still in its infancy'.

These words brand the doctor as a first-class charlatan. Micro-photography is a specialized branch of a photographic art which involves the *reduction* of large scenes to minute proportions on film or photo-plates. Think of micro-dots, beloved of spies, as an up-to-date example. The micro-photographic process is excellent for the storage of bulk information but in 1888 would have been useless for the careful study of documents. No one with any knowledge of photography would have used that term to describe the system used by microscope societies, including the one Dutton had belonged to. The system they used was a very different one called photomicography, aimed at obtaining enlargements of microscopic objects by photographing them through a microscope attached to a camera. It was ideal for photographing grains of pollen, blood cells, flies' eyes, and other microscopic delights . But even in modern criminology it has only a limited use in the study of documents; it is used to blow up individual letters on cheques, passports and so on to reveal possible alterations or superimpositions.

If, in 1888, the doctor had really been allowed to photograph 'the Ripper correspondence', then his task at that time was simple . He only needed to take along a whole or half-plate camera, with extendable bellows, to carry out the work. This would have given him exact-size negatives of the letters and preserved all the fine details. The plates could be enlarged as needed or studied, as positives, by projection. Neither micro-photography nor photomicography could offer any advantages – indeed to use them would have been a retrograde step.

If final proof of charlatanism is needed it can be provided. Dr Dutton says he micro-photographed the writing at Goulston Street. If he did, he would know exactly what the writing said. But he obviously didn't, since McCormick renders it: 'The Jewes are not the men to be blamed for nothing', which is wrong in its words and wrong in the crucial mis-spelling. It is no more than a botched version of one of the already botched reports circulating after the inquest on Catherine Eddowes. And Dutton condemns himself as a liar when he says of Jack : 'He wrote "Jewes" with an extra e when he scrawled his messages in chalk on the wall, and which the police so stupidly washed off.' If Dutton had so much a looked at that writing he would have known that the spelling took the curious form 'Juwes'. This was confirmed at the time by Sir Charles Warren and is so shown on the copy kept in the Scotland Yard file.

There you see why McCormick's theory is quite untenable. It asked far too much in the first place, for there is a limit to the valid use of unsupported testimony – and McCormick has well exceeded that limit. When unsupported testimony is found to be flagrantly false, then new doubts arise, and fresh research now makes these doubts take on a further disquieting aspect.

The research involves the article quoted by McCormick in his chapter 'The End of the Quest' which appeared in the *Sunday Chronicle* soon after Dr Thomas Dutton's death in 1935. Up to now, McCormick's version has been taken on trust by everyone. But my discovery of the column tells a very different story. The column was based on an interview given by Miss Hermione Dudley. McCormick calls her a patient of the doctor, but she was more than that, as the column shows: she was also a friend of Dutton's, and that is important. Why conceal it? McCormick has this to say of Miss Dudley: '. . . the patient [Miss Hermione Dudley] did not reveal the name of the killer. Indeed it is doubtful whether she knew very much more than Dutton's claim to have established the identity of the Ripper, for her subsequent story (given in an interview) resembled very much the theory of Leonard Matters. Possibly she had read Mr Matters' book and confused his version with that of Dutton.'

This is a clear attempt to belittle Miss Dudley's knowledge, yet she states with certainty that she knows the contents of Dutton's diaries. How can she be so certain? Because the lady was not someone standing on the sidelines, but the actual *owner of the diaries*. These are her own words: 'My father was one of the few men to whom he showed this document [the diaries] and owing to my own interest in it, Dr Dutton gave it to me some time ago.' (*Sunday Chronicle*, 17 November 1935.)

And what does Miss Dudley, owner of the diaries, tell us about them? She says this: 'Often he told me and he repeats it in his diary – that he knew the identity of Jack the Ripper. He described him as a middle-aged doctor.' She then makes it clear that although the doctor knew the identity of Jack, he never gave the name to her, nor put it in the diary. What is more, the diary account of the Ripper's actions and motives in no way resembles the Pedachenko story. Dutton's nominee was, in fact, simply a doctor out to take revenge on prostitutes.

And that, I'm afraid, kills stone dead the Pedachenko farrago. As dead as Rasputin himself.

7

The Body in the River Thames

For many years after the last reputed murder two main theories held sway: the killer was either in an asylum, or had committed suicide in a moment of lucid repentance. The latter theory usually named drowning as the chosen form of death. There were strong reasons for this widespread acceptance of 'the drowned man' as the Ripper, for police sources had repeatedly leaked fragments of information all pointing towards the River Thames as the place of penance.

The most explicit reference to a watery end was first given by Major Arthur Griffiths in Volume One of his *Mysteries of Police and Crime*. Griffiths was a former Inspector of Prisons and as such was well connected with the higher echelons of the police, including Mcnaghten. This gives his observations a certain weight; he's not dealing with gossip, but is reporting firm opinions, with perhaps some good reasoning behind them.

Griffiths states that after the last murder, the police came to the point of strongly suspecting several persons:

> . . . all of them known to be homicidal lunatics, and against three of these they held very plausible and reasonable grounds of suspicion. Concerning two of them the case was weak, although it was based on certain suggestive facts.
>
> One was a Polish Jew, a known lunatic, who was at large in the district of Whitechapel at the time of the murders and who having developed homicidal tendencies, was afterwards confined in an asylum. This man was said to resemble the murderer by the one person who got a glimpse of him – the police constable in Mitre Court.
>
> The second possible criminal was a Russian doctor, also insane, who had been a convict in both England and Siberia. This man was in the habit of carrying about surgical knives and instruments in his pockets; his antecedents were of the very worst, and at the time of the Whitechapel murders he was in hiding, or, at least, his whereabouts was never exactly known.
>
> The third person was of the same type, but the suspicion in his case was stronger, and there was every reason to believe that his own friends

Did the Ripper seek atonement in the river's depths?

entertained grave doubts about him. He was also a doctor in the prime of life, was believed to be insane or on the borderland of insanity, and he disappeared immediately after the last murder, that in Miller's Court; on the 9th of November, 1888. On the last day of that year, seven weeks later, his body was found floating in the Thames, and was said to have been in the water a month. The theory in this case was that after his last exploit, which was the most fiendish of all, his brain entirely gave way, and he became furiously insane and committed suicide.

Years later Macnaghten endorsed the suicide theme when he said: 'I became a detective officer six months after Jack the Ripper committed suicide, and never had a go at that fascinating individual.' Yet another ex-police officer boosted the suicide explanation at great length, this time in the 1930s. Former Detective-Sergeant Edwin T. Woodhall was more explicit than either Griffiths or Macnaghten; no name was advanced, but a full description of the suspect was offered.

The man first came to the notice of the police when they compared complaints received from Stepney and Spitalfields. A tall man with a 'frightful face' kept leaping out of doorways scaring the wits out of passing women. He was finally 'caught in the act but only subdued after a struggle'. Then, strapped down to one of the hand ambulance trucks of the period, he was carted off to the police station. Woodhall reports that it was obvious

> . . . before even the doctor saw him, that the man was insane, but it was the kind of insanity that was intensely dangerous and cunning; for from a raving, violent 'human animal' he changed at once to a mild – apparently sane – polite 'human being'. What impressed everyone present was the prisoner's eerie appearance. His face was entirely black, and, circling in wide rings, both eyes were painted white. This commenced from the forehead, including the eyes, the nose, the moustache and mouth, which were all of the same colour, giving an impression, when seen in the dark, of some weird-looking skull or death mask.

If the black-faced man was strange, stranger still was the notice taken of him. For Woodhall's story continues by stating that Scotland Yard ordered the East End police to bring the suspect west, to headquarters, for expert questioning, a most unusual step. When the man arrived at the Yard he was ushered into a room and confronted by two unnamed government officials who were left alone with the now placid suspect. But as soon as the door closed the madman reverted to type, grabbed a large cylindrical ebony ruler from the desk and used it as a truncheon. He savagely struck the officials and while they were reeling from shock and pain, darted out of the room, rushed down the corridors and escaped from the building.

Three weeks later, a paddleboat tied to the Waterloo Pier was shifted. There, lodged under the paddlewheel was a swollen corpse. It surfaced and was fished out by the river police. 'The black burnt cork and the white paint on the already decomposing features were hideously evident. Who he was, and where he came from, or anything at all about him, is . . . a complete mystery, for not a detail of correspondence or a clue of any kind was found on the corpse. Nor did any person come forward to claim him.'

Woodhall even claimed that he'd seen a police mortuary photograph of this drowned Ripper suspect. No one else, however, has ever seen it. So is there any contemporary support for this strangest of tales? There is in part. The *Illustrated Police News* for Saturday, 17 November 1888 carried this report:

> Great excitement was caused shortly before ten o'clock on Sunday night [11th], in the East End, by the arrest of a man with a blackened face, who publicly proclaimed himself to be 'Jack the Ripper' . . . Two young men, one a discharged soldier, seized him and the crowds . . . raised a cry of 'Lynch him!' Sticks were raised, and the man was furiously attacked and but for the timely arrival of the police he would have been seriously injured. The police took him to Leman Street Station. He refused to give any name, but asserted that he was a doctor at St George's Hospital . . . It took four constables and four civilians to take him to the station and protect him from the infuriated crowd. He is detained in custody, and it seems that the police attach importance to the arrest, as the man answers to the police description of the man who is wanted.

After that brief reference, the black-faced man disappears from the scene. Could the fiasco at Scotland Yard have been too painful to make public at the time? Do the limited newspaper reports really underpin Woodhall's claim? And are there any hints anywhere else about this mystery within a mystery? Well, some lines of Macnaghten's could be construed as a guarded confirmation, and we'll consider them later. For the moment, we can conclude that the suicide theory had a strong tradition behind it and that this tradition was further strengthened by the new information that Woodhall had divulged in 1937.

Matters rested there until 1959 when a fresh chapter opened, thanks to the enterprise of Daniel Farson. His interest in the Ripper began when he interviewed Colin Wilson, then embroiled in his Ripper-derived novel, *Ritual in the Dark*. Farson was wooed by his infectious enthusiasm and found himself becoming a Whitechapel addict. Farson's move to the East End in 1958 landed him in Ripper territory. What, then, was more natural than his inclusion of the murders in his television series, *Farson's Guide to the British*. One sequence included an appeal for information and the letters poured in. Most showed an eager interest, but little else, yet among them was a letter that later became of prime importance. It came from a Mr Knowles who had spent some time in Australia in the 1920s. While there, he had seen a document called *The East End Murderer – I Knew Him*, privately printed at Dandenong by a man called Fell. The author's name was confused in Knowles's memory, but it was either Lionel Druitt, Drewett or Drewery.

To this day I'm sure Dan Farson periodically kicks himself. Instead of dashing off a reply by return post, bristling with questions, he put the Knowles letter in a folder and did nothing about it. Sadly this folder, packed with other letters and material on the case, was stolen from Television House. Technically, the folder was 'borrowed' by an unknown person, but since no receipt was given and since it has never been returned, it was theft without doubt.

The significance of the Knowles letter hit Farson in 1959. He was staying with Lady Rose McLaren and mentioned that he was assembling some programmes on the Ripper. By one of those extraordinary strokes of fate Lady Rose was due to visit her mother-in-law that afternoon, and her mother-in-law was Christabel Aberconway, daughter of the late Sir Melville Macnaghten. Lady Aberconway was more than sympathetic. She dug out her copy of her father's private notes on the Ripper case. Dan Farson was allowed to make his own copy, and new possibilities beckoned.

When his programmes were finally screened, the name of the suicide in the river was withheld in deference to Lady Aberconway's wishes. But the man's initials were given. They were M.J.D., and they fitted no one mentioned in any of the known published accounts. The identity of this mystery man was finally revealed in 1965 and it was then shown that he figured as one of three main suspects as surmised by Griffiths. Macnaghten's notes, in the form owned by his daughter, declare that '. . . no proof could in any way ever be brought against anyone, although very many homicidal maniacs were at one time or another suspected. I enumerate the case of three men against whom the police held very reasonable suspicion. Personally, and after much careful and deliberate consideration, I am inclined to exonerate two of them. But I have always held strong opinions regarding No 1 and the more I think the matter over, the stronger do these opinions become. The truth, however, will never be known, and did, indeed, at one time lie at the bottom of the Thames, if my conjectures be correct.'

Following that brief preamble Macnaghten then introduces his suspects:

No 1 Mr M. J. Druitt, a doctor of about 41 years of age and of fairly good family, who disappeared at the time of the Miller's Court murder, and whose body was found floating in the Thames on 3 December, i.e. seven weeks after the said murder. The body was said to have been in the water for a month, or more – on it was found a season ticket between Blackheath and London. From private information I have little doubt but that his own family suspected this man of being the Whitechapel murderer and it was alleged that he was sexually insane.

No 2 Kosminski, a Polish Jew, who lived in the very heart of the district where the murders were committed. He had become insane owing to many years' indulgence in solitary vices. He had a great hatred of women with strong homicidal tendencies. He was (and I believe is) detained in a lunatic asylum about March 1889. This man in appearance strongly resembled the individual seen by the City PC near Mitre Square.

No 3 Michael Ostrog, a mad Russian doctor and convict, and unquestionably a homicidal maniac. This man was said to have been habitually cruel to women, and for a long time was known to have carried about with him surgical knives and other instruments; his antecedents were of the very worst and his whereabouts at the time of the Whitechapel murders could never be satisfactorily accounted for. He is still alive.

There are minor errors in the transcription of these notes in Farson's book and in Tom Cullen's book as well. In particular the date of Druitt's

Montague J. Druitt, named by Macnaghten, defamed by others.
Did Macnaghten (right) really know just who the Ripper was?

death is wrongly given as 3 December and wrongly again as 13 December (in Farson's revision), but these errors in no way detract from the fact that Macnaghten is definitely nominating Druitt as the probable murderer – but only in these notes. A major difference exists between this copy and the official notes left by Macnaghten in the Scotland Yard file.

The file notes open by referring to an article in the *Sun* in 1894 that had sensationally named Thomas Cutbush as the killer. Macnaghten counters the *Sun* by saying '. . . I may mention the cases of 3 men, any one of whom would have been more likely than Cutbush to have committed this series of murders.' In other words, Druitt is simply presented as one of three possibles, and the notes avoid making a choice of the man most likely to be guilty. No one is exonerated. All three are just placed side by side as potential culprits. Yet, if these official notes say one thing, Macnaghten's memoirs contradict them. There he comes down on a suicide as the killer.

Are there grounds, though, for accepting Druitt as the chief candidate? If there are, Macnaghten fails to provide them, and police records are empty. Indeed his reference to private information implies that he is not drawing on police records but on something supplied by outsiders, perhaps Druitt's family. Even so, the only damning thing he says about Druitt is that the man was sexually insane. But what does that mean? Macnaghten is hardly the fittest person to make judgements on sexual matters. Just look at his slating of Kosminski: he claims that the man went insane through masturbating too much. If he accepts such a hoary old pseudo-medical illusion, then how sound is his diagnosis of Druitt's oddities? In those days, for some respectable families, anything except the heterosexual missionary position was regarded as a wild perversion.

Apart from that, there is the jarring conflict between Macnaghten's notes and the statements in his autobiography, *Days of My Years*. In this book he says: 'I incline to the belief that the individual who held up London in terror resided with his own people; that he absented himself from home at certain times, and that he committed suicide on or about the 10th of November 1888 . . .' This is not Montague Druitt. Druitt did not live at home with his own people, but in chambers in London, and his suicide took place on or after 1 December – the date on the train ticket in his pocket. Who then is Macnaghten referring to? His final words seem to present us with a conundrum. He says that his nominee committed suicide '. . . after he had knocked out a Commissioner of Police and very nearly settled the hash of one of Her Majesty's principal Secretaries of State.'

Compare those words with Woodhall's 1937 story of black-face and the assault with the ebony ruler. Woodhall said his story was confirmed by Macnaghten's autobiography, so are these the give-away sentences? Not a bit of it. Woodhall's account was nothing but melodramatic fiction. He made it all up himself. For in truth the black-faced man was identified and released within hours by the East End police, and the *Globe* for 12 November 1888 tells us who he was. He was a Dr Holt, living in Willesden and working at St George's Hospital. He fancied himself as an amateur detective and had rubbed his face with soot to make himself less conspicuous. Clearly Macnaghten is not party to Woodhall's follies, but how reliable is he with any of his Ripper theories? Was he consistent? Did he, at a later date, revise his theories by replacing Druitt with some other suicide? These were questions never asked by Farson.

Looking at it now, it all made for a poor start for any candidate. Yet, when he first started on his hunt, Farson was confident that there *was* extra evidence linking Druitt with the murders. Despite the loss of the Knowles letter the Australian trail looked exciting, for an independent linking of the names – Fell, Druitt and Dandenong – came in a letter written by Maurice Gould of Bexleyheath.

Maurice Gould, 'an amateur criminologist', had been in Australia from 1925 until 1932. Whilst there he had met two men who knew the identity of Jack the Ripper – or so they said. Their knowledge came from papers owned by a Mr W. G. Fell of Dandenong. The story is a bit woolly, but the men said Fell had once housed a man named Druitt who had left papers proving the Ripper's identity. Fell had been willing to part with these papers, but only for £500. One of the men, Edward MacNamara, was a freelance journalist and would obviously have loved to secure the papers, but £500 was way beyond his means. So the golden opportunity passed and no one else ever seemed to take up Fell's offer. This is well worth remembering.

Whatever doubts Farson had were secondary. He discovered that a Dr Lionel Druitt was Montague's cousin. Dr Lionel had practised in London for some years – an important point, this – then in 1887 had resettled in Australia. The implications were breathtaking. The cousin of the chief suspect had known just who the murderer was. Had he shared the same information that had convinced Macnaghten? In 1961, Dan Farson flew to Australia, with high hopes that the answers could be found there.

Once in Australia he mentioned his search to the newspapers and on television. Then, accompanied by Alan Dower, special correspondent of Melbourne's *Truth*, he drove out to the Dandenong Ranges. At Lang-Lang, where W. G. Fell had been said to live, Farson actually traced a storekeeper with the same name, but it was a dead lead. Storekeeper

Fell knew nothing of printer Fell, the man behind Lionel's secrets.

On the positive side, Farson did locate an elderly woman who remembered Dr Lionel. The lady – a Miss Stevens – lived at Drouin, near Lang-Lang, and said that the doctor practised in her town in 1903, recalling that he had a daughter named Dorothy. Later research confirmed that Dorothy had been born in 1899 but it also showed that in 1903 Lionel had two other daughters – one born in 1889, the other in 1891. It was odd that these were somehow forgotten by the lady; still, a connection with the key area had been established. At that point, however, all progress came to a halt. Fell could not be traced. The documents failed to surface. No one with any first-hand or even second-hand knowledge of the affair came forward.

In the years that followed a number of people made separate searches for the elusive Fell and his evasive document. It should have been quite straightforward. Fell lived at a time when registration of births and deaths was compulsory. There were electoral rolls as well, to supplement those basic entries, and added to these were the various town, area and trade directories. So, logically, one could have expected to find a number of entries relating to W.G. Fell. Not one, though, could be found. When Paul Bonner of the BBC asked for help from the Australian Broadcasting Commission, he received the following reply: '. . . A search of directories around 1890 reveals no such person as W.G. Fell.' A search through death records between 1933 and 1937 failed to unearth a death certificate, even though Fell was supposed to have died in 1935.

Of the document itself, not a single mention could be found anywhere. The ABC researchers filed the following report in April 1973: '. . . *The East End Murderer – I Knew Him* . . . have checked Sidney libraries and spent three days in Melbourne checking every available source including libraries, historical societies, criminologists, archivists, private collectors, publishers and newspapers. Druitt's publication is not listed in Australian bibliographies . . .'

It could be argued that the document was a private affair and would escape public notice and listings. But a private publication is not a *secret* publication. The moment an individual has more than one copy made it's obvious that the knowledge is meant to be shared. Why is it then that no one *anywhere* appears to have read the text? Knowles claimed he saw this document, but failed to give even the most elementary description of its format. Was it a four-folded leaflet, or a pamphlet, or a small book? As for the contents, he supplied – nothing. Are we to believe that he read the startling title and didn't read further? That stretches credulity to the very limits.

The only other person in the whole world who seems to have some knowledge of the Druitt papers is Maurice Gould. But is Mr Gould a reliable witness? Judging by his other statements, I'd say not. Consider the curious affair of the Head Librarian of Poplar. Gould is an enthusiastic student of the Whitechapel murders; when he first wrote to Farson he even sent him a manuscript he'd written about Jack: his nominee was a nameless cleric. So Gould was certainly aware of the importance of names, dates and places in tackling this problem. On learning that Farson had found a link between the Druitts and the Minories in the City of London, he made '. . . numerous inquiries, including a considerable time spent with an ex-head librarian of Poplar who was a fervent Ripperphile . . . From some recess in the library he produced an old either Voters' list or a Directory, which listed an M.J. Druitt as living in the Minories. This fact, together with the information you unearthed about Druitt, made such a link that I think we took it for granted that he was the man we sought. Although this Druitt lived in the Minories he was not listed as a doctor as far as I can recall.' These are Gould's own words quoted from his letter to Farson on 6 April 1971. But Farson was later unable to trace this important listing, and the ex-librarian had died.

Again we confront an incredible story. After numerous inquiries, and after spending considerable time in the search, Gould was shown just the evidence he'd been seeking. But did he note down the name, date and place of publication of the important list? Did he take a photocopy as proof? He did neither of these things. That in itself erodes his credibility. To be frank, such a casual attitude after investing so much time and devotion is unbelievable. How can unsubstantiated statements by Gould be used to prop up any theory?

With Knowles, it is somewhat different. The man is presumably dead and not able to add to his original recollections. If we accept Farson's recall as correct, Knowles was able to yoke the name Druitt with Jack's years before the connection had been made public, so hindsight is ruled out. But how could these names become interlinked before the disclosure of the Macnaghten paper? Farson didn't know the name; neither did any other Ripperphile who can be traced.

One answer to this quandary must involve the existence of yet another Ripper hoax. It is possible that the Druitt-Ripper theory was first exported to Australia by ex-Detective Leeson. Leeson had been injured during the famous Sidney Street seige of 1911, injured too severely for him to stay in the force, so he was pensioned off. He stayed in England until after the trials of the Sidney Street suspects, then left for Australia and the pleasures of a healthy climate.

His fame travelled with him. It seemed everyone wanted to hear him yarn away about English crime. Australians were then newly intrigued by the notion that Jack had actually been a citizen of Melbourne: this followed on the publication by Forbes Winslow of his letter from 'Jack's Melbourne lady friend'. Thus many of Leeson's conversations inevitably veered around to the question of the Ripper's identity.

It so happened that Leeson had an especially strong interest in the Ripper murders. One chapter in his book, *Lost London*, explains why. In 1891, he was in uniform and patrolling in the neighbourhood of The Mint. A police whistle shrilled out and Leeson headed for the sound. He found PC Thompson standing guard over a still-living woman – Frances Coles. Her throat was cut and her body mutilated. As far as the two constables were concerned, this showed that the Ripper was still at work.

Leeson's personal involvement with 'the Ripper' led him to think often and deeply about the sort of man who could be so barbarous. This, naturally, led him to discuss the many candidates put forward as the killer. Since Druitt was amongst the names he'd encountered, it would come to mind whenever he ran through a roster of the suspects. When he talked about Whitechapel, in Australia, some enterprising journalist may have noted the name and wondered if the late Dr Druitt could have been connected: the surname, after all, is a rare one. From that small beginning a spurious 'exposure document' could have been evolved, the ultimate object being to sell the 'inside story'.

If this conjecture holds good, then the spurious story must have lacked conviction, for no one snapped it up, and if it had had some power behind it, the papers would have fought each other for the rights. According to Gould's two informants, the asking price was only £500. In 1931, as we shall see later, the *Daily Express* had been prepared to pay that much simply for *the name* of the Ripper and nothing more.

For the moment, this must all stay on the plane of conjecture. Yet if we opt for the contrary explanation, that there was a genuine document written by Dr Lionel Druitt and privately printed by Fell in 1890, the problems become insurmountable.

For a start, what was the point of publishing, when the Druitt family desperately wanted secrecy, so much so that Montague's brother, solicitor William Druitt, had even lied before the Coroner's Inquest on his brother. William swore that he was the sole relative, so concealing the fact that there was another brother and also sisters. Obviously he was trying to protect the others, to spare them the anguish of having to give evidence and face cross-examination. But why? Possibly because 'the sexual insanity' we've heard of was too shameful a thing to have to discuss in public or private. There's also a possibility that Montague's oddness may have aroused suspicions within the family about his involvement with prostitutes and in the murders. Many other families entertained similar illusions about their own wayward members. In this case, the suicide may have been seen as a confirmation of suspicions.

Add to this the fact that Montague's younger brother, Captain Edward, arrived in Australia in 1889 to take up service with the Queensland Defence Forces, staying in Australia until 1892. Is it feasible that his cousin Lionel would publish anything which would not only distress the family back in England, but at the same time endanger Edward's military career?

If the alleged document named Montague and if it really was published by Lionel, then it would count as a cruel, heartless and completely uncalled-for piece of vaporizing, branding Lionel as irresponsible in the extreme, for there was no possible way he could prove his cousin was the Ripper. Any information he had was of necessity second-hand, gleaned from his family in England. Yet they wanted privacy above all things, privacy to nurse their suspicions because suspicions, in the end, were all they had. Even Macnaghten was able to say only that they 'believed', that they 'suspected'. Not once does he state that they possessed an atom of proof. Nothing that can be learned about Lionel marks him as capable of inflicting such suffering on his family. That, together with the complete absence of both the document and its printer in all known records, means the 'Australian evidence' has to be discounted completely.

Not much is then left, except a manufactured mystery surrounding the Druitts and the Minories. Daniel Farson felt he had hit on 'a piece of crucial evidence' when he discovered that Dr Lionel had once had a surgery in the Minories. Yet this was back in 1879: what possible connection has that with the Whitechapel murders? For Farson, though: 'This is the first link between [Montague] Druitt and the East End of London, the absence of which has been so baffling until now'.

Farson found 'the association beyond coincidence'. Association? That there *is* an association evades most people, but Farson tries hard to make a case by saying: 'There is every reason to believe that Montague and Lionel knew each other. Lionel was four years older than Montague and might well have felt it his duty to look after the boy when they were both in London. Lionel, a doctor, lived in the Minories at number 140, assisting Dr Thomas Thynne. It is reasonable to assume that Montague might have visited Lionel there, and this would explain his knowledge of the district. It is conceivable that he lived there himself after Lionel had left, and that at some time Lionel had grounds for suspicion.'

All this is more than puzzling. It is possible to visit the Minories every day of one's life and still know nothing of the rest of the East End. Apart from that, the evidence in the 1879 Medical Register only shows that Lionel worked for a short while in the Minories, perhaps just a few months. He was there in that year only, as an assistant to the regular practitioner, but his permanent address was elsewhere, at 8 Strathmore Gardens, W8, near Kensington Church Street.

What is it then that impels Farson to push this tenuous Minories connection so hard? The simple answer is faulty research. A failure to spot significant leads gave him false confidence and also allowed him completely to misinterpret some bogus Ripper letters, drawing the following conclusion: 'The importance of the Minories is not simply their position in the East End. They have a particular significance in the story of the Ripper. On 29 September 1888, the Ripper wrote from Liverpool: "Beware, I shall be at work on the 1st and 2nd inst., in Minories at twelve midnight, and I shall give the authorities a good chance, but there is never a policeman near when I am at work." '

For Farson, this is telling, since Catherine Eddowes was murdered on 30 September at Mitre Square, and Mitre Square is just a short walk from the Minories. He calls it '. . . one minute's walk' – which is doubtful, but unimportant. What is important is his quotation from the second letter from Liverpool. His incomplete quote reads: 'What fools the police are. I even give them the name of the street where I am living.' This gives the impression that the street referred to is the Minories of the first letter. Nothing of the sort. Farson has left out the first part of this jibe: the missing part is the street referred to. It reads: 'Prince William Street, Liverpool.'

By making these two letters important, Farson is claiming that Druitt either had them posted for him in Liverpool, or went to that city to post them himself. Both suggestions are preposterous. With post-boxes all over London, why bother to leave the metropolis? Farson also makes the assumption that the letters are genuine, yet there is nothing to distinguish them from the hundreds of hoax and crank letters sent to the press and the police. Even so, the Minories is the slender thread that Farson seeks to strengthen. In his original book he reiterates its importance twice more and sums up: '. . . The Minories was referred to in one of the "letters from the Ripper" and lies within a few minutes' walk of the various murders.' That helps along his assumption that 'Montague Druitt kept in touch with the Minories and possibly rented a room there himself.'

There was a certain recklessness about Farson's reasoning which led him to grab at anything to aid his weak case. This is shown in the postscript of his 1973 Sphere edition, where he includes two hilarious stories about Jack and the Minories.

One story involved a Mr Herbert Rowley and a family yarn about a great-aunt. The aunt was a nurse at the London Hospital but lived out, in the Minories. One foggy night in 1888 an outbreak of fever led to a shortage of staff at the hospital. A messenger boy called on the off-duty aunt and summoned her back to the wards. She stepped out into the fog and walked up the deserted Minories. After she had covered only a short distance, a man came from the shadows, questioned her and offered to walk with her to the hospital. She accepted, and they walked together in silence, until the hospital gates were reached. Then, in his educated voice, the man said, 'I see that you are a respectable woman.' He turned away, paused and then said, 'I am Jack the Ripper,' and hurried off. The nurse fainted and by the time she grew coherent, it was too late to intercept the man. Though the police were called and the hunt was made '. . . it was "gone to ground" or *that small room in the Minories*' (Farsons's italics).

What small room? A story which simply places a nurse in the Minories ends by placing Jack there as well, without a particle of evidence, and Farson takes it seriously.

More comic still is the '. . . exciting new evidence from Frederick Pocock of Romford, Essex'. This involved a fried fish shop in the Minories next to the railway arch. The shop was owned by Pocock's relatives and from them his mother learned that '. . . this man Druitt had an attic room (on the third floor) and after the murders he used to burn a lot of rubbish in the cellar in the furnace under the pans and stewed eel copper.' Farson summarizes the story by saying: 'Pocock's mother was accosted by a man at the Aldgate East end of the Minories and she suspected him of being the Ripper. When she mentioned the incident to her relative at the fried fish shop, her description was surprisingly like the lodger in the attic room above.'

A fishy story indeed. Frederick Pocock wasn't born until 1892, so he obtained this gossip years after the last murder. He was eighty-one when he retold it all to Farson. By that time he could easily have absorbed the name Druitt from the newspaper and television publicity and muddled it in with his recollections of his mother's fancies. But Farson is blind to this. He solemnly comments: 'Mr Pocock's story provides yet another link with the Minories and the noose around Montague tightens. "Beware," wrote the Ripper on 29th September. "I shall be at work . . . in Minories at twelve midnight." And later the contemptuous boast: "What fools the police are. I even give them the name of the street where

I am living." ' If nothing else, Dan Farson tends to lay it on thick.

One of the *Punch* Ripper cartoons is entitled *The Nemesis of Neglect*, a phrase that could well be adopted to describe the Minories myth. By neglecting to scour the contemporary papers hard enough, Farson fell into a trap. There *was* a connection between Jack the Ripper and the Minories. And it *was* firmly established in September 1888. But it has nothing whatsoever to do with Montague Druitt. It involved the arrest of an aggressive individual on Tuesday 18 September.

The *Penny Illustrated Paper* for 22 September gives this account:

> Charles Ludwig, forty, a decently-attired German who professed not to understand English, and giving an address as 1, Minories was charged on Tuesday, at the Thames Police-Court with being drunk and threatening to stab Alexander Finlay of 51 Leman Street, Whitechapel. The prosecutor said that very early that morning he was standing at a coffee-stall in the Whitechapel-Road when Ludwig came up in a drunken condition. In consequence, the person in charge of the stall refused to serve him. Ludwig seemed much annoyed, and said to the witness, 'What are you looking at?' He then pulled out a long bladed knife, and tried to stab witness with it. Ludwig followed him round the stall, and made several attempts to stab him, until witness threatened to knock a dish on his head. A constable came up, and he was then given into custody . . . Witness and constable Johnson had previously received information that Ludwig was wanted on the City ground for attempting to cut a woman's throat with a razor. On the way to the station the prisoner dropped a long-bladed knife, which was open, and when he was searched a razor and a long-bladed pair of scissors were found on him . . . Considerable excitement prevailed in the neighbourhood, owing to a report that the prisoner, a German barber, was connected with the recent murders in Whitechapel, and that some important discoveries would result from his capture . . .

For days the rumours circulated that Jack the Ripper was the man from the Minories. Eventually, there were other suspects to replace Ludwig. But the Ripper-Minories conjunction was aired in the national press ten days before the first Liverpool 'Ripper' letter was penned. That letter simply reflected the state of play at the time, and nothing more.

So that has to be the last word on the Druitt theory, but in dismissing it, let us agree that it was different. For a while it did seem to have some merit, if only because of Macnaghten's papers. That made it well worth pursuing, but only up to a point, the point at which the hoax element became clear. And that was reached a long time ago!

8

The Chicago Connection

'The Third World War did not break out in November 1970, but the newspaper headlines in every country could not have been bigger or blacker. WAS JACK THE RIPPER OF ROYAL BLOOD? The question was repeated again and again.'

Those are the words of Nigel Morland, whose magazine the *Criminologist* created this storm by advancing a totally unexpected candidate for the role of the Ripper. More than 3,000 newspapers took up the story and a new era for Ripper-hunters dawned. But this fresh trail cannot be intelligently explored without proper bearings, and these have to be taken from a point as far back as 1895.

On 28 April 1895, the Chicago *Sunday Times-Herald* printed an astonishing article which claimed that the Ripper had been detected, trapped and incarcerated in 1888. This piece, 'The Capture of Jack the Ripper', was destined to have a crucial and malign influence on future research. Here, for the first time since 1895, is the complete text of this essential account:

> The story recently told by Dr Howard, a well-known London physician to William Greer Harrison, of the Bohemian Club, in San Francisco, in regard to the fate of Jack the Ripper, and which is at last given to the world, unseals the lips of a gentleman of this city, who is thus enabled to give the *Times-Herald* a full and exhaustive account of that exhaustive search by London detectives, which at the conclusion of years of unremitting labor, has resulted in fixing the identity of the famous Whitechapel murderer beyond the shadow of a doubt.
>
> The Dr Howard referred to was one of a dozen London physicians who sat at a court of medical inquiry or as a commission in lunacy upon their brother physician, for at last it was definitely proved that the dreaded 'Jack the Ripper' was no less a person than a physician in high standing, and in fact was a man enjoying the patronage of the best society in the west end of London. When it was absolutely proved beyond peradventure that the physician in question was the murderer, and his insanity fully established by a commission de lunatico inquirendo, all parties having knowledge of the facts were sworn to secrecy. Up to this time of Dr Howard's disclosure this oath had been rigidly adhered to.

THE CHICAGO CONNECTION

A London clubman, now in Chicago, who is acquainted with Dr Howard, is of the opinion that, being in a foreign country and perhaps under the influence of wine, Dr Howard has permitted his tongue to wag too freely. Coupled with this conjecture he said yesterday to a reporter of the *Times-Herald*:

'I notice that Dr Howard has not revealed the name of the physician who committed the murders. For this he has reason to be thankful, as such an act would have resulted in the total destruction of his London practice. As it is, he will doubtless be privately reprimanded by the Royal College of Physicians and Surgeons, as an oath administered under such circumstances is considered of the most sacred and binding nature.'

The story of Dr Howard is substantially correct, as far as it goes. When 'Jack the Ripper' was finally run to earth it was discovered that he was a physician in good standing, with an extensive practice. He had been ever since he was a student at Guy's Hospital, an ardent and enthusiastic vivisectionist. Through some extraordinary natural contradiction, instead of the sight of pain softening him, as is the case with most devotees of scientific experiments, it had an opposite effect. This so grew upon him that he experienced the keenest delight in inflicting tortures upon defenceless animals. One of his favourite pastimes was to remove the eyelids from a rabbit and expose it for hours, in a fixed position, to a blinding sun. He would take a seat near it, totally forgetful of meals, of the passage of time and of everything except the exquisite sensations he experienced in watching the agonized contortions of his victim.

This passion for inflicting pain so grew upon the man, who was afterwards to rank as a disciple of cruelty with Nero or Ghengis Kahn, that as he approached manhood and his softer nature impelled him to seek a wife he could hardly restrain himself from an indulgence in his barbaric pursuits long enough to woo and win her. He had scarcely been married a month before his wife discovered that he had a mania for inflicting pain. In testifying before the commission she gave the following extraordinary evidence:

'One night we were sitting in the drawing room. It was quite late. I arose to go to bed. When I arrived upstairs I remembered that I had left my watch upon the drawing room mantelpiece. I descended the stairs. As I approached the drawing room I heard the sounds of a cat mewing piteously. Looking through the door, which happened to be open, I was horrified to see my husband holding a cat over the flame of the moderator lamp. I was too frightened to do anything but retreat upstairs. When my husband came to bed along toward daylight I felt that I was occupying the same couch with a monster. I discovered later that he had spent almost the whole night in burning the cat to death.

'The next day he was as kind and loving as possible. I discovered later that he was subject to an unconquerable mania for inflicting pain. It was quite possible for me, as I studied him closely, to tell when these moods were coming on. On such occasions some apparently trivial act would put me on my guard. He was apt at such times to begin by catching a fly and twirling it impaled upon a pin. He was a strange contradiction. When our little boy, only four years old, imitated him once in this respect the father was actually shocked and was so indignant that he gave the child a sound whipping. As the boy screamed with the pain of the punishment the ferocious side of my husband's nature asserted itself. He would in all probability have beaten the child to death if I had not interfered. In his normal moods he was an excellent husband and father and one of the gentlest and most tractable of men. I have frequently heard him express sincere sympathy with persons in misfortune.'

The circumstances which led to the detection of this inhuman monster with a dual nature are extraordinary and altogether unparalleled in the history of crime. As the fact of the arrest and imprisonment of Jack the

Robert Lees – a master of psychic fiction.

Ripper has now been divulged by Dr Howard, it is only right that proper credit should be given to the man who put the London police upon his track. He himself has sacredly observed his promise – he refused to take any oath on the ground of religious scruples – not to divulge the identity of the Ripper.

Robert James Lees, the gentleman to whom the unfortunate of the east end of London owe their present immunity from the attacks of a monster who for long years made every one of them venture out at night literally with her life in her hands, is the person entitled to the credit of tracking Jack the Ripper. Mr Lees is at present the proprietor of a novel institution for the higher education of the workingmen at Peckham, a suburb of London. Over 1,800 workmen attend his classes and he has invested a large sum of money in the enterprise which is now on a paying basis. Mr Lees is recognised today as one of the most advanced labor leaders in England and is an intimate friend of Kier Hardy, the leader of an independent labor party. He at present resides at 26 The Gardens, Peckham Rye, London S.E.

In his early years Mr Lees developed an extraordinary clairvoyant power, which enabled him to discern, as with the eyes of a seer, things hidden from the comprehension of ordinary men born without this singular gift. At the age of 19 he was summoned before the queen at Birmingham, where he gave evidence of his powers as a clairvoyant which excited her majesty's utmost astonishment. Having considerable means of his own, however, he devoted himself to literary pursuits, became a profound theologian and ultimately took up the study of spiritualism and theosophy. He is at present the recognised leader of the Christian Spiritualists in Great Britain.

At the time of the first three murders by the ripper, Mr Lees was in the height of his clairvoyant powers. One day he was writing in his study when he became convinced that the ripper was about to commit another murder. He tried in vain to dispel the feeling. As he sat at his table the whole scene arose before him. He seemed to see two persons, a man and a woman, walking down the length of a mean street. He followed them in his mind's eye and saw them enter a narrow court. He looked and read the name of the court. There was a gin palace near this court, ablaze with light. Looking through the windows he saw that the hands of the clock in the bar pointed to 12.40, the hour at which the public houses are closed for the night in London.

As he looked he saw the man and the woman enter a dark corner of the court. The woman was half drunk. The man was perfectly sober. He was dressed in a dark suit of Scotch tweed, carried a light overcoat on his arm, and his light blue eyes glittered in the rays of the lamplight which dimly illuminated the dingy retreat the pair had chosen.

The woman leaned against the wall and the man put one hand over her mouth. She struggled in a feeble manner, as if too much overcome by liquor to make any effectual resistance. The man then drew a knife from his inside vest pocket and cut the woman's throat. The blood streamed out from the wound, some of it spurting over his shirt-front. He held his hand over the woman's mouth until she fell to the ground. Then divesting the lower limbs of his victim of their apparel, the butcher inflicted sundry gashes upon her with his long knife. These were delivered in a scientific manner, and resulted in the ripper's laying certain organs beside the body of his victim. He then deliberately wiped his knife upon the clothes of the woman, sheathed it and, putting on his light overcoat deliberately buttoned it up so as to hide the blood stains on his shirt-front, after which he walked calmly away from the scene of the murder.

Such was the extraordinary clairvoyant vision presented to the second sight of Mr Lees. So impressed was he by what he had thus miraculously witnessed, that he at once went to Scotland Yard and detailed the whole matter to the detectives. As they regarded him as nothing short of a lunatic, and had been for some months visited by all sorts and conditions of cranks with Jack-the-Ripper theories, he naturally received little attention.

By way of humoring one whom they considered a harmless lunatic, the sergeant on duty took down the name of the place where Mr Lees said the crime would be committed and also noted that the hands of the clock in the mythical public house had pointed to 12.40. at the moment when the Ripper and his victim had entered the court.

At 12.30. on the following night a woman entered the public house facing on the court in question. She was quite under the influence of liquor, and the bar keeper refused to serve her. She left the place swearing and using vile language. She was seen by another witness to enter the court again at 12.30. in company with a man dressed in a dark suit and carrying a light overcoat upon his arm. Witness thought the man was an American because he wore a soft felt hat, and added that 'he looked like a gentleman'.

This was the evidence given before the deputy coroner, who held an inquest on the body of a woman who had been found in the very spot described by Mr Lees 'with her throat cut from ear to ear and otherwise indecently and horribly mutilated' – to quote the coroner's records. Mr Lees himself was indescribably shocked when he learned of the murder the next day. Taking with him a trusted man-servant he visited the scene of the outrage. To use his own language – 'I felt almost as if I was an accessory before the fact. It made such an impression upon me that my whole nervous system was seriously shaken. I could not sleep at night and under the advice of a physician I removed with my family to the continent.'

During his visit abroad Mr Lees was no longer troubled by these strange hallucinations, notwithstanding the fact that while he was absent the 'ripper' had added to his list of crimes no less than four additional atrocious murders. It then became necessary for Mr Lees to return to London.

One day, while riding in an omnibus from Shepherd's Bush in company with his wife, he experienced a renewal of the strange sensations which had preceded his former clairvoyant condition. The omnibus ascended Notting Hill. It stopped at the top, and a man entered the interior of the vehicle. Mr Lees at once experienced a singular sensation. Looking up he perceived that the new passenger was a man of medium size. He noticed that he was dressed in a dark suit of Scotch tweed, over which he wore a light overcoat. He had a soft felt hat on his head.

Over a year had elapsed since Mr Lees' clairvoyant vision, but the picture of the murderer had been indelibly impressed upon his mind.

Leaning over to his wife he remarked earnestly, 'That is Jack the Ripper,' his wife laughed at this, and told him not to be foolish. 'I am not mistaken,' replied Mr Lees, 'I feel it.'

The omnibus traversed the entire length of the Edgware road, turning into Oxford street at the marble arch. At this point the man in the light overcoat got out.

Mr Lees determined to follow him. Bidding his wife continue on her journey in the direction of home, he followed the man down Park lane. About half way down the thoroughfare he met a constable, to whom he pointed out the man in the light overcoat informing him that he was the dreaded 'ripper' and asking that he be arrested. The constable laughed at him, and threatened to 'run him in'.

It seems that the 'ripper' must have entertained some apprehension that he was in danger, for on reaching Apsley House he jumped into a cab and was driven rapidly down Piccadilly. A minute later Mr Lees met a police sergeant to whom he confided his suspicions.

'Show me the constable who refused to arrest him!' exclaimed the sergeant. 'Why it was only this morning that we received news at the Bow Street station that the "ripper" was coming in this direction.'

That night Mr Lees again received premonitions that the 'ripper' was about to commit another murder. The scene of this outrage was not so distinct as on the former occasion, but the face of the murdered woman was clearly defined. Mr Lees noted with great particularity the aspect of the 'ripper's' victim. A peculiarity of the mutilations, which were somewhat similar to the first, was that one ear was completely severed from the face and the other remained hanging by a mere shred of flesh.

As soon as he recovered from his trance and the consequent shock he experienced in witnessing this dreamlike tragedy, Mr Lees hastened to Scotland Yard, where he insisted on having an immediate audience with the head inspector of police. The functionary listened with a smile of incredulity to the first portion of his visitor's story, which died away at once, however, upon his reaching that portion of his narrative, which spoke of the victim's ears being severed from her head.

With a trembling hand and a face which plainly betokened the effect of Mr Lees' communication, the officer drew a postal card forth from his desk and laid it before his visitor.

It was an ordinary postal card, written in red ink. In addition it bore the marks of two bloody fingers, which had been impressed upon it by the writer, and which remained as a kind of bloody sign manual upon its calendered surface.

This postal card read as follows:

> Tomorrow night I shall again take my revenge, claiming from a class of women who have made themselves most obnoxious to me my ninth victim.
>
> JACK THE RIPPER
>
> P.S. To prove that I am really 'Jack the Ripper' I will cut off the ears of this ninth victim.

Dr Lees was no sooner confronted with this awful confirmation of his second vision than he fainted dead away and remained as one absolutely insensible to what was going on around him.

It must be recollected that at this time the entire British metropolis, comprising within a radius of twenty miles of Charing Cross a population of nearly 7,000,000 souls, was completely terrorised by this awful series of murders, which shocked indeed the whole of christendom by their unparalleled barbarity, the frequency of their occurrence and the apparent complete immunity enjoyed by their inhuman perpetrator.

The inspector himself, who was a religious man, looked upon the extraordinary coincidence of the receipt of the post card – with the contents of which he alone was familiar – and the story of Mr Lees, as a warning sent from heaven, and as a divine intimation that he must leave no stone unturned to bring this monster to justice. All that day he concentrated his entire energies upon the problem of how best to cover the intricate territory known as 'the Whitechapel district'. He had at his command a force of nearly 10,000 constables. By dusk of the next day no less than 3,000 of these in citizens' clothes, in addition to 1,500 detectives, disguised as mechanics and dock labourers, were patrolling the courts and alleys of Whitechapel.

Notwithstanding these precautions 'Jack the Ripper' penetrated the cordon, slew his victim and made his escape. The inspector, when told that this victim had been discovered with one ear completely severed from her body and the other hanging from her head by a mere shred of flesh, turned deathly pale and it was some time before he recovered his usual self possession.

Mr Lees was so affected by this last tragedy that he at once removed to the continent. While he was thus abroad, the 'ripper' completed his sixteenth murder, and had coolly informed the Scotland Yard authorities that he 'intended to kill twenty and then cease'.

Shortly after this Mr Lees returned to England where he made the acquaintance of Roland B. Shaw, a mining stockbroker, of New York and Fred C. Beckwith, of Broadhead, Wis. who was then the financial promoter of an American syndicate in London.

These three gentlemen were dining one day in the *Criterion* when Mr Lees turned to his two companions suddenly and exclaimed:

'Great God! Jack the Ripper has committed another murder.'

Mr Shaw looked at his watch and found it was eleven minutes to eight. At ten minutes past eight a policeman discovered the body of a woman in Crown court, in the Whitechapel district, with her throat cut from ear to ear and her body bearing all the marks of the Ripper's handiwork.

Mr Lees and his companions at once went to Scotland Yard. The news of the murder had not yet reached the inspector, but while Mr Lees was relating his story, a telegram arrived giving full details of the outrage.

The Inspector, taking with him two men in plain clothes, at once drove to Crown court in company with Mr Lees and the two Americans. As they entered the court Mr Lees exclaimed:

'Look in the angle of the wall. There is something written there.'

The inspector ran forward, and not having a dark lantern with him struck a match. As the tiny flame flared up the words 'Seventeen, Jack the Ripper' done in chalk upon the wall were distinctly visible.

The inspector by this time was in a condition closely bordering on insanity. It must be borne in mind that this madman had for years baffled all the resources of the greatest police force in the world – that rendered desperate at last, the British authorities had summoned to their assistance the most experienced detectives in France, Germany, Holland, Italy, Spain and America, that they had lavished immense sums in an endeavour to trace the fiend, that there was then pending an aggregate reward of £30,000 together with a life pension of £1,500 per annum, all to go to the man who should first deliver to justice the terrible 'Ripper'.

As before stated, the inspector seemed to recognise in Mr Lees an instrument of providence – and he determined then and there to avail himself of his marvellous, though altogether incomprehensible powers.

After an earnest appeal from the inspector, Mr Lees consented to try and track the 'Ripper' – much in the same way as the bloodhound pursues a criminal. There seemed to be some magnetic wave connecting an impalpable sense he possessed with the fugitive. All that night Mr Lees submitted himself to his strange magnetic influence and traversed swiftly the streets of London. The inspector and his aids followed a few feet behind him. At last, at 4 o'clock in the morning, with pale face and bloodshot eyes, the human bloodhound halted at the gates of a west end mansion, gasping with cracked and swollen lips, as he pointed to an upper chamber where a faint light yet gleamed.

'There is the murderer – the man you are looking for.'

'It is impossible,' returned the inspector. 'That is the residence of one of the most celebrated physicians in the west end.'

The most extraordinary part of this well nigh incredible narrative is now to come. The inspector had been so strongly impressed with the clairvoyant powers of Mr Lees that he determined to put them to the crowning proof.

'If you will describe to me,' he said, 'the interior of the doctor's hall I will arrest him, but I shall do so at the risk of losing my position, which I have won by over twenty years' faithful service.'

'The hall has a high porter's chair of black oak on the right hand, as you enter it, a stained glass window at the extreme end, and a large mastiff is at this moment asleep at the foot of the stairs,' replied Mr Lees without any hesitation.

They waited then till 7 o'clock, the hour at which the servants begin to stir in a fashionable London residence. They then entered the house and learned that the doctor was still in bed. They requested to be allowed to see his wife. The servant left them standing in the hall, and Mr Lees called the inspector's attention to the fact that there was no mastiff visible as he had described, though his description of the hall in all other respects tallied exactly. Upon questioning the servant as to the whereabouts of the dog she informed Mr Lees that it generally slept at the foot of the stairs, and that she let it out into the back garden every morning.

When the inspector heard this he exclaimed:

'Great heavens!' adding in an undertone to his companion, 'It is the hand of God.'

In the course of half an hour's searching examination the doctor's wife, who was a beautiful woman, confessed that she did not believe her husband was of sound mind. There had been moments when he had threatened herself and her children. At such times she had been accustomed to lock herself up. She had noted with heart-breaking dread that whenever a Whitechapel murder occurred her husband was absent from home.

An hour later the inspector had completed his arrangements for the examination of the doctor, and had summoned to his aid, two of the greatest experts on insanity in the metropolis. When accused, the doctor admitted that his mind had been unbalanced for some years and that of late there had been intervals of time during which he had no recollection of what he had been doing. When told that they believed he had been guilty of the Whitechapel murders during these intervals, he expressed the greatest repugnance and horror of such deeds, speaking as if the murderer was quite a different person to himself, and expressing great willingness to bring him to justice. He told the physicians that he had on one or two occasions found himself sitting in his rooms as if suddenly aroused from a long stupor, and in one instance he had found blood upon his shirt front, which he attributed to nosebleed. On another occasion his face had been all scratched up.

On hearing this the inspector caused a thorough search of the house to be made, when ample proofs were found that the doctor was the murderer. Among others the detectives brought to light the famous Scotch tweed suit and soft felt hat, together with the light overcoat. When convinced of his guilt, the unfortunate physician begged them to kill him at once, as he 'could not live under the same roof with such a monster'.

As stated in the early part of this article, an exhaustive inquiry before a commission in lunacy developed the fact that while in one mood the doctor was a most worthy man, in the other he was a terrible monster. He was at once removed to a private insane asylum in Islington, and he is now the most intractable and dangerous madman confined in that establishment.

In order to account for the disappearance of the doctor from society a sham death and burial were gone through, and an empty coffin, which now reposes in the family vaults in Kensal Green, is supposed to contain the mortal remains of a great west end physician, whose untimely death all London mourned.

None of the keepers know that the desperate maniac who flings himself from side to side in his padded cell and makes the long watches of the night hideous with his piercing cries is the famous 'Jack the Ripper'. To them and to the visiting inspectors he is simply known as Thomas Mason, alias No. 124.

Now, the colouring may be melodramatic, but apart from that it all seems so precise. Here are the details of the events all set down in easily verifiable chronological order. Here we find times pinpointed, people named, and locations clearly indicated. But despite this air of exactitude, are we really looking at an authentic summary?

9

The Ananias League
Steps In

The Chicago revelations bear blatantly false credentials. The very first paragraph strains one's belief. We are asked to accept that Dr Howard's few brief remarks in San Francisco were enough to unseal the lips of a confidant of Lees in Chicago. In turn this implies that Lees had violated his promise of secrecy and confided in a man of dubious ethics. This line of reasoning could be taken further, but it would be a sheer waste of energy. The fact is that this story, from start to finish, is a massive hoax. Not only that, but it is deliberately constructed as a self-revealing hoax. Every paragraph proclaims its bogus nature. Not a single paragraph, in truth, deals with *any* of the real Jack the Ripper murders.

Let us take the chronology for a start. The murders are depicted as taking place over a period of years, but the real Ripper murders were committed in a short period of just over ten weeks. Then take the number of victims. In reality five women died at the hands of the Ripper, yet the Chicago piece clocks up seventeen deaths. As for the carefully logged times, these are equally absurd. Lees's 'initial vision' recorded a murder happening at 12.40 at night – none of the murders took place at that time. His remarkable clairvoyant experience of the last murder, witnessed by two Americans, placed the Crown Court murder at eleven minutes to eight. Again, no murder took place at that time, and it is equally certain that no Ripper murder took place at Crown Court.

The episode of the bloodstained postcard is yet another droll invention. No such card was ever received by the police; but the hoaxer had credited Lees with a vision which involved the severance of an ear, and the card gives weight to that vision and to the sequel of the 'ninth victim' being discovered '. . . with one ear completely severed . . . and the other hanging from her head by a mere shred of flesh'.

Another glaring absurdity is built into the Park Lane episode. Lees loses his quarry due to the disbelief of the patrolling constable. Shortly afterwards an enlightened and indignant police sergeant fumes: 'Show me the constable who refused to arrest him! Why it was only this morning that we received news at the Bow Street station that the "ripper" was coming in this direction.'

So the West End police 'knew' that the Ripper was due in their territory that day. But why that day? According to the Chicago story itself, the Ripper lived and practised *in the West End*, so he was there every day, in and about their territory, never needing to come in from an area outside.

Daft? Of course – but then the hoaxers were intent on making their brain-child as grotesque as possible, gleefully piling on the absurdities to see just how much they could get away with. So who were these hoaxers? What were their motives? Well, before answering those specific questions, we need to look at the long tradition of newspaper hoaxing that prevailed in the USA.

Five years before this Chicago hoax was fashioned, American writer Henry Clay Lukens wrote: 'Hoaxing of the too credulous reading public has been nowhere so successfully practiced as in this country . . . Ananiases have not been infrequent . . . the *New York Herald's* startling bogus, half-column-headlined story of the escaped menagerie at Central park, and a Brazilian Monte Cristo wedding, detailed with reportorial gravity and precision in the *New York Times*, are both classics of their simulative kind.'

Just four months after Lukens made those comments the Chicago *Daily Tribune* published a convincing study of the Indian rope trick. Apparently a Mr S. Ellmore had investigated the phenomenon and found it absolutely genuine. Drawings and photographs backed up his reports and, for a while, believers in the occult and the paranormal were triumphant. Here was the splendid proof! Four months later the excitement waned, when on 6 December the paper admitted that the whole thing was an invention launched to boost its circulation. The very name of their fictitious investigator had been a give-away to an intelligent reader. But the paper had wanted to sell more and they did so by concocting the reports of S. Ellmore.

This hoax tradition flourished well into the twentieth century. Indeed, William Salisbury's *The Career of a Journalist* is a veritable encyclopaedia of fakes in which the author participated or had intimate knowledge, while Curtis MacDougall in his book, *Hoaxes*, deals with some 180 newspaper hoaxes, most of them of American origin. Added to this tradition, and often closely intertwined with it, was the American love of tall story pow-wows, and Ananias or liars' clubs. Nowhere was this eccentric passion more cherished than in the various Bohemian clubs of the land, and in the case of the 1895 Chicago story, the initial impetus stemmed from San Francisco's Bohemian Club, one of the most famous.

When it came to tall tales of the Ripper-kind, Chicago couldn't afford to be outdone, for it was in Chicago that the earliest grotesque theory about the murders had been devised. On 3 October 1888, Dr J. G. Kiernan, editor of the *Medical Standard*, proclaimed that the Whitechapel murderer was a cannibal pure and simple. And it was in Chicago that the earliest full-length fantasy on the murders was published: in 1889, Chicago's Eagle Publishing Company issued E. O. Tilburn's *The Whitechapel Mystery: Jack the Ripper, A Psychological Problem*. In it, the killer was identified as an English doctor aided and abetted by an American policeman. From then on, Chicago's Bohemians seemed to take the London mystery very much to their hearts.

Nowhere else in the States was the subject more debated and theorized over. As a logical consequence, the devotees created a unique club dedicated to Jack the Ripper; and logically, they named it The Whitechapel Club. Newspaper editor Julius Chambers gave a little whiff of the atmosphere of the club when he wrote: 'The Whitechapel Club, Chicago . . . entertained me at dinner sitting under a noose and wearing a black cap that "was said" to have covered the face of a murderer hanged at Joliet. Quaint, frolicsome chaps were the Whitechapellers of that period.' What Chambers forgot to mention was that the dining table was made in the form of a huge coffin with one coffin-nail for each member.

Journalist James Milne went one better when he revealed that: 'In Chicago, I was taken one night to a Whitechapel Club, which the literary and artistic Bohemians had so christened, because it sported an atmosphere of the "horrible and awful", as well as a kindly hospitality. In particular it invited "tall stories" from its members, and would then shout them down with a weird chorus, of which one verse ran:

> In the days of old Rameses; are you on?
> They told the same thing, they told the same thing.
> In the days of old Rameses, the story had paresis –
> Are you on, are you on, are you on?

We need look no further to find the culprits behind the 1895 hoax. This strange, frolicsome club was not only the focal point for knowledgeable Ripperphiles, but it was also a tall story workshop. As well as that, it was a favourite club of many of the editors and reporters on the *Sunday Times-Herald*, with its premises actually at the rear of the *Times-Herald* building. The combination of these three elements makes it certain that club graduates united to draft this spoof report. For oddly enough, it needed real expertise to write a Ripper yarn that *avoided* using a single fragment of the authentic information. It would have been far easier to

Above and opposite: The Whitechapel Club, Chicago,
where hoaxes were burnished to perfection.

take the real events and add some bogus bits and pieces to them, but that would have diminished the value of the tall story. For in all such good spoofs a dashing boldness is called for: only this ensures that the exploit wins the unstinted admiration of the boon-companions who are party to the secret.

The enthusiasts who crafted the piece were not only bold, but they took special pleasure in building in clues and allusions easily understood by students of the crimes. It was, in a way, something on the lines of the knowledgeable games present-day Sherlockians play with each other. There, behind the gross parodies in the article, you can spot the newspaper references that served as inspiration. For example, the mad doctor's sadistic pursuits – impaling flies, roasting a cat, blinding rabbits and so on – are based on the hypothetical portrait of the Ripper printed in the *Illustrated Police News* on 6 October 1888. The article said:

> 'There can be no doubt, however, that human beings are met with who . . . manifest from their infancy an enjoyment in inflicting cruelty which is certainly congenital. Dr Savage has known children of the tenderest ages who, from pulling off the wings of flies, proceed to the baking of live frogs and to the boring out of birds' eyes. Their exploits have culminated in the kicking of cats and dogs to death, and in the pouring over

them of boiling water or burning them alive . . . it can be no matter of
surprise if they grow up to be the murderers of their fellow beings . . . The
apparently purposeless character of the crimes by which we have lately
been shocked goes far to suggest that their perpetrator . . . is really one of
these unhappy creatures.

In turn, the lurid postcard threatening to cut off the ears of the 'ninth
victim' is based on the two famous epistles posted on 25 September and 1
October 1888. The initial letter promised to '. . . clip the ladys [*sic*] ears off
and send to the police officers'. It was written in red ink. While the postcard that followed said apologetically: 'had no time to get ears for police.'

Similarly, the writing on the wall item, with its inflated number of
victims, is based on the reports surfacing after the Chapman killing. A
message was rumoured to have been found scrawled on the door of 29
Hanbury Street: 'This is the fourth. I will murder sixteen more and then
give myself up.' This 'writing' was nothing but the product of an inflamed
imagination. So, ironically, one phantom message later served to inspire
yet another phantom message.

The Chicago clowns were fortunate. It was then the heyday of so-called
'yellow journalism'. At that time, sensational columns were eagerly
sought after by the newspapers, and journalistic ethics were callously
neglected. Professor Edwin Emery notes this in his history of journalism,

The Press and America. Of the yellow-pressmen he writes: 'Theirs was a shrieking, gaudy, sensation-loving, devil-may-care kind of journalism which lured the reader by any possible means. It seized upon the techniques of writing, illustrating and printing which were the prides of the new journalism and turned them to perverted uses. It made the high drama of life a cheap melodrama, and it twisted the facts of each day into whatever form seemed best to produce sales for the howling newsboy. Worst of all, instead of giving its readers effective leadership, it offered a palliative of sin, sex and violence.'

'Sin, sex and violence' – the Ripper feature offered all three, plus the added bonus of the supernatural element and a mysterious, high-placed mad doctor. There was an additional incentive to run the story just then. The pressmen had learned that the talkative Dr Forbes Winslow was due in New York to chair the mental diseases section of the International Medico-Legal Congress. Winslow had earlier been courted by the *New York Herald*, which recorded his views on the Ripper-hunt, so once he was actually in New York, it was certain he would be chased after for further copy, including the latest on the Whitechapel mystery. Thus forewarned, the Chicago paper marketed their 'Ripper exclusive' six days before Forbes Winslow docked in the States.

It was all beautifully in line with the philosophy summed up by Hearst's editorial lieutenant, Arthur McEwen: 'What we're after is the "gee-whiz" emotion. We run our paper so that when the reader opens it he says: "Gee-Whiz." '

And it was all so very, very good for the circulation. Cash, not quality, was the great god of those times, as Professor Emery confirms, using the *New York Journal* as his example: '. . . Journalistic historian Willard G. Bleyer cited these headlines of the *Journal* published during the fall of 1896, and undoubtedly was justified in linking them with a circulating jump of 125,000 in a single month: "Real American Monsters and Dragons" – over a story of the discovery of fossil remains by an archaeological expedition. "A Marvellous New Way of Giving Medicine: Wonderful Results from Merely Holding Tubes of Drugs near Entranced Patients" – a headline which horrified medical researchers. "Henry James' New Novel of Immorality and Crime: The Surprising Plunge of the Great Novelist in the Field of Sensational Fiction" – the *Journal's* way of announcing publication of *The Other House*.'

Everything, then, favoured the hoaxers, but how did they expect to get away with their involvement of Dr Howard and R.J. Lees? Did they blindly trust that both men would keep silent and see their reputations soiled?

10

Medium Rare?

In the case of Dr Howard, an avenue of escape lay open, for no Christian name was ever given, not even an initial to work on, and no address was supplied. Even so, knowledgeable readers took the doctor to be Dr Benjamin Howard who lived at the St George's Club, Hanover Square, London. This is certainly what the English paper, the *People*, thought, for on 19 May 1895 it commented on the Chicago feature and wrote:

> Not long ago there appeared in a London weekly a terribly realistic description of a criminal lunatic who was confined in one of our penal establishments. The man had degenerated into an inarticulate beast. He was said to be the fiend known as 'Jack the Ripper' . . . It was only regarded as a fanciful narrative from the pen of a clever novelist. It may have been true nevertheless, and colour is given to this possibility by a statement which has recently been made in San Francisco by Dr Howard, an Anglo-American physician not unknown in London, and who is, I believe, a member of the Royal College of Surgeons. I knew Dr Howard very well at one time, and always regarded him as a man of intellectual power. He has been telling the Bohemian Club of San Francisco a remarkable story, no other than the true and particular account of the capture and confinement of 'Jack the Ripper', who, he declared, was no other than a well-known London physician, now supposed to be dead. For the sake of the profession and for other reasons he was wiped out by a mock death and burial, but at the present time is under restriction as a dangerous lunatic. It was, according to Dr Howard, one Robert James Lees, a philanthropist and advanced labour leader, and a friend of Keir Hardie, who, through his extraordinary clairvoyant powers, led the London detectives to the home of the murderer. Mr Lees is mentioned as still residing at 26 The Gardens, Peckham Rye. At present he is the leader of 'the Christian spiritualists in Great Britain'. A commission de lunatico inquirendo established the facts against the criminal who confessed to mental aberrations, during which he lived some other life and awoke to find himself in strange places under strange circumstances. Dr Howard affirms that he was a member of the commission that sent 'Jack the Ripper' to an asylum for the rest of his days. Dr Howard will have to answer for the breach of a vow which he made in common with his colleagues never to reveal what had passed. The story is told with remarkable circumstantiality, and Chicago publishes a portrait of

Mr Lees, who might well be interviewed on the subject. If the narrative with which he is credited is true, it is one of the most striking of hypnotic revelations.

When this damning piece appeared Dr Benjamin Howard remained silent. So was this an admission of guilt? Far from it. It simply meant that Dr Howard was out of the country and never saw the libel. When he returned he quickly acted to set things right and wrote the following letter to the editor and publisher of the *People*:

> St Georges Club,
> Hanover Sqr, W.
>
> Jany 26-96
>
> Sirs
>   A number of persons have called my attention to 'A startling story' in your widely read 'The People' – May 19. 1895 directly charging me with 'the breach of a vow' etc.
>   In this publication my name is dishonourably associated with Jack the Ripper – and in such a way – as if true – renders me liable to shew cause to the British Medical Council why my name with three degrees attached should not be expunged from the Official Register.
>   Unfortunately for the Parties of the other part – there is not a single item of this startling statement concerning me which has the slightest foundation in fact.
>   Beyond what I may have read in newspapers, I have never known anything about Jack the Ripper. I have never made any public statement about Jack the Ripper – and at the time of the alleged public statement by me I was thousands of miles distant from San Francisco where it is alleged I made it.
>   In my absence from London this statement has passed uncontradicted so long that the damage has multiplied beyond private methods of correction.
>
> I am Yours Truly
> B. Howard

Dr Howard received a prompt reply from the journalist who'd written the story. It read:

> January 31st, 1896
>
> Dear Dr Howard,
>   I took the 'Jack the Ripper' notes from a two-column report in the *Chicago Times*. It was published in such evident good faith that I never thought of doubting it. You will observe that I spoke of you not only with respect but with admiration.

I hope at all events that the incident may lead to a renewal of our friendship.

Tell me what you would like me to do and I shall only be too glad to comply with your wishes.

I always remember you as an appreciative acquaintance of the dear son whom I lost and of whom you predicted great things.

Won't you come to see me?

Joseph Hatton

That correspondence successfully killed off the initial part of the hoax: significantly, no one came forward to nominate a rival Dr Howard as the San Francisco culprit. But the Lees case was rather different. He knew enough about the murders to demolish the hoax with a few facts and figures, but the man stayed tight-lipped and his pen stayed dry. There were good reasons for Lees's silence, for he shrewdly recognized that the article was taking a rise out of him. At the same time he saw that his fantasies had caught up with him with a vengeance, for he had privately boasted that he had secret information about the Ripper's end. Far better then, to maintain a dignified silence and leave others to picture him as a man able to guard solemn secrets. In that way he stayed safe.

Lees was no liar in the ordinary sense of the word. He believed he had a mission to elevate people's thoughts: all his organizing and preaching was dominated by that belief. But, like many others with an urgent sense of mission, he lost touch with reality. The things he longed and hoped for became much more than mental pictures. For Lees, they became concrete experiences and achievements. If he thought about a problem and its solution, he very often ended up asserting that his mental intervention had actually solved the problem. This grotesque process is well illustrated by the assorted psychic tales he told.

Among these tales was one involving his actions as a government agent years *before* the Ripper murders. He assured his daughter Eva that, back in 1883, he'd even been responsible for the capture of a Fenian bombing team, the group masterminded by the Irish revolutionary, Dr Gallacher. Lees's feat was performed after he had guided some American visitors around places of interest in London. Apparently a psychic voice had urged him to report these tourists to Scotland Yard. He did so, calling on his 'old friend Anderson', the police chief. The police acted, raided the address in Villiers Street given them by Lees, and the bomb-plot was squashed.

Unfortunately for Lees's yarn, this particular affair is extremely well documented. The records show that the bomb-plot was foiled as a result of the astuteness of George Pritchard, a strictly non-psychic storeman in

Birmingham. The bombers had set out to manufacture nitro-glycerine at 128 Ledsam Street, Ladywood, Birmingham, approaching Pritchard's firm with an order for a quantity of glycerine, stating that they were about to manufacture a hair oil. But they demanded a quality of chemical purity that was way above that needed even for a luxury hair oil. Pritchard guessed they were lying. He checked on their workshop and found enough incongruities to justify a visit to the police, and the police used skeleton keys to enter the place. Once inside they discovered a bomb factory but realized that it was far too soon to pounce, so they made their exit, leaving the materials intact. From then on, careful observation and the study of seized letters led to the arrest of the whole gang, including the London team headed by Dr Gallacher.

Another fantasy claim involved the writing of Lees's books. According to him, these were dictated to him by spirit guides. Not disembodied, invisible guides. On the contrary, these departed spirits actually materialized in Lees's study and as flesh and blood creatures sat on chairs, cleared their throats and dictated each line in sonorous tones. Lees even asserted that he had a photograph showing one of them. There was a photograph, certainly, that showed Lees with an odd, white-draped, semi-transparent figure at his side. This was the picture that appeared in the *Illustrated Leicester Chronicle* on 28 November 1929. A curious interview accompanied it.

In this interview, Lees affirmed that the photograph was taken by a Mr Boursnell of Shepherd's Bush, a photographer interested in spiritualism but without experience of taking spirit photographs. Mr Lees encouraged him to try and sat in front of his camera. As Boursnell was focusing, Lees became aware of the spirit of one of his greatest friends, and this prompted him to watch the photographic plate being developed. The two men watched in awe, as a strange shadow first appeared on the plate and then, slowly, developed into a clear picture of the spirit of Lees's friend, standing by the side of the studio chair.

And there we have two more fantasies, for Boursnell had been taking (or rather faking) 'spirit pictures' long before Lees sat for him, and the 'spirit' that appeared on the photographic plate was no friend or guide, but simply a stock Boursnell prop – a picture of a painting, superimposed by double exposure. There is no doubt about this. I happen to own a set of photographs that once belonged to Boursnell. They were taken by one of his assistants and show Boursnell himself, hamming it up with various 'spirit extras' surrounding him. Among this collection is one of Boursnell posing with the alleged 'guide' in the Lees picture. In this shot, the drapery is arranged differently, there's less of it, and the stock picture has

The Birmingham plot of 1883: the kitchen of Whitehead's house at Birmingham,
used as a nitro-glycerine distillery.

been reversed, so that it faces from right to left, but more of the clothing is
visible, showing the 'guide' to be a portrait dating from about the
mid-nineteenth century.

It hardly needs much more proof to demonstrate that none of Lees's
wild claims can be taken seriously. In fact, Lees's own diary entries for
1888 vanquish the claim that he had cooperated successfully with the
police for years, and that he had worked with Anderson as early as 1883.

This diary (preserved at Stansted Hall) shows that Lees did not approach the police until 2 October 1888, two days after the murders of 30 September. The diary records:

> Tuesday 2nd October. Offered services to police to follow up East End murders – called a fool and a lunatic. Got trace of man from the spot in Berner Street. Wednesday 3rd October. Went to City police again – called a madman and fool. Thursday 4th October. Went to Scotland Yard – same result but promised to write to me.

Now those are obviously not the words of someone already involved with the police, neither are they the words of someone who has already forecast two murders. His reception confirms this. With two correct predictions to his credit, as given in the Chicago newspapers, he would have been received with awe and respect, and welcomed. But he was simply treated by the exasperated police like any of the other psychics who were then clamouring to have their 'special knowledge' recorded and acted on. It was arrogant of Lees to expect special treatment, to have his fantasies thought of value. In fact, for over 40 years, hardly anyone except for his adoring followers ever took Lees's illusions to be valuable. But then, following his death in 1931, came a dramatic change of attitude.

It had all begun with an article published in Lees's local paper, the *Illustrated Leicester Chronicle*.

Richard Boursnell and Robert Lees (right), using the same prop, a hovering 'spirit guide', only reversed.

11

Fleet Street Joins the Frolics

The article that turned the tide on 23 November 1929 was an account of an interview given by Lees. The vital passage in the text read:

> As a young man he was a Government agent, and his psychic powers enabled him to unravel many important mysteries which defeated the brains of Scotland Yard. In fact, he is one of the few people who know the identity of the notorious 'Jack The Ripper' . . . He was sworn to secrecy, and on oath promised not to divulge the name, and as a Government servant refusing to give information which was badly wanted, he was banished from London to St Ives for five years.

This choice morsel alerted the popular press in Fleet Street and a bevy of determined reporters made the trip to Lees's Leicester home, each convinced that he could wrest the name of the killer from Lees. But Lees refused to talk, even when cheque books were flourished, and the national press stayed frustrated. Fellow-spiritualist Conan Doyle tried his best as well, but even he couldn't persuade Lees to divulge the name, so the flurry of interest died down for a while. Then, in January 1931, Lees died and the *Daily Express* seized the chance. Perhaps the secret could be wormed out of Lees's daughter, Eva? She'd shared a home with him until his death, and she had been the closest to him of all his children. The possibility was alluring.

The man who set out to uncover the secret was crime-reporter, Cyril Morton, a man good at both cajoling and wheedling. He called on the ever-garrulous Eva Lees and talked to her for hours about her father's life and works but when he finally came round to asking for the name of the Ripper, Eva held back. She felt it was far too soon. For the time being she didn't want her father's death overshadowed by an association with the sordid horrors of Whitechapel.

Morton offered her £500 (quite a sum at the time), but Eva refused to budge and he came away empty-handed. Before leaving, though, he did glance through the batch of newspaper clippings on Eva's table, among which was a copy of the Chicago *Sunday Times-Herald* article.

He returned to Fleet Street smarting and thwarted. For once his persuasive techniques had flopped. His dreams of an exclusive Ripper feature were stone dead. Then, remarkably, fortune positively beamed on the *Express*. A 'close friend of Lees' suddenly turned up with a secret document dictated by Lees and left for safe keeping until after his death. Well, that's what the *Express* said, for on 7 March 1931 it ran the following story:

> The 'Daily Express' is to publish an astonishing document, which has long been kept a close secret, and which purports to describe how a clairvoyant solved the mystery of the 'Jack the Ripper' crimes and enabled the ferocious murderer to be identified and arrested.
>
> The recent death of Mr Robert James Lees, the famous spiritualist and clairvoyant, who died in Leicester at the age of eighty-one, will revive and possibly answer the question, 'Who was "Jack the Ripper"?'
>
> A document was placed in the hands of the *Daily Express* shortly after his death by a close friend who was known to have enjoyed Mr Lees' complete confidence. Mr Lees had left word that the text of this document should not be revealed in this country until after his death. That request was observed.
>
> This document is one of the most remarkable narratives that has ever reached a newspaper office. Point by point, giving time and date and place, the late Mr Lees tells how, through his clairvoyant powers, he was able to identify 'Jack the Ripper' and to lead the police, 'like a bloodhound', to the murderer's home where he was apprehended.
>
> The document, as he dictated it, is an authorised account of the part claimed to have been played by Mr Lees in this amazing drama.

There is much more in the same vein and the piece ends: 'Certainly nothing more thrilling on the subject has been given to the world than the story of this remarkable, brilliant man, with his great zeal and faith in his supernatural powers.' Part one of the secret document appeared on 9 March 1931 and part two on the following day.

In recent years the public has been treated to some noteworthy hoaxes. Think back to the Mussolini papers, the Howard Hughes memoirs, and the Hitler diaries as prime examples. But in those cases the bogus material was deftly handled and a great deal of imaginative skill was involved, especially in the preparation of the Hughes and Hitler documents. In 1931, though, no such high, exacting standards were aimed for. The *Express*'s 'secret document' was just an appallingly cheap con trick. It wasn't secret, it wasn't new, it wasn't dictated by Lees, and it wasn't supplied by a friend of the medium. It was nothing but a crafty, space-filling sensation engineered by Morton.

Before leaving Leicester, crafty Cyril had noted the issue date of the Chicago paper. He then secured a copy of the text from the USA and chopped out all the bits that revealed its American origin. Out went the opening section, and with it, Dr Howard. Out went the give-away sentences that linked the story with 'a gentleman of this city', that is, Chicago. The past tense replaced the present tense where appropriate, and a new nine-line introduction was added. Then, unbelievable as it may seem, this cosmetically tarted-up version of the 1895 Chicago hoax became the 'secret document'. Tiny amendments apart, the text as printed in the *Daily Express* is word for word the exact text of the *Sunday Times-Herald* piece of 28 April 1895.

One would have expected this double hoax to be denounced within days, but far from it. Eva Lees fumed away to her friends, but never went public. All the crime reporters in the land seemed to suffer a collective amnesia concerning the real Whitechapel affair. Unbelievably, the story acquired a new vigour and went on gaining in strength.

The French embraced it when it was reprinted in their papers. In Australia it was circulated by the spiritualist movement and later published in a pamphlet by James O'Neil, whose introduction says, in awe: 'Surely, insight into the ghastly mystery surrounding the Jack the Ripper atrocities, was granted to the late Mr R. J. Lees, for the purpose of giving the truth to the world, concerning this ghoul.' William Boyle Hill retold it in 1938 in his book *A New Earth and a New Heaven* and has his inquirer, Rupert Elsmore, bowled over by the tale: 'Rupert sat in his chair, overcome with horror, and speechless with amazement, at last he spoke . . . "I have only to say that what you have read to me tonight has absolutely converted me to a belief in clairvoyance and its astounding powers and possibilities." ' Even Dr Nandor Fodor incorporated a digest of the account in his weighty *Encyclopaedia of Psychic Science*, reproduced without reservations as if it was an accurate, trustworthy piece of real-life history.

More important still was its earlier endorsement in 1935 by ex-Detective Sergeant Edwin T. Woodhall in his book *Crime and the Supernatural*. In retirement the wily Woodhall had found a fresh source of income. Big money could be made by spinning tales about his police days and his war-time experiences in Army Intelligence. It didn't matter too much if some of the yarns were a bit thin – he could always fall back on his imagination.

Woodhall promptly made capital out of the *Express* story; worse still, he gave it an added spurious authority when he wrote:

In a black-japanned box, somewhere in the archives of the British Home Office, are the confidential papers concerning the identity of the most mysterious and spectacular murderer of the past hundred years . . .

Speculation has always been rife as to 'Jack the Ripper's' identity. He was never brought to justice, and it is commonly believed that the police were as ignorant as were the public as to who this prowling, maniacal butcher really was.

But, even in those early days, there were officers at Scotland Yard possessed of vision and imagination; and when, completely baffled and in despair . . . a well-known clairvoyant put certain information at their

Edwin T. Woodhall, a tall story merchant.

disposal, it was investigated, corroborated and seized upon as affording Scotland Yard a new avenue to their enquiries . . .

I am now about to make one of the strongest claims in regard to crime and the Supernatural ever made in this country. In making this claim I have the support of one of the most powerful daily national newspapers of this country. My claim is that 'Jack The Ripper' was tracked down by a clairvoyant, and that his identity was actually known to the authorities . . . The circumstances which led to the detection of this unhuman monster, are extraordinary and altogether unparalleled in the whole history of crime.

Then, in relating the Lees legend, Woodhall added his own quota of chicanery. Whether or not he knew the piece was spirited hoax rather than sordid untruth, he certainly knew the chronology was nonsensical, so he deliberately altered sections of the published text to make it fall more in line with the actual events of 1888. The nebulous, unnamed location of the medium's first vision now became 'George Yard Buildings'. The original lack of date was now remedied so that it read: '. . . late on the night of August Bank Holiday'.

Woodhall, like the hand-on-heart rogue he was, ended his piece:

I have no actual proof of its truth, but during my years at the Yard it was more than once recounted to me as I have related it, and I have not the smallest doubt that it is true, and that psychic science was, even forty-five years ago, enabled to step in where police work had lamentably failed, and lead to the detection and incarceration of one of the world's worst criminal lunatics.

This rejigged version of Woodhall's gave the myth even greater credence. His piece was reprinted in the magazine *Prediction*; in Odhams's *Fifty Strangest Stories Ever Told*; and in the Mellifont paperback *Jack the Ripper or When London Walked in Terror*. Thus throughout the 1930s, the Lees story became inescapable for anyone intrigued by the Whitechapel enigma, and it was in the 1930s that Dr Stowell began working out his own outlandish West End solution to the East End mystery.

12
Gullibility Takes the Field

It was Dr Thomas Eldon Stowell's solution that had seized the headlines in November 1970. His article in the *Criminologist* gave that magazine more unasked-for publicity than could have been bought for a million pounds. Stowell gave no name to his suspect – he simply called him S – but his article gave so many details of the suspect's life and family that it was obvious the Duke of Clarence was being singled out. Stowell wrote:

> He was the heir to power and wealth. His family, for fifty years, had earned the love and admiration of large numbers of people by its devotion to public service to all classes, particularly the poor, but as well to industry and the workers. His grandmother, who outlived him, was very much the stern Victorian Matriarch, widely and deeply respected. His father, to whose title he was heir, was a gay cosmopolitan and did much to improve the status of England internationally. His mother was an unusually beautiful woman with a gracious personal charm and was greatly beloved by all who knew her.
>
> After the education traditional for an English aristocrat, at the age of a little over 16 years, 'S' went for a cruise round the world with a number of high-spirited boys of approximately his age group. He was, perhaps, too popular and gregarious for his own safety. It is recorded that he went to many gay parties ashore . . . and I believe that at one of the many shore parties which he enjoyed in the West Indies on his world journey, he became infected with syphilis.

In Stowell's view it was this dread infection that affected the brain of 'S' and turned him into a criminal lunatic, the slaughterman of Whitechapel. But his guilt was covered up. Stowell surmised:

> It seems obvious that all the efforts of Sir Charles Warren and the police were primarily directed towards preventing further murders and secondly to avoid the embarrassment that would be caused by bringing to trial for these murders, the heir of a noble and prominent family. Clearly he was a lunatic, and was not responsible for his actions. Such however was the indignation of the public that it would have been satisfied with nothing less than a capital sentence.

His activities were probably known to his family after the second murder, perhaps even after the first. After the murder of Annie Chapman he disappeared and nothing was heard of him until letters first posted from Liverpool were received from him one or two days before the murder of Stride and Eddowes and in these he announced his intention.

I believe that within an hour or two of the murder of Eddowes on 30 September, he was apprehended and certified to be insane and was placed under restraint in a private mental home in the Home Counties. But the police were busy with preparations for the Lord Mayor's Show. The murderer escaped from his custodians and got to his Whitechapel haunt, where he murdered Mary Jane Kelly and left the scene an hour and a half before sunrise on 9 November.

According to Stowell, 'He was throughout, under the care of the great physician Sir William Gull.' This disclosure had a regrettable side-effect, for the popular view had it that the Ripper must be a surgeon: the removal of kidneys and other organs seemed to confirm this. As a result of this fantasy '. . . it was not unnatural for the rumourmongers to pick on a most illustrious member of my profession of the time – Sir William Gull, Bt, MD, FRCP, FRS. He was physician to Guy's Hospital, Physician in Ordinary to Her Majesty Queen Victoria, to HRH the Prince of Wales, and physician to a large number of the aristocracy and the wealthy, including, if I am right in my deductions, the family of Jack the Ripper . . .'

As Stowell saw it, there was a good reason why some people could entertain such a wild notion: 'It was said that on more than one occasion Sir William Gull was seen in the neighbourhood on the night of a murder. It would not surprise me to know that he was there for the purpose of certifying the murderer to be insane, so that he might be put under restraint as were the other lunatics apprehended in connection with murders.'

Having introduced Gull into the scenario, Stowell then went further and made Gull's house the possible 'doctor's mansion' of the Lees story. He reasoned along these lines:

> Fred Archer in his book [*Ghost Detectives*] tells an interesting story that Lees, the medium, was asked by the police to 'use his uncanny gifts to help them'. Lees led them to 'an impressive mansion in the West End'. The house was the home of a fashionable and highly reputable physician . . . It interests me to speculate whether the 'imposing mansion' to which Lees led the police was 74, Brook Street, Grosvenor Square, the home of Sir William Gull, and whether Mr Archer's story is a variation of one told to me by Sir William Gull's daughter Caroline . . .
>
> Mrs Acland's story was that at the time of the Ripper murders, her mother, Lady Gull, was greatly annoyed one night by an unappointed visit

from a police officer, accompanied by a man who called himself a 'medium', and she was irritated by their impudence in asking her a number of questions which seemed to her impertinent. She answered their questions with non-committal replies such as 'I do not know', 'I cannot tell you that', 'I am afraid I cannot answer that question' . . .

Later Sir William himself came down, and in answer to the questions, said he occasionally suffered from 'lapses of memory' since he had had a slight stroke in 1887; he said that he had once discovered blood on his shirt. This is not surprising, if he had medically examined the Ripper after one of the murders.

Stowell may have been gripped by strong convictions, but is there any firm evidence to justify them? Here we run into a problem, for Stowell's papers were destroyed the day after his death and since then his family has consistently refused to discuss the affair with reporters, researchers or anyone else. This is understandable, perhaps, for the affair brought them a massive amount of unwanted publicity and harassment. They may also feel that the uproar following publication served to shorten Dr Stowell's life, for he died just eight days after his theory went into print. However, despite this lack of access, careful probing shows that Stowell's story is without substance, and that Stowell himself is a consistently unreliable advocate.

In his lengthy article, he is repeatedly inaccurate about the dates and duration of events – so much so, that you have to marvel he could be so wrong so often. At one point he makes a great show of judging Clarence's character from his clothing: 'I have seen a photograph of my suspect which suggests paranoia by the extravagance of his dress, for which I am told he became a butt. In this photograph he is seen by the riverside holding a fishing rod, wearing a tweed knickerbocker suit of perfect cut, not a fold misplaced and without a crease. On his head is a tweed cap set far too precisely, and he has a small moustache. He is wearing a 4in. to 4½in. stiff starched collar, and is showing two inches of shirt cuff at each wrist (I was told by my elders that he was given the nickname of "Collar and Cuffs").'

You can well imagine Stowell poring excitedly over this picture, inspecting it minutely, dragging from it every tiny fragment of information that suited his purpose. Yet for all that, he was incapable of reporting what he saw. In all the photographs of Clarence there is only one of him with a rod by a river, and in that photograph Clarence is not wearing knickerbockers; his bare knees stick out from underneath a kilt adorned by a badger-headed sporran. That Stowell could miss, or ignore, such an ultra-prominent feature says much for his state of mind.

Just how trustworthy was his mind? Nigel Morland found him 'a sane

The photo of the Duke of Clarence – Eddy – that trounces Stowell's description.

and courteous man' and was impressed by 'the careful research, the quiet authority, and the absolute certainty expressed by him as to the Ripper's identity'. But I'm afraid Nigel Morland was far too trusting, easily deceived and erratic in judging the quality of anyone's research, as his enthusiasm over the Frank Spiering fiasco will show.

Though we can accept that Stowell was gentlemanly and most likely an exemplary medical man, we have to face the truth that when he tangled with the Ripper mystery he lost his standards, falling victim to the same influences that corrupted earlier theorists like Forbes Winslow, Leonard Matters, Le Queux, Woodhall and others. The verdict on Stowell has to be a harsh one. In short, he became both a liar and a fantasist.

Of his lies there can be no doubt whatsoever. All the information he gave, despite its inaccuracies, involved one person and one person only: Eddy, Duke of Clarence. Just the photograph and its interpretation alone would be conclusive, but a full ten years before he published his article, he even *told* Colin Wilson, among others, that Clarence was the Ripper. Then, on 2 November 1970, after publication, he appeared on television and allowed interviewer Kenneth Allsop to speak of Clarence as the murderer. Not once did he contradict him. Yet, on 5 November, he sent the following letter to *The Times* (published on the 9th): 'Sir, I have at no time associated His Royal Highness, the late Duke of Clarence, with the Whitechapel murderer or suggested the murderer was of Royal blood. It remains my opinion that he was the scion of a noble family . . . Yours faithfully, a loyalist and a royalist, Thomas E. A. Stowell.'

These lies were only summoned up to protect his cherished obsession, the belief that he had successfully deciphered esoteric information understood by only a few. Fortunately, almost every fantasy preserves clues as to its origins, and in looking for those clues we have a useful starting date: in 1960 Stowell admitted that his initial revelation came to him in the early 1930s.

There were only two new published pieces of interest to Ripper hunters in that period. First came the *Express* story and its repetition by W.B. Hill and Woodhall. Next came Michael Arlen's satirical Ripper novel, *Hell! Said the Duchess*. But how, exactly, did *they* affect his thinking?

Stowell's true state of mind can best be understood by thinking of those scholars who embroil themselves in passionate lost causes, like the Bacon-Shakespeare controversy or the Britain Is Israel myth. The protagonists on these wondrous battlefields go to extreme lengths to find suggestive references, hidden allusions, even complete cyphers, which support or reinforce their beliefs. Sad to say, such dedication can often lead to fanaticism and deviousness.

Devious indeed had been Stowell's casual mention in 1970 of Fred Archer's book. He gives the impression that he has only just met up with the Lees legend, though, as I've shown, this had been inescapable for Ripperphiles for almost forty years. In the 1930s when Stowell first met it, it had provided the impetus for his runaway speculation. A West End doctor? A physician in high standing . . . enjoying the patronage of the best society? Such a man would of necessity have been known to Stowell's friend and teacher, Theodore Dyce Acland. But who could it be? The questions were soon to be echoed by a crop of tantalizing references in Arlen's novel.

Hell! Said the Duchess has a contemporary setting. A few real life characters are introduced, like Oswald Mosley and Winston Churchill, but all the others are, in the author's words, 'curiously enough, imaginary'. The story revolves around a series of Ripper-style murders in the West End, but the killer is, or seems to be, a woman. Central to this story of Jane the Ripper is a large house in Grosvenor Square, lived in by the suspect, the Duchess of Dove, and her cousin Miss Gool. One incident involves the theft of a photograph of the Duchess taken by a photographer named Clarence. At another point the suspect is taken, for her own safety, to a nursing home and put under the charge of old Dr Lapwing. At the conclusion it is discovered that the sexually voracious murderer is a male, able to transform himself into the exact double of Mary Dove before each killing.

Stowell's fantasy may well have started off as a lighted-hearted piece of mental theatre: the suspect, and the suspect's doctor bear the names of birds, the significant house is set in Grosvenor Square. Grosvenor Square? But that was where dear Caroline Acland lived when she was Caroline Gull, along with her father. And her father, Sir William Gull, was undoubtedly 'a physician in high standing – enjoying the patronage of the best society'. Were the bird names, then, a clue? Was the name Gool, so suggestive of Gull, a reinforcing clue? And the killer – could the bi-sexual aspect be a pointer to the real Ripper of the last century? Could this real Ripper have been a mentally disturbed patient of Gull's? A man so highly placed that when caught, he had to be spared a trial, taken to a nursing home and cared for by old Dr Gull? Could it have been his eminent patient, bi-sexual Clarence? If it was, what could possibly have driven him to murder?

In the primary stages something along these lines was evolved. Yet if it began light-heartedly, it terminated, years later, as a grimly dogmatic certainty.

We can never be sure of Stowell's exact trains of thought, but we can be certain that an unreal mental tableau was eventually built by him. This is proved beyond question by his initial statement in 1970 about Gull: '. . . it was not unnatural for the rumourmongers to pick on a most illustrious member of my profession of the time – Sir William Gull . . .' There is not a grain of truth in this whatsoever, no trace of any rumour linking Gull's name with the murders in the whole of the 82 years leading up to Stowell's claim. I have searched and others have searched; our collective verdict is – nonsense.

Stowell's most specific reference is nonsensical as well. He wrote: 'It was said that on more than one occasion Sir William Gull was seen in the neighbourhood on the night of a murder.' But who saw him? Where is their testimony? Again, extensive searches fail to bring a single such sighting to light. No one, anywhere, has ever testified to seeing Gull in Whitechapel in the whole of 1888, let alone on the specific dates of the killings. But, of course, without these inventions Stowell's grand fantasy would lose its quaint internal logic. It was essential for Stowell to resolve the contradiction between the two component parts of his theory. The Lees story could not be taken intact, otherwise he was saddled with a killer-doctor: of Gull that was unthinkable. But if Gull could be presented as simply the victim of rumours, if he could be *innocently* linked with Whitechapel – then the problem might vanish. Even so, something extra was called for, some direct testimony from Gull's own family to complete the exoneration. Caroline Gull had married Stowell's friend, Acland, who was adviser at a London sanatorium. So Stowell invented a new ending to the Lees saga and attributed it to Gull's daughter.

One thing is certain. There is nothing in the least far-fetched in pointing to the fictional sources of Stowell's brainwaves. Seekers after the unusual have often found their 'revealed truths' in openly fictional writings. Take the various 'hollow earth' factions as a prime example. In Nazi Germany, Bulwer Lytton's novel *The Coming Race* was taken seriously by initiates as a work of supreme importance. A Vril Society was formed, named after Lytton's superhuman psychic power, an imaginary power mastered by a civilization living *inside* the earth. Vril Society members believed 'they had secret knowledge that would enable them to change their race and become equals of the men hidden in the bowels of the earth'. Other 'hollow-earthers' found their 'hidden evidence' in novels like Willis Emerson's *The Smoky God*, or the grotesque magazine horror stories, *The Shaver Scripts*.

On a loftier plane, *Alternative Three*, a novel based on an Anglia TV April Fool's Day documentary, is now being used by a number of cults to prove that scientists are being forcibly abducted to staff a colony on Mars.

116

On the lowest plane, we have the example of the wretched anti-Semitic *Protocols of the Elders of Zion*, based on a fictional political satire, but believed in and used to cause immense misery. The *Protocols* have even been used to bolster up wild theories about the Ripper murders, as we shall see later.

Dr Stowell was not the first Ripperphile to be carried away by the urgings of a fevered imagination, but he was far and away the most influential. It was due to his inspiration that a new wave of outlandish theorists now emerged.

Lord Lytton, better known as Sir Edward Bulwer Lytton,
author of *Zanoni* and *Master of the Mage, Tautriadelta*.
White magic, black magic – the real Ripper met both through Lytton.

13

A Royal Champion Challenges

Heading this exotic new wave came Michael Harrison. In theory he should have made an ideal advocate. He is a leading Sherlockian and by 1972, when his biography of Clarence came out, he had a string of over 40 books to his credit. Sadly though, prolific writers often skimp on research, as in Harrison's case; and he has a record of ignoring findings likely to upset his pet theories.

Still, for all that, Harrison's basic ideas were certainly novel. He took Stowell's arguments and tried to show that his suspect could not have been Clarence. Yes, Clarence was involved in the true story, but only because the suspect '. . . must have been close enough to Eddy in some important particular . . . to excuse his being confused with Eddy.' Harrison located the vital clue to that suspect's identity in the letter S used by Stowell. This is his reasoning: '. . . I was struck by one curious fact: if Stowell was hinting that Eddy was the Ripper, why did he say: "Now for my suspect. I prefer not to name him, but to call him S." Why S?'

Harrison then goes on to make a profound observation, yet ends with a naive conclusion. He writes: '. . . in all deformations of an original truth, something of the original remains. It is this truism that, in embellishing a tale, the human mind clings on to one *fact*, which has enabled folklorists to retrieve, from the most fanciful of legends, that underlying truth that we call "historical fact". So with his choice of S.'

By hurriedly accepting this initial as the key, Harrison donned the fool's cap. Had he bothered to ask Nigel Morland about the mysterious letter S, he would have found out that his guess was wild and worthless. It turns out that Stowell had originally wanted to refer to the Ripper as X, but Morland was fed up with this worn-out device and asked Stowell to use any other initial, even his own. So Stowell obliged by using his own initial. Thus the letter S is totally without significance. It leads nowhere. But for Michael Harrison it led straight to the second son of one of Britain's most famous judges, a man who had once been Eddy's tutor at Cambridge, James Stephen.

Harrison presented his proofs stage by stage. First he listed '. . . a few of Stowell's "facts" which *cannot* apply to Eddy.' He then demonstrated that the dates and the duration of visits made by S would not fit in with Eddy's recorded life. But if they didn't fit Eddy, did they fit anyone else? This question Harrison evades, leaping instead to these words of Stowell's: 'Jack the Ripper was obviously Sir William Gull's patient, and Mrs Acland told me that she had seen in her father's diary an entry, "informed Blank that his son was dying of syphilis of the brain".' This, to Harrison, is unacceptable. He asked: 'Would such an entry have been made in the diary of *any* physician in the year 1889? For it was not until 1913 that Hideyo Noguchi demonstrated that paresis is produced by the surviving spirochetes of syphilis.'

From that stage Harrison argued: 'The fact is – the fact *must* be – that Mrs Acland, not being herself a doctor, but merely connected with doctors, was "remembering" for Dr Stowell in the light of knowledge acquired long after the death of her distinguished father in 1890. What she had seen was that initial S, but not the entire name, for then Stowell could not have hinted that Eddy was the Ripper.' Harrison then wrote down the qualifications and characteristics that S was required to have. They included the following:

> S, quite apart from being intimately connected with Eddy or Eddy's family, must have been important in himself, to provide powerful motives for hushing up his crimes.
>
> If, however, S were not so important that the revelation of his crime(s) could threaten the social order, then perhaps his family or some other member of his family might be of great importance in the State.
>
> Assuming that S was the Ripper, then an analysis of the Ripper's mentality, as revealed not merely by the murders, but by the vast exhibitionistic literature originating from this maniac, should help to disclose his identity.
>
> Some link appeared to have been established between the Government in general and the Ripper, as a 'poem' of the Ripper's appears to contain an allusion to a letter that Queen Victoria wrote to the Home Secretary. This could only have happened if the Ripper was either highly placed socially, or his family were in a position to discuss the Queen's letter.

This last proposition is incredibly naive. Harrison has in mind a so-called Ripper poem sent to Macnaghten in 1889. It runs:

> I'm not a butcher, I'm not a Yid
> Nor yet a foreign skipper,
> But I'm your own light-hearted friend,
> Yours truly, Jack the Ripper.

Oddly enough Colin Wilson, too, takes this seriously when he comments: 'Queen Victoria had suggested that the police should check on all foreign skippers coming ashore. This was not public knowledge but Stephen could easily have found it out through the Duke of Clarence.' Really? A little extra thought would have shown that the verse does no more than sum up three of the speculations that were widely toyed with at the time. Seamen, especially foreign seamen, were certainly objects of suspicion. And if you want a nautical crew term to rhyme with Ripper what else are you going to choose but skipper? It's as simple and as insignificant as that. But, skippers apart, that was Harrison's human blueprint. So whom did it fit? He had no doubts at all:

> . . . the only S who fitted all these requirements was an S who had been intimate with Eddy since the summer of 1883: Jim Stephen. It is clear also that, homosexual or not, an intimacy, jealously possessive on Stephen's side, and lazily tolerant on Eddy's, sprang up between these two in those 'golden weeks' whilst Stephen was endeavouring to fit Eddy for entrance to Trinity.

Having identified Stephen, Harrison then suggested that the intimacy between the two men 'had an element in it perhaps even stronger than sexual attraction'. He argues that the Stephen family was greatly ambitious and James Stephen falsely assumed that he had in some way captured Eddy for himself. This illusion was shattered when Eddy left Cambridge for the Army and scarcely bothered to keep in touch. A fit of sulking on Stephen's part could have been expected, but something much more bitter and sinister resulted. It was brought on by a severe blow on the head. The blade of a windmill struck James, says one version; another has it caused by the door of a moving train. But whatever the cause, the blow led to a personality shift and a maniacal thirst for revenge. Out of revenge, Stephen became Jack the Ripper.

Put baldly the thesis looks too absurd to be entertained, yet Harrison battles manfully to support his case. Every fraction of his Sherlockian ingenuity is brought into play. He rakes through Stephen's verses to show that he has an irrational hatred of women, and a sadistic attitude towards punishment. This is not hard to accept; consider these few lines:

> O may'st thou suffer tortures without end:
> May fiends with glowing pincers rend thy brain,
> And beetles batten on thy blackened face!

Those lines were addressed to an anonymous Belgian. His crime? He accidentally stepped on Stephen's toes – so the punishment hardly fitted the crime. Harrison's second point about attitudes seems made.

Unfortunately, this poem was written in July 1882, a year before Stephen's involvement with Eddy, and four years before the accidental blow to the head. If anything it shows that Stephen's personality defects were there all along. More significantly, it shows that his aggression was purely verbal: he didn't assault the clumsy Belgian, and there's no evidence that he ever assaulted anyone else.

James Stephen – dread slayer of cottage loaves.

Stephen's apparently real hatred of women was confined to words as well, as in his poem 'A Thought':

> If all the harm that women have done
> Were put in a bundle and rolled into one,
> Earth would not hold it,
> The sky could not enfold it,
> It could not be lighted nor warmed by the sun;
> Such masses of evil
> Would puzzle the devil
> And keep him in fuel while Time's wheels run.

Much more vicious was his verdict on a nameless woman:

> I do not want to see that girl again:
> I did not like her: and I should not mind
> If she were done away with, killed, or ploughed.
> She did not seem to serve a useful end:
> And certainly she was not beautiful.

121

After emphasizing those last lines, Harrison comments: 'No plainer revelation of Stephen's murderous values could ever have been made public.' Perhaps so, but we are still dealing with nothing but words. Did they lead to actions? Harrison insists they did, but to back his claims resorts to nothing but pages of word-play. He starts by conjuring up the fact that Stephen knew the obscene students' song 'Kaphoozelum'. And 'Kaphoozelum', he insists, '. . . is about "the harlot of Jerusalem", a term which, without straining meaning, might well apply to any East End whore of the 1880s'. He dwells on eight of the stanzas and of one says, '. . . the next stanza deserves our deepest attention':

> For though he pays his women well,
> This syphilitic spawn of hell,
> Struck down each year and tolled the bell
> For ten harlots of Jerusalem.

What, though, is the significance of these lines? For Harrison, it all revolves around the fact that the poem refers to 'ten harlots'. This leads him to query '. . . why, then, does Jack the Ripper, in one of his thirty-four attested letters, talk of "*eight* little whores"?' At once we see what Harrison is up to. We have already met the fictitious 'thirty-four attested letters' in the Dr Dutton yarns. By accepting this bogus story, Harrison is able to quote the 'Ripper's poem' found in the 'Dutton Papers', which runs:

> Eight little whores, with no hope of heaven,
> Gladstone may save one, then there'll be seven.
> Seven little whores, begging for a shilling
> One stays in Henage Court [*sic*], then there's a killing.
>
> Six little whores, glad to be alive,
> One sidles up to Jack, then there are five.
> Four and whore rhyme aright.
> So do three and me,
> I'll set the town alight,
> Ere there are two.
>
> Two little whores, shivering with fright,
> Seek a cosy doorway in the middle of the night.
> Jack's knife flashes, then there's but one,
> And the last one's the ripest for Jack's idea of fun.

This poem allows Harrison to draw these odd conclusions:

> Now there were two murders of women earlier in 1888 that most Ripper 'experts' deny as forming part of the Ripper series. Yet if we add these two murders to the five that all are agreed that the Ripper committed, and the three which came after . . . thought by some to be Ripper murders, we do arrive at the figure ten. Ronald Pearsall . . . states definitely that 'there were eight murders by Jack the Ripper in 1888 . . . the first murder was in April, but it did not receive wide publicity.' This would make Jack's 'Eight little whores, with no hope of heaven' fit beautifully.

Confusing? Certainly, and to compound this confusion Harrison then adds: 'But I feel that however many may be attributed to the Ripper the murders were initially planned to be ten . . .' Then follows his stunning proof: '. . . because that [10] is the number of harlots that "the syphilitic spawn of hell" struck down.'

So the whole dramatic theory rests on nothing more tangible than the lines of a bawdy student song. However, we have to bear with our theorist, since he has more proofs to flourish. Harrison solemnly states that the '. . . reference to Heneage Court implies knowledge which can have come to the Ripper only through an association with officialdom.' Not so. Since this poem is drawn from the unacceptable Dutton Papers, there is an alternative explanation. I suggest that it was concocted after the publication in 1931 of ex-PC Spicer's letter about the Heneage Court incident. Let me emphasize that there is no trace of these verses before their publication in 1959, thus they have no bearing on events in 1888.

But this still leaves Harrison with his two ultimate proofs. The first rests on the slender observation that only one of the ten killings (he counts the double killing on 30 September as a single event) took place in Cambridge term time: all the others took place in college vacations or half-term holidays.

The second proof involves '. . . new evidence which can hardly be coincidental'. This new evidence makes Harrison think that there *were* ten and what's more that Jack originally set out to get ten. The proof consists of a list of victims and their death dates, and a matching list of suggestive Royal or 'classical' occasions falling on those dates.

In his eagerness to make it all fit, Harrison names the seventh victim as Annie Farmer, but unhappily for his theory, she wasn't killed on 21 November 1888. On that date she had picked up a man and shared a bed with him at the common lodging house at 19 George Street. At 9.30 in the morning she started screaming and staggered down the stairs bleeding from a throat wound. There was no sign of her attacker. Later it was found that her wound was superficial and it is extremely doubtful if any 'attack' ever took place. The police found some coins hidden in her mouth, so it looks as if her client had objected to being robbed and the 'attack' had been staged as a quick way out of an awkward confrontation. Yet, despite these easily established facts, Annie Farmer appears on Harrison's list as one of the slain.

The list in full is too tedious to consider name by name. It all looks like an exercise in misplaced ingenuity. Nothing about it rings true. Harrison even tries to pinpoint the anguish that triggered off the serial slaughter. He imagines James catching Eddy womanizing: 'The trauma of detecting Eddy with a woman may have been an actual experience or a symbolic one: "the harlot" may have been a real harlot or she may have been a woman who stepped in between Eddy and Stephen; in all probability, the Princess of Wales. (The removal of the uterus from the slain woman is symbolical of an attack on women, not as whores or even females, but as *mothers*).'

It's all so empty and worthless. Yes, James was mentally unstable, but so eventually was his father Sir James Fitzjames Stephen and others of his family as well. Even so, at no time was he found to be a homicidal maniac, and at no time was he spotted in the Whitechapel area on the fatal days.

Even Harrison's later finding – that Stephen habitually carried a sword-stick – has no bearing on the murders. Such swords are designed for piercing, not for ripping open. The Ripper used an easily concealed slashing knife, not a lengthy fencing blade: of that there's no doubt. But it doesn't deter Harrison from exulting over his remarkable find, for he knows of a time when James actually *used* the blade. Admittedly, it was only thrust into a cottage-loaf but for Harrison that was enough. The loaf was 'a representation of the female human figure – and Stephen was symbolizing his wish to kill all females . . . when he plunged the sharp point of his sword into the bulging "bosom" of the cottage-loaf'. And *that* is possibly the high point of Harrison's reasoning!

It was all an overblown display in misplaced cleverness, but its author just wasn't clever enough. Harrison allowed himself to be taken in by the bogus Lees account, by the Stowell fantasy and by the Dutton hoax. Out of these combined muddles came the gloriously tragic figure of James Stephen, dread slayer of cottage-loaves.

Just who on earth could be expected to take such a tale and treat it with respect? Well, surprisingly enough, one American writer did. But only in parts; for he, in turn, had his own weird disclosures to make.

14
A Republican Strikes Back

'For almost ninety years, the British establishment's fear of the truth being known has led Prime Ministers, members of Royalty, and Scotland Yard officials, to conspire in hiding the identity of the world's most infamous mass murderer.' So states the American writer, Frank Spiering, in his *Prince Jack – the True Story of Jack the Ripper*. The book's cover displays the State Crown sitting on a scarlet cushion. In front of it rests a large, single-edged butcher's knife. Spiering's message is unmistakable.

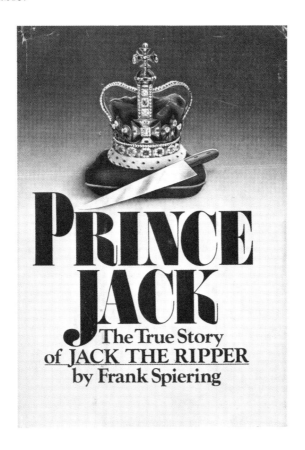

Prince Jack was heralded by powerful claims. The publisher asserted that Spiering backed his case with 'impeccable research' and this included 'a copy of the notes of Sir William Gull . . . The papers relate in detail Sir William's sensational and suppressed discoveries after examining the young prince.' In his Introduction Nigel Morland seems to concur, writing: '. . . I am *very* impressed by Frank Spiering. He is a dedicated writer, a man who's put authenticated research above anything else. He has probed into the Ripper case, probed with a mind unimpressed by baseless facts, and while I fear he is going to revive the whole violent controversy, he will do so unintentionally. This book is an important one and, I suggest, the last word on Jack the Ripper.'

When I first flicked through this book I was at once struck by the full-page photograph of 'Police Commissioner Charles Warren'. There he is, resplendent with medals, thoughtful and determined, behind his large drooping moustache. Unfortunately, it happens to be a photograph of Major-General Sir Hector MacDonald, the famous 'Fighting Mac'. This blunder sets the tone for the rest of the book, for despite the accolades, the research throughout is abysmally poor. And its conclusions? To be fair, let us first see what Spiering has to say.

He admits that his book is mainly a reconstruction of what he feels did happen, yet it is all based on everything he read, officially and unofficially. He maintains, too, that he interviewed staff members at Buckingham palace and people at Scotland Yard, to make sure his conclusions would be exact.

Spiering opens his story by picturing Eddy wandering after midnight through the Spitalfields quarter of Whitechapel. Eddy had apparently strayed from the company of his homosexual friends and was now making a solitary descent into the area's hellish slums. Near Buck's Row he caught sight of Barber's Horse Slaughter House and found himself drawn towards this gaslit hall of agony.

The slaughterhouse was crowded with butchers. Eddy watched almost mesmerized as their knives flashed and with each slash there was a scream '. . . but not a human scream, as the blood poured from the throat of a stallion, then a mare. More horses were brought in . . . and the ritual continued – as the men in their blood-soaked leather aprons slashed away . . .' Eddy stayed unable to look away: '. . . organised slaughter was intoxicating'. He stood watching and unnoticed for ages. He could sense the horses' thoughts: 'The bewilderment, the terror, the suffering agony. He had dreamed of such a place, but had never been inside one. There were knives everywhere, lying on stools, on the floor. He picked one up. It was a long cutting blade. No one noticed him leave the place, taking the knife with him . . . He touched the edge of the knife . . . He smiled as it gave him a sudden sense of power.' With the knife hidden under his coat, Eddy waited to exercize that power. Mary Anne Nichols died that very night, and at 5.36 a.m. Eddy fled the district by the first underground train that clanged out of Whitechapel Station. He still clutched the knife under his coat.

The appetite had been roused and the hunger grew once more. On 8 September, Eddy slunk back to the East End and hung around the Jewish abattoir in Aldgate High Street. He watched the preparations for slaughter, noted how the captive beasts were despatched with a single expert slash to the throat. Straight through to the bone went the razor-edged knife and then the carcasses were slit open to release the intestines and organs and expose the heart and lungs for inspection.

Several hours of watching brought on a high state of excitement. Then, when Eddy at last crept away, he took with him one of the butchers' leather aprons. No one saw him steal it. Now he was ready for a second sacrificial victim: this time the ritual would be spectacular . . . A few coins lured his victim into the deserted yard at the rear of Hanbury Street, and there she looked on, puzzled, as Eddy removed his coat to reveal the leather butcher's apron tied around his waist. It was a short-lived puzzlement. The knife slashed across the neck – straight through to the bone. She sank to the ground. Then, imitating the actions of the Jewish slaughtermen, Eddy slit and ripped her torso open. Again he made an easy escape. The only clue he left behind was the leather apron, placed a few inches away from the backyard water-tap. When it was found it was so saturated with water that it was quite free of blood.

At this point we should pause and take stock. At last a piece of verifiable evidence has been introduced – the leather apron. It was stolen by Eddy; worn ritually by Eddy; and abandoned by Eddy. Let us now nail that lie. The apron and its ownership were fully investigated by Coroner Wynne Baxter on the first day of Annie Chapman's inquest. Mrs Richardson, the cat's meat woman, testified that the apron belonged to her son John; it was used by him in his work. Baxter then asked: 'Can you explain to us how the apron happened to be under the water-tap in the backyard where it was found by the police?' Mrs Richardson replied: 'Yes I can, last Thursday I found the apron in the cellar, where it had got mildewed. My son had not used it for a month – so I put it under the tap intending to wash it, and left it there.' A further question established that the apron had been there from Thursday to Saturday, so it had no bearing on the murder. Its role as Clarence's cast-off was pure invention on Spiering's part.

More examples of such 'impeccable research' are found at the point where James Stephen is dragged into the story. Spiering had read Michael Harrison's *Clarence* and decided to go along with his reasoning, for part of the way. Eddy is made to visit Stephen's house bearing with him a mysterious package. Alone with James, Eddy opened the packet and brought out 'the bloody portion of a human body'. James laughed at first, believing that some elaborate practical joke was involved. Then he realized that Eddy was intensely serious.

Eddy needed to confess, to share his dread secrets with his most intimate friend. So he poured out his story: 'He had murdered two women, two common women who had approached him in the stews of Spitalfields.' The first had been killed 'in a sudden moment of agony within himself'. It was almost a casual killing. But the second woman was different. He needed to kill her because he wanted everyone to know about the pain and the agony he felt inside. He had found something special with that woman. It was better than making love to anyone. That violent act of destruction '. . . had no meaning other than he felt afterward tremblingly afraid, yet wonderfully free, as if that person were part of himself, some awful burning part that he could cut out and leave there.'

James would understand some of these feelings for he had poured such emotions of agony and frustration into his poems. And after a while James did understand. Initially he had believed Eddy to be the victim of an hallucination – the newspapers had certainly given enough details to nourish nightmares – but then he gradually came to accept that he was listening to a murderer, and an unrepentant one at that.

Without the slightest remorse, Eddy declared that the women were of no value to society: they had no prospects, no hope and no hearts and they were a menace. Years before, one such prostitute had infected him. It was better for them that he killed them – they would have died anyway.

With James, revulsion was replaced by amazement and then by a calculating opportunism. He alone shared the secret. The knowledge gave him more power than he had ever imagined. And yet –

> Eddy's story had filled him with dread for himself. He was aware that the unreality and the real were somehow merging inside him, that he soon would not be able to distinguish between the two . . . There had long been insanity in his family and it was inevitable that he should inherit some of

Opposite: 'Prince Jack the Ripper' – the cry of one fervent camp.
True or False?

Hay.

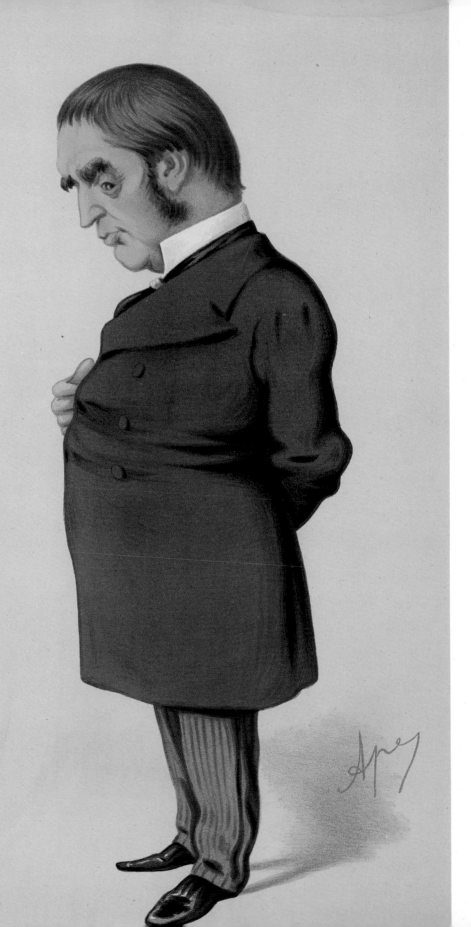

it . . . Eddy was real, had seemed real, and was now completely unreal. He was a murderer, no longer a prince, he roamed through Whitechapel destroying whores. It was inconceivable, ludicrous, yet James, himself, felt that he should join in . . . it was time to add something himself to the furore – a bit more notoriety, that he could control with his pen. He would use red ink . . .

At that stage, Frank Spiering has James sit down and write the famous 'Dear Boss' letter to the Central News Agency. He pictures James toying with the problem of a signature: 'He needed a name that could be connected with the past. Scores of famous criminals came to mind: Jack Shephard; Spring-Heeled Jack; Three-Fingered Jack; Slippery Jack. He signed it "Jack the Ripper".' The letter was then shown to Eddy, who made no comment; but James knew what Eddy's plans were, for he only struck at weekends. So the letter was sent. A few days later, a second message was penned and 'on September 30 he mailed a postcard to the Central News Agency . . . at the bottom of the card James added his own red ink-stained thumbprint'.

Once again, we are presented with a checkable clue: the date of the postcard. Is Spiering revealing something that arose out of the special research he made? Not a bit of it. He's simply repeating the errors of earlier writers, for the card was in fact mailed on 1 October. Predictably, all the events leading up to this historic correspondence are sheer make-believe, Spiering-style. But then Spiering has very little time for things as boring as facts, as witness his handling of Stephen's poems. He raced through Harrison's text and missed the point of his reference to the anonymous harlot song. In *Prince Jack* Spiering displays his ignorance by saddling James Stephen with the *authorship* of 'Kaphoozelum'. Five stanzas are cited, each one allegedly showing Stephen's frame of mind when he wrote it!

Yet if Spiering is hopelessly wrong so far, there's always the promise of his master-card: he, alone, has the text of Gull's notes to draw on, the papers that '. . . relate in detail Sir William's sensational and suppressed discoveries after examining the young prince.'

Gull first enters on the afternoon following the murders of Elizabeth Stride and Catherine Eddowes. Queen Victoria was greatly concerned with her grandson's health: his hands were trembling, his face pale, he complained of severe headaches. A medical check was obviously called for, so Eddy was sent to call on Sir William at 74 Brook Street, Grosvenor

---

Opposite: 'Dr Jack the Ripper' – Sir William Gull,
the 'Masonic Madman' of the Sickert/Knight fantasy.

Square. The visit was a timely one, for according to Spiering the royal physician diagnosed obvious signs of extreme dementia, and the chronic suppuration about the ear was a symptom of syphilitic cachexia – which could affect the brain. But what lay behind the dementia? Gull decided to use hypnosis to find out.

Under hypnosis Eddy told him first about James, then about the anger he felt towards his father. Finally, his eyes 'became like glass as he recalled another image, one that filled Gull with alarm. It was "the knife" he referred to and the woman in the darkness. Gull watched in horror as Eddy showed him how he slit the woman's throat. The phantom knife descended with a sudden thrust down.' Now Gull knew the underlying cause of Eddy's demented state: syphilis was pushing him into fits of fantastic rage. The violence was the outpouring of his pain. Eddy had passed beyond fantasy: 'He had reenacted the obsessions that he felt. The madness which had overtaken his being was a perpetual state of delirium. He was not mentally responsible, yet the acts had been committed. Gull had no alternative but to let this information be known. That is why he communicated to Sir Charles Warren that he had to see him immediately.'

According to Spiering, who, remember, has 'Gull's testimony', Warren called on Gull and listened to his account of Eddy's confessions. He learned that the prince had '. . . implicated his former tutor, James K. Stephen, as the author of the letters to the Central News Agency which bore the signature "Jack the Ripper".' Warren listened carefully and then '. . . confronted Gull with an astonishing revelation. Not only was he aware of Prince Eddy's murderous activities; this knowledge had been shared with the Home Secretary Matthews and with the Prime Minister as well.'

From then on Gull was drawn into this top-level conspiracy of silence. The Queen could not be informed, but it was essential to isolate Eddy until his father could be alerted and 'appropriate measures be taken'. Could Sir William help? Sir William could. Immediate medical care was called for and this could be given in complete secrecy at a private sanatorium known to Gull, the House of Rest Sanatorium in Balham, where Theodore Dyce Acland advised. Acland was not only a reliable friend, but was actually engaged to Gull's daughter Caroline. Who better to keep the dread secret?

With Warren's agreement, Eddy was moved into the sanatorium and treatment commenced with iodide of potassium, electrical therapy and drugs. At first the patient seemed subdued and incoherent. By the second week he became increasingly wildly delirious and extremely violent in his actions: it seemed that the syphilitic condition could be controlled, but not the inner torment and madness which turned him into the dreaded Ripper. Still, he was now out of circulation and out of further harm.

Thus the Ripper vanished from the scene for some six weeks. Then on 8 November, Sir William received disheartening news from the director of the Balham House of Rest: Eddy had suffered a violent fit of rage and made good his escape from the hospital. He was on the loose once more.

Once free, in Spiering's view, Eddy's confused mind churned over two thoughts. His father's birthday fell next day, on Friday. Motherdear and Georgie would be celebrating at Sandringham; he wanted to be with them. First, though, he had to tell James about his imprisonment, about the doctors who were plotting against him. So he made his way through the bleak night and headed for De Vere Gardens. Hours later, safe inside James's house, he broke down and wept as he made his bitter accusations. Then, at first light, he fell asleep and was still asleep when a small, hand-picked group of men turned up at De Vere Gardens. Sir William had roused Sir Charles Warren and suggested that Eddy would make straight for the Stephens' house. James had no option but to let them in, but when they searched the rooms they found that Eddy had slipped out without making a sound. After the police left, James checked the pantry and noted that one of the long knives was missing.

The rule of secrecy still applied, and Gull felt that the burden of recapture fell on him. With help, he climbed into his carriage and had his coachman take him east and through the mean streets of Whitechapel. It was a thankless task, with only a slender chance of success, yet what else could the old doctor do? But Gull failed, Eddy struck and Mary Kelly died in her grimy room. Once his frenzy was over Eddy burned his blood-soaked clothes in her fireplace: 'He then dressed himself in a woman's dress and shawl which he'd brought with him in the black hand bag.' He escaped through the window and arrived at Sandringham in time to celebrate his father's birthday, explaining away the women's clothes by pretending '. . . that he had attended a costume party the night before. He privately joked that he had gone to the affair dressed as his grandmother.' But shortly after luncheon the Prince of Wales sent Eddy back to London by coach. At Gull's house the doctors were waiting for him. The confinement had to begin once more.

At this juncture, Spiering also involved R.J. Lees in the Ripper hunt. Earlier on he had introduced the medium by relating the standard spiritualist story of Lees's meeting with Queen Victoria. Now the story is taken one step further, yet it is easy to see that no new documents are drawn on: the account is basically an amalgam of the *Daily Express* version and Stowell's additional tale 'gained from Caroline Gull'. Even so, Spiering embellishes the tale with some imaginative detail of his own, following the example of Edwin Woodhall. He writes: 'On the afternoon of November 9th, while riding in an omnibus, [Lees] saw a man enter a house in the fashionable Grosvenor Square area . . . Lees quickly got off the bus and found a constable. He related to him that he had just seen Jack the Ripper enter the house at 74 Brook Street. The constable laughed at him threatening to "run him in". Lees hastened to Scotland Yard, where he found an inspector who was willing to accompany him to 74 Brook Street the following morning.'

The visit takes place and the Stowell version is spliced into position with this conclusion: 'There was nothing that could be done, however, as Gull was not the man Lees had seen enter the house, and Gull insisted that neither he nor his family had any knowledge who that person was. Lees later claimed that he received payments from the Privy Purse to keep silent. Like so many others, records of these payments have disappeared.'

In embellishing his version, Frank Spiering didn't bother to check either on the bus routes of the time, or the geography of the Park Lane area. Had he done so he would have learned that no buses ran along Brook Street, or through Grosvenor Square, while Gull's house, in fact, could not have been spotted from any of the buses that passed by Marble Arch or ran down Park Lane.

Despite these absurdities, Spiering insists that he has the telling papers left by Gull, and from that position of strength he goes on to explain that Eddy was kept stable under a regime of drugs and hypnotic suggestion. With time, the prince's condition improved so much that 'As long as he was watched, and never allowed to venture anywhere on his own, he could attend state dinners, greet foreign royalty, and superficially appear as if he were as free as any royal prince . . .' In that improved state he visited Egypt and toured and hunted in India; 'Meanwhile, six thousand miles away, the London press noted that there had been no Ripper murders for over a year'.

On his return from India Eddy fell in love with Princess Hélène of Orléans, a disastrous choice. Hélène was a Roman Catholic and her father's Royalist political ambitions were anathema to Republican France. Since Eddy's father was determined to weld a permanent bond between France and Britain – an Entente Cordiale – Eddy had to be prised away from the troublesome Orléans family. The Pope helped by lecturing Hélène on her duties as a member of the One True Faith, Eddy's family pressures mounted, and in the end his own instability brought about the collapse of the courtship. There were other ladies who caused Eddy's heart to skip, but the promise of love proved too weak to smother the insane hate inside the prince. On 13 February 1891, Eddy took to the streets once more and slew Frances Coles, and at this point the Establishment closed ranks to end the drawn-out, menacing affair.

James Stephen was silenced first. On 21 November 1891 he was '... committed by the powers who ruled England, to the lunatic ward of St Andrew's Hospital, Northampton'. Eddy was then progressively weakened in body. Spiering argues that –

> as the last cycle of Eddy's life was pushed towards its finality, it is reasonable to imagine that certain means were introduced to bring it to a swift conclusion. In place of the regular administrations of iodide of potassium, Eddy was most probably given daily injections of morphine. It effected relief from his pain and produced deep sleep ... Finally, when he was confined to a rest home in Ascot, the dosages were steadily increased until the sleep condition became permanent.

Officially, Eddy died at Sandringham on 14 January 1892 and the cause of death was given as influenza. Spiering regards this as the inevitable cover-up and notes: 'Shortly after the deaths of Eddy and his lover, James Stephen in 1892, the official Jack the Ripper file was sealed by the Metropolitan Police and Home Secretary Matthews' office ... the file's cover was marked with the profoundest verification of the murderer's identity: CLOSED UNTIL 1992.'

In the USA, *Prince Jack* is widely believed to be true but it is not published in Great Britain. Spiering would have it that the Establishment conspired to keep the truth from the British public. So, in fairness to his major claims, let us for a brief interval forget the absurdities and ask instead if at any point Spiering has reasoned from genuine sources? Is he using hitherto suppressed evidence? If so, his thesis could still be of importance.

A meticulous search shows that nowhere in the book is a single sentence quoted from any palace or police official that backs up his story, so we can eliminate them at once as sources. Everything then *must* hinge on the papers left by Sir William Gull, but what Gull actually *wrote* can't be determined from the text: nowhere is a single, direct quote offered. At least, though, Spiering does tell us where the decisive papers can be found. He says: 'I was extremely fortunate in locating a copy of Dr William Gull's notes, bound in an ancient portfolio, kept in, of all places, the New York Academy of Medicine.'

I have written to Frank Spiering offering to pay for a copy of these notes. I naturally assumed that such momentous writings would hardly

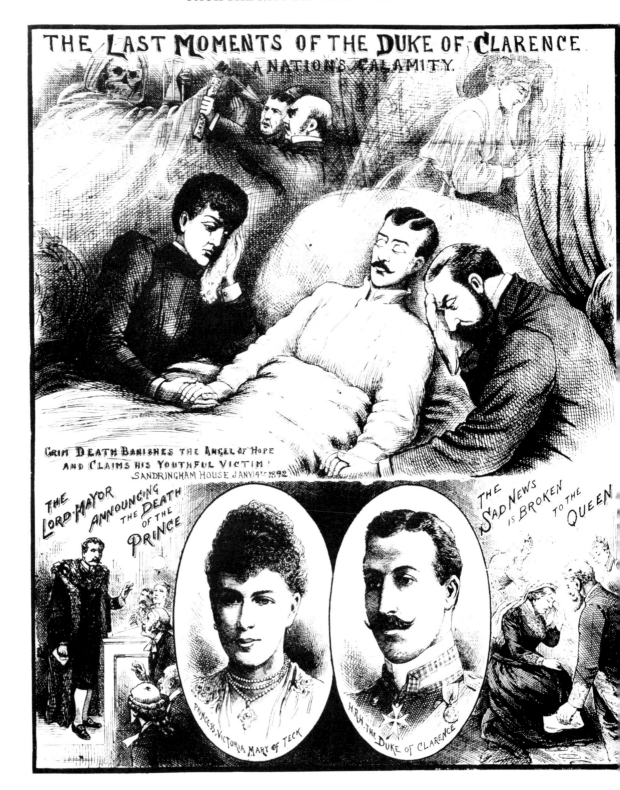

be treated casually by anyone and it seemed only logical to deduce that he had kept a copy for himself. But no reply was ever received from him, which is more than strange. Surely Spiering should have been proud to demonstrate that his account rested on strong foundations – but he stayed silent.

There is good reason for this silence. As a double-check, I asked the librarian of the New York Academy of Medicine to supply me with photocopies of the Gull papers. Their staff searched and I later received a letter dated 20 November 1986. It reads:

Dear Mr Harris,

To the best of our knowledge, the Library does not contain a portfolio with notes of Sir William Gull referring to the Whitechapel murderer. All of the material in our collection which is available to researchers is cataloged. None of the entries in our catalog for works by or about Sir William Gull contains the material referred to by Mr Spiering.

In a library the size and age of ours, it is possible that a set of notes bound with a larger work or other works could have gone unnoticed by our catalogers, but it is highly unlikely. Mr Spiering was never able to remember or reconstruct the catalog entry he submitted for retrieval from our stacks and in which he allegedly found the notes by Gull. Thorough searches by staff also proved fruitless.

Sincerely yours,
Brett A. Kirkpatrick, Librarian.

Only one conclusion is possible – we are faced with yet another elaborate hoax. At the start we were promised the 'solution to the ultimate murder mystery where the enigmatic outlines of Jack the Ripper are filled in and a royal figure emerges'. But instead of that boldly sketched portrait we find nothing but a collection of worthless Yankee Doodles.

15

Enter Knight in Glass Armour

'Jack the Ripper was not one man but three, two killers and an accomplice. The facts surrounding their exploits have never before been teased from the confused skein of truths, half-truths and lies which have been woven around this case. Falsehoods deliberate and accidental have hopelessly enmeshed the truth.' With those provocative words Stephen Knight opened his presentation of *The Final Solution*.

His search for the truth began when the BBC planned a series on the Whitechapel murders. Early in 1973, a tip to the BBC team from an official at the Yard led to a meeting with an artist named Joseph Sickert, known as the illegitimate son of the famous painter Walter Sickert. From his father Joseph had picked up an elaborate and chilling tale about the killings. The BBC team were eager to listen to this, for they already knew that Walter Sickert had had a long-standing interest in the Ripper case. The story that was unfolded involved Joseph's mother, Alice, and *her* mother. It also brought in the Duke of Clarence as a major figure, but this time with a marked difference. Clarence was no longer cast as the Ripper or even as the Ripper's playmate; he was portrayed as the pathetic cause of the mayhem but totally innocent of any other involvement.

In its early, truncated form, the story was that Clarence had fallen for a shop assistant in Cleveland Street. A secret marriage ensued and a child was born. All of this, of course, raised problems for the palace and the state, so the foolish union had to be smashed. Smashing it seemed easy, but a friend of shop-girl Annie's escaped the official trap and fled to Whitechapel where she shared her secret with a handful of fellow prostitutes. They dreamed of blackmail. They ended up on mortuary slabs. The Masons took good care of that!

In this raw state 'the Sickert version' was slotted into the final episode of the BBC's *Jack the Ripper* series screened on 17 August 1973. One month later Stephen Knight visited Joseph Sickert to interview him on behalf of the *East London Advertiser*, the sole surviving paper covering the Whitechapel area. At first he thought of a newspaper feature only, but as he listened to Sickert, he began to realize that the story was too great to be left to stray newspaper articles. At the end of four hours Knight decided that it cried out for a book-length treatment.

When all objections were stilled, Knight began to co-operate in earnest with Sickert and the background research began. There were many doubts and queries, but the initial searches began at Cleveland Street, W1 – all roads led there.

It was in Cleveland Street, at No 15, that Walter Sickert had kept a studio; not his only one, by any means, but the tragically crucial one. It became crucial because of a chain of events stretching back to Denmark of the 1850s. In those times, Walter Sickert's father, Oswald, had apparently made friends with many members of the Danish royal family. As a court painter, he came to know the future Queen of England – Alix, daughter of King Christian IX. In 1863, Alix married Edward, Prince of Wales, and came to live in England. Five years later Oswald moved to London and settled there, keeping up his old friendship with Alix: in time, his son Walter joined him in her privileged circle.

By the early 1880s, Alix grew concerned about her eldest son Eddy's personal development. His father disliked him. The boy seemed dim and lacking in vitality, and the restricted court circles failed to stretch him or fire his imagination. She decided that he had an undeveloped artistic soul; perhaps the world of art would give his personality the chance to grow, would stimulate a sense of responsibility.

With these thoughts in mind, Alix turned to young Walter Sickert and asked him to 'take Eddy under his artistic wing'. Sickert was only too anxious to help. He passed off Eddy as a younger brother, Albert, and as Albert and Walter the pair would wander freely around the pubs, coffee-houses and studios of the Bohemian village of North Soho. A royal coach, with its unmistakable coat of arms, would carry the prince from the palace. At a pre-arranged and quiet spot, Eddy would slip out and continue his journey in an undistinguished coach driven by trusted John Netley.

The arrangement, according to Knight, worked smoothly. Eddy thrived and relaxed and none of his early adventures troubled the court. Then, in the summer of 1884, came a doom-laden meeting. Sickert introduced Eddy to one of his young models and Eddy fell for her. The girl was Annie Elizabeth Crook (also known as Cook) who worked at the tobacconist's shop at 22 Cleveland Street. She was illiterate and no beauty, but she had a winning charm and she won. As proof, she gave birth to Eddy's daughter, Alice Margaret Crook.

After the birth in April 1885, Annie continued to live in the basement of

6 Cleveland Street; she even kept on her job at No 22. This was possible because Sickert paid an Irish girl to act as the child's nanny. The nanny's name was Mary Kelly. At first, the parties involved kept the royal secrets close, Kelly included. Even when Eddy and Annie went through a marriage ceremony, no word leaked out, though the ceremony was conducted at the private chapel of St Saviour's and St Saviour's was Roman Catholic, thus in direct conflict with the faith upheld by the Royal Family.

What 'happened next' can only be entertained if we suspend judgement for a while and ride along with the Sickert view of the political climate in the 1880s: that the monarchy was in such disrepute that republicanism was flourishing, as was, even more sinister, the socialist movement. Anything and everything that these twin menaces could use against the crown was welcome. Any royal scandal would be grist to their mill and a scandal involving Eddy would be a godsend. Why?

According to the Sickert line, as endorsed by Knight, 'Eddy seemed the only hope of salvaging some last vestige of the common man's affection for his Royal Family. Young and attractive, he was popularly regarded as the one King who might make the throne secure again. If he too slid onto the downward path of immorality and dissipation, (Prime Minister) Salisbury feared, the end of the monarchy was surely nigh.'

What, though, was so special about Eddy's folly? In Sickert's eyes Eddy

> . . . had created a danger worse even than if he'd followed in his father's mucky footprints . . . The age was bedevilled with an anti-Catholic feeling so intense that even without the prevailing threat of Socialism, Eddy's marriage could have precipitated a revolution . . . the monarchy and the very structure of British politics seemed on the brink of collapse . . . Eddy's behaviour was enough at this perilous moment of history to fire the fuel of revolution.

Prime Minister Salisbury decided to act swiftly. The troublesome union had to be shattered, once and for all. So, on 2 April 1888, a band of plain-clothed police gathered at the Howland Street end of Cleveland Street. They were all dressed as ruffians and in true ruffian-fashion they staged a street brawl. While the locals were captivated by the mêlée, two hansom cabs drew up at the studio end of the street. Walter Sickert was outside at the time and saw what happened. Two men in brown tweeds leapt from one cab and went into his studio at No 15, the place where Eddy and Annie used to liaise, emerging again with Eddy between them. Meanwhile, the other coach had stopped outside No 6, and a man and a woman had descended into Annie's basement rooms. Together they dragged Annie out into the street and despite her struggles forced her into the cab. Then the two cabs raced off in opposite directions.

Walter Sickert never saw Eddy again, but he gathered he had been taken back to court and placed under strict supervision, almost house arrest. As for Annie, though he met her once or twice afterwards, the carefree girl he'd once known no longer existed. Following the raid, she had been taken to Guy's Hospital, confined there for 156 days and only released after an operation had rendered her epileptic and feeble-minded. From then on, she wandered the streets and ended up in a series of workhouse beds, until she died insane in 1920.

In that callous way the union was neutralized, but even so, a threat still remained, for Mary Kelly had escaped the net, together with Annie's child Alice. The pair were now in hiding, somewhere in the slums of Whitechapel. Worse still, Kelly had broken silence and confided in a group of low-grade harlots, who, quickly sensing money in her secrets, hatched a blackmail plot.

Salisbury now had two secrets to safeguard. Coupled inexorably with Eddy's blunders was the inhuman treatment meted out to Eddy's innocent bride, and now only the most drastic action could end these new threats. That action could not be Government-inspired: it would be engineered by the secret brotherhood that really counted – the Freemasons.

> For Masonry was the power behind the Throne and Government alike. If the Throne went, and Britain became a republic, the Masons went too. Kelly and her cronies had to be silenced if the reins of power were to remain firmly in Masonic hands . . .

Freemason Salisbury called in Freemason Sir William Gull to mastermind the silencing operation. Sir William, we're to understand, had already proved his worth by operating on Annie Crook. Scalpel in hand, he was fully prepared to operate on each of the harlots in turn. This time no hospital theatre would be involved, for the risks were too high:

> One poor woman shrieking for her truths to be heard and begging inspectors, doctors and visitors to believe she was the wife of a prince could easily have been dismissed as mad. But four apparent lunatics crying out the same tale, even though they were mere East End whores, would have produced a pattern that many would have been eager to interpret. If to certify or imprison them was out of the question, and to leave them at large was clearly unthinkable, to kill them was the only practical alternative to Gull's ruthless mind.

The equally ruthless John Netley was chosen to drive Gull's coach around the East End. Netley was of course already involved, having known of the Cleveland Street assignations for years. He'd shown that he could keep

Sir Robert Cecil, Marquis of Salisbury, KG: did this patriarch direct the hand that held the knife? Could the noble head of Sir William Gull, Bart, MD (right) have housed a killer's brain?

secrets, and now he became party to some of the most ghastly secrets of the day. Inside the shelter of his coach he saw harlots butchered; then he followed Gull's orders and dumped the bodies wherever the doctor felt they should rest. Netley's sadistic side was so inflamed by the bloodshed that he despatched Elizabeth Stride himself and later went on to inflict the long-drawn out mutilations on the whores' ringleader, Mary Kelly.

Before the blackmailers could be slain they had to be located and that's where the accomplice came in. He was none other than Sir Robert Anderson, Assistant Commissioner of the Metropolitan Police, a high-ranking Freemason belonging to the same lodge as Gull and Salisbury. Officially he was on sick leave at the time, spending his days on the Continent; in 'truth', he was skulking around the backstreets seeking out information.

Up to there, the Sickert-Knight disclosures set the mind reeling. Could there be even more extraordinary things to emerge? Certainly. For we learn that the whores' deaths were staged as a proclamation. To the general public, the murders seemed to be just the frenzied actions of a deranged mind, but to those in the know, they could be seen as ritual killings carried out according to the directives of the Masonic Codes. That's why the throats were cut from left to right, as in the penalty clause of the Masonic Entered Apprentice. The Apprentice swears to keep the secrets revealed to him '. . . without evasion, equivocation or mental reservations of any kind, under no less a penalty, on the violation of any of them, than of having my throat cut across, my tongue torn out by the root and buried in the sands of the sea . . .'

This, according to Knight, is only one of the Masonic parallels. He refers to Chapman's corpse and notes that the intestines had been placed on the shoulders. For Knight this is 'definitely Masonic'. He compares it with the Masonic myth of the murder of Hiram Abiff. The three murderers were caught and executed 'by the breast being torn open and their heart and vitals taken out and thrown over the left shoulder.' Unfortunately for the comparison, Eddowes' intestines lay over the right shoulder. Still, that was no problem for Knight, who argues that '. . . it is possible that the point about *which* shoulder was overlooked' – because of the hurry, of course.

Other details are brought forward to show the Masonic connection; much ingenuity is displayed in this hunt for prints of the Hidden Hand. Even Hogarth is dragged in to provide some extra substance to the theory: his engraving, 'The Reward of Cruelty', is painstakingly analysed to show '. . . similarities between the killing of Mary Kelly and a Masonic ritual murder'.

Yet that engraving does no more than show a standard eighteenth-century medical dissection of a hanged criminal. All the so-called significant features – removal of the heart and intestines, the use of a screw and pulley to raise the head, the mutilations – were common to the anatomy classes of that period. But Knight has a wild case to plead and wild examples naturally follow.

Even if we agree that Stephen Knight became reckless at times, his *complete* case, which after all vindicates Eddy, must still be viewed impartially. There may be some solid truths there. Indeed, the whole basic story might just be true. So we urgently need to return to the starting point, to Cleveland Street in 1884. Perhaps enlightenment awaits us there?

16

The Cracks Begin to Show

Nineteenth-century Cleveland Street was well served by directories, electoral registers and rate-books, yet none of those for 1884 shows an entry for either Walter Sickert or Annie Elizabeth Crook or Cook. This in itself does nothing to scotch the story; if Sickert simply rented rooms, he would not show as a rate-payer or voter and could easily be unlisted in a street directory. No women had votes at that time, so Annie wouldn't appear on that register, and if she too rented the basement at No 6 she might not appear on the rate-returns. Thus in both cases the absence of any form of listing proves nothing one way or the other.

There is, though, independent proof of Annie's presence in Cleveland Street. Her daughter's birth certificate, dated 18 April 1885, records the child's name as Alice Margaret Crook. The father's name is not given but the mother's is stated as 'Annie Elizabeth Crook, confectionary assistant from Cleveland Street'. That in itself upholds some of Joseph Sickert's claims about his grandmother, but there is an extra entry on the certificate which goes even further. Annie was illiterate, as Sickert stated, so she needed to make her cross, and in witnessing this cross the registrar himself wrote: 'The mark of Annie Elizabeth Crook, Mother, 6 Cleveland Street, Fitzroy Square'. So the early part of Joseph Sickert's story seems to be confirmed. Later searches in the rate-books, conducted by Karen de Groot, seemed to underscore this proof by showing that in 1888 the basement of 6 Cleveland Street was occupied by an Elizabeth Cook; by then she was obviously in an improved position, to reach the stage of being a rate-payer, if in fact the two women were one and the same.

Now the slight variation in the surname had earlier been pointed out by Joseph Sickert. It was the sort of error an illiterate woman making her cross on the rate-payment receipts would never notice. In all, then, the certificate is satisfactory in establishing residence, but at the same time it raises legitimate doubts about the place of Alice's birth. It is shown as Marylebone Workhouse, yet if the unnamed father *was* Eddy, why did he allow his beloved to have their child in the pitiless wards of a workhouse? Compared with Annie or Walter or any of the throng in Cleveland Street, Eddy was an extremely rich man and he had a full eight to nine months in which to pass money on to Annie. Mother and child could have had a discreet, safe and comfortable confinement in some quiet nursing home. But, if we believe this story, Eddy callously looked the other way, which is just not believable. Interestingly enough, Knight never once considered this problem.

The alleged marriage is just as unbelievable. It took place at a St Saviour's Infirmary Chapel and Mary Kelly was the witness. In Knight's book, BBC research assistant Ian Sharp describes at length how he searched in vain for this St Saviour's. He tried Southwark Cathedral, which had once been named St Saviour's, but their records for the 1880s failed to show a marriage involving Annie. An infirmary of that name in Osnaburgh Street no longer existed and its successor, St Saviour's Hospital, in Hythe, Kent, had no records for the period. Prolonged searches at the central index of births, marriages and deaths failed to bring to light any marriage that could be remotely connected with Annie. Reluctantly, the St Saviour's lead had to be abandoned.

I know nothing of Ian Sharp. When he undertook his search in 1973 he may not have been fully steeped in the literature of the Whitechapel murders; if so, he could easily have missed the warning signs that he was in the presence of a hoax. With Stephen Knight, though, no such allowance is possible. In the bibliography to his book he includes *three* editions of Donald McCormick's *Identity of Jack the Ripper*, but nowhere in his own book does he indicate this point: *that St Saviour's Infirmary formed an important part of an earlier and irreconcilable theory peddled by McCormick.*

Fittingly, this Infirmary is the Workhouse Annexe located in the spurious yarns attributed to Dr Dutton. In McCormick's book, Dutton is quoted as saying: '. . . Martha Turner, Annie Chapman, Mary Nichols, and Mary Kelly all attended a clinic at St Saviour's Infirmary in Westmoreland Road, Walworth, right up to the time of their death.' McCormick comments: 'The doctor stated that he made this discovery from Dr J.F. Williams, who lived in Camberwell and attended the St Saviour's Infirmary.' It was at this clinic that the doomed whores met Jack the Ripper. For Jack, alias Pedachenko, worked there part-time as an assistant to Dr Williams.

This connection between Kelly, St Saviour's and the Ripper allows McCormick to say: 'A reconstruction of the Miller's Court murder now takes on a different aspect. Kelly had been to the clinic at St Saviour's

Infirmary. She would, therefore, possibly be known to Pedachenko. He may have found out her address and made a rendezvous with her . . . if Kelly knew Pedachenko already, she would have no qualms about taking him back to her room; she could reasonably assume that an assistant at a clinic would be respectable enough.'

And there we have it. For over thirteen years before Joseph Sickert wrought his mischief it was firmly in print that Kelly died *because* of her involvement with a St Saviour's Infirmary. It is impossible that Knight could have missed this: after all, he'd read three editions of McCormick's book, and one would have been enough. So was the knowledge subconsciously pushed to one side? Did facing the jarring facts threaten the whole viability of his *Final Solution*?

Since Stephen Knight is dead, many such queries will never be answered. His quirky ideas may have been completely governed by devotion to his conspiracy theories, or the brain tumour that killed him may have played its part by producing erratic thought patterns. Who can tell? What is certain is that he evaded problems that threatened his 'solution'. With trying difficulties out of the way, he then used worthless documents to give his theories substance. His political portrait of the times, for example, became distorted, then unreal.

The riots of Black Monday 1886 had been troublesome, but only for the mollycoddled householders and clubmen of Mayfair and its fringes. The demonstrations that followed were purely a London affair and highly localized at that. Even Bloody Sunday had been occasioned only by the understandable anger of the long-term unemployed, but these angry men weren't revolutionaries, by any means. They wanted 'something now' – palliatives to take away the worst pressures that crushed body and spirit. The ruling class, the power-wielders, call them what you will, had no illusions about the upheavals. Timorous duchesses and soft-handed manufacturers may have trembled in their beds for a while but the knowledgeable men of power knew that 'Revolution' was nothing more than an emotive slogan. The 'Reds' who used Marxist jargon were derisively small groups, like Hyndman's Social Democratic Federation and Morris's Socialist League. The masses, though, were different. At heart they were acquiescent. They could be calmed eventually by measured doses of social reform.

How right the rulers were; they correctly divined the discontent. But in

---

Opposite: The Two Nations: 'The Whitechapel murderer has been so successful in calling attention for a moment to the social question' – G. B. Shaw

Stephen Knight's scenario, the rulers are depicted as being in a state of genuine fear for their very future. Out of fear they turned for guidance to a secret code of conduct, a type of terrorist handbook. It was called *The Protocols of the Learned Elders of Zion*.

Knight introduces these *Protocols* by stating that they give an indication of the plans and ambitions of at least some of the leaders of Freemasonry. He says:

> ...absolute power is the ambition, at least of the Freemasons in the highest degrees, and nothing, not even human life, must stand in its way...With such fanatical writings set down as 'protocols' by high Masons, it needs only an extreme or lunatic fringe to take them absolutely literally. Of all the hundreds of thousands of Freemasons in England in the 1880s, there were bound to be these lunatic fringes. And a peculiar sort of lunacy did inspire the Ripper killings...

Knight quotes one protocol as: 'Only sheer force is victorious in politics... *Violence must be the principle*, cunning and hypocrisy must be the rule of those governments which do not wish to lay down their crown at the feet of the agents of some new power.' He then comments that it '...describes almost exactly the dilemma facing Salisbury with the misconduct of Eddy and the blackmail from Mary Kelly and her cronies. He was surrounded by "the agents of some new power" – socialists, anarchists, republicans – and he dealt with the problem, said Sickert, in just the way prescribed in the protocol. Violence, indeed, became the principle, and cunning and hypocrisy coalesced in a near-perfect cover-up.'

His next illuminating protocol reads: 'In order to obtain our ends we must have recourse to much slyness and artfulness.' Having absorbed such an original and profound directive, Knight comments: 'Once again, so much slyness and artfulness has been brought into play on the murderous field of the Ripper, that no one has been able to get near the truth working, as all previous investigators have, from the outside. It has taken Walter Sickert, reconnoitring from within the tangled web, to point the way and show that the spider at the centre is in reality a horde of tarantulas.'

A further protocol includes the words '...in order to demonstrate our enslavement of the Gentile governments in Europe, we will show our

---

Opposite above: Was 'Ripper Druit' drugged and dumped in the Thames at this spot?
Below: Sandringham House, Prince Eddy's *official* place of death. Rumours, though, nominate a mental home...

A LOST WOMAN
MARY KELLY
IN MILLER'S COURT

The fairest of the five. The most foully butchered.

power to one of them by means of *crimes of violence*, that is to say by a *reign of terror*.' Knight thrills to this, and declares:

> The documents containing the *Protocols* were stolen thirteen years after the Whitechapel murders, but they were not new even in 1901. Had the reign of terror . . . already happened by the time the documents were stolen? *Had it happened in Whitechapel in 1888? . . .* Was the murder of the five whores perpetrated not only for the motive of self-protection already described, but also to demonstrate the far-reaching power of Freemasonry to initiates the world over?

Others of the *Protocols* are treated in the same incredible fashion – for Knight actually *believes* in the documents. He says they were '. . . in existence a long time before they were actually published. And they bear such uncanny resemblance to the events surrounding the Ripper case, it seems inescapable that they exerted an influence.' He alludes vaguely to the doubts about the *Protocols'* authenticity but insists that:

> Forgeries or not, the product of fanatical minds or not, the fact is that they have been taken in deadly seriousness by thousands of people. It will be shown that Sir William Gull, fanatically inclined and almost certainly insane toward the end of his life, was just the sort of high Mason to take the *Protocols* literally, as he did the whole of Freemasonry's allegory and ritual. And it is Sir William Gull's alleged conduct *as a result* of the *Protocols* and other Masonic lore, not the genuineness of that lore itself, which is under discussion.

Intoxicated with his conspiracy angle, Knight sums up: 'If Masonic supremacy appears in jeopardy, it is re-established by a show of strength, by crimes of violence . . . the strength of Masons high in the Government was being threatened by the self-interest of Mary Kelly . . . Kelly and her confederates would have received the penalty meted out to those who betray the brotherhood. This is exactly what happened.'

A great deal has been made of these protocols – so what is their real status? Unequivocally I can state that they are blatant fiction, appallingly bad fiction at that. They were never known to Gull or any of the other Masons of the 1880s, because they never existed: they are a twentieth-century concoction, crude and muddled passages first included in a Russian pamphlet published in Moscow in 1905. The author, Sergei Nilus, was a fanatical believer in the impending coming of the Anti-Christ. In his pamphlet's epilogue he wrote:

> It is nearly four years since the Protocols came into my possession. Only God knows what efforts I have made to bring them to general notice – in vain – and even to warn those in power, by disclosing the causes of the storm about to break on apathetic Russia . . . One can no longer doubt it, the triumphant reign of the King of Israel rises over our degenerate world as that of Satan, with his power and his terrors. The King born of the blood of Zion – the Anti-Christ – is about to mount the throne of universal empire.

Many other fanatics were just as certain that the Pope was the Anti-Christ, but their diatribes had no lasting ill-effect. Nilus's crudities, though, were used to justify pogroms and hatred towards the Jewish people: in Tsarist Russia such anti-Semitic propaganda was welcome. After 1918 these words of hate were exported and eagerly reprinted by the Nazis in Germany and by their imitators elsewhere. By using them, Knight demonstrated the shallowness of his thinking and the damning defects of his research.

For this misconduct no excuses are possible. There is an extensive literature dealing with the *Protocols* and their origins, yet not one of these essential books, pamphlets and articles is mentioned in his text or bibliography. He had a responsibility to check the provenance of these strange and 'once hidden' edicts, which he avoided. Sadly, it's an age-old story: believers in the Hidden Hand gain such a tremulous inner excitement from their discoveries that their reason is by-passed. They inhabit a mental world of whispers and dark broodings over dimly glimpsed secrets. Light is anathema to this murky world. It stays rigorously shuttered.

Had Knight delved into the background of the *Protocols* he would have encountered M. Maurice Joly, a French Roman Catholic lawyer living in Paris in the 1860s. A writer of philosophical articles, Joly came to nurse strong liberal, political ideas which naturally put him at odds with the despotic tendencies of Napoleon III. This ruler's rigging of elections, his press censorship, his curbs on free speech, his use of informers and spies, made Joly seethe, so he composed a satirical attack on the dictator.

Hampered by fears of the censor, Joly's attack was hardly an open one and suffered as well from his stodgy, philosophical style. Even so, in 1864, it went to press. *Dialogues aux Enfers entre Machiavel et Montesquieu* allows Machiavelli to put forward his cynical and opportunist views on manipulation; his opponent tries to counter them. The book was obviously destined not to reach the best-seller ranks. Yet, best-seller or not, it gained immortality when its text was picked over and used to create the *Protocols*: the greater part of the *Protocols* consists of no more than revamped versions of Machiavelli's views as invented by Maurice Joly. Some other works of fiction make up the remaining parts, but Joly is pre-eminent.

So much for the documents that are alleged to have inspired Sir Ripper Gull. In the hands of other interpreters, they have been blamed for causing the Russian Revolution, for the defeat of Germany in World War I, and for the take-over of the White House by 'anti-business minded' Jews. For the sake of completeness, let us note that they have even been seen as the mainspring of the French Revolution. In a way, it's quite a come-down to have them linked with the Masonic Fiend of Whitechapel; but for Knight, this link was a certainty.

17
The Breastplate Shatters

I am not, and never have been, a Freemason, but I can state categorically that nothing links Masonry with the Whitechapel murders. Neither does anything, save Stowell's and Walter Sickert's fantasies, show that Gull was in any way involved. How is it, then, that Stephen Knight is able to present the semblance of a case for two murderers and an accomplice?

He starts by stating: 'Surprisingly, there are more people than Sickert who point an accusing finger at Gull . . . For instance, in the Chicago *Sunday Times-Herald* of 28 April 1895, there appeared a story . . . told by a well-known London physician, Dr Howard. Howard, his tongue loosened by drink, claimed he was one of the twelve London physicians who had sat . . . as a commission in lunacy upon a brother physician, who had been responsible for the Jack the Ripper murders.'

Having quoted sections of the article, Knight concludes with its finishing words: 'None of the keepers knows that the desperate maniac . . . is the famous "Jack the Ripper". To them and to the visiting inspectors he is simply known as Thomas Mason, alias No 124.' Knight pounces on this to declare: 'Allowing for the sensational treatment which any such story is bound to have received in America at that time, there is still a hard core of provable fact. There was, for instance, an asylum in Islington – called St Mary's – but its records have been destroyed. And in 1896 an Islington 'pauper' called Thomas Mason died – at exactly the age Gull would have been had he lived.'

If you accept that reasoning, you also have to accept that in 1895 British newspapermen suddenly put their brains into hock. There, without cost to them, was one of the hottest tips of the century. They learned that the Ripper was alive and howling away in Islington. They even knew his asylum name and number – and yet they did nothing about it. In the previous year a bold reporter of the *Sun* had even penetrated Broadmoor in the hunt for a Ripper story, but suddenly all initiative and competitive drive were forgotten.

It is just not acceptable. Within hours of hearing the story every live-wire journalist in Fleet Street and the provinces would have been on the track. Easily hidden spy-cameras – and there were plenty about – would have been tucked into bowler hats, pinned beneath cravats or stuffed under waistcoats. Bribes would have been offered, and gladly accepted. Within days No 124, Thomas Mason, would have been featured on front pages, together with his mug-shots. But that didn't happen. Why? Because the newspaper world at least must have quickly realized that the story was hokum and wouldn't bear close scrutiny.

Knight was a newspaperman himself, so one might expect that his training would immediately alert him to the absurdity of the asylum story. But of course he needed to believe that part to be true: the name 'Mason' fitted right into his Hidden Hand jigsaw. With the confidence of the zealot, he concluded that:

> The name under which the physician in Howard's story was certified – Thomas *Mason* – brings to mind the Freemasonic tradition that in certain circumstances a Mason will die by his greatest achievement. Gull, said Sickert, was in his element removing the troublesome by certifying them insane. Now there is completely independent evidence that this was the ultimate fate of Gull himself. What more appropriate name for a certified Freemason than Mason, a pun horribly consistent with the humour described in the Masonic *Protocols* as so essential?

The very same point is made twice more at later stages. For Knight, its significance outweighs logic. Hasty acceptance supersedes careful appraisal.

This haste is a constant factor throughout his *Final Solution*; he didn't even read the Chicago piece with care, which is why he refers to it as Dr Howard's. As the text shows, only the opening two paragraphs were based on 'Howard's revelations'; the rest was attributed to the anonymous gentleman of Chicago whose 'lips were at last unsealed'. Having mis-read the article, he then promptly fathered the entire piece onto Dr Benjamin Howard. But then, he needed to prove that:

> Howard, almost certainly a Freemason . . . could well have been one of the several Masonic members of the St George's Club who connived in Annie Elizabeth's elimination after she and Prince Eddy were parted. As such, Howard would have been an ideal choice to serve as one of the twelve doctors needed to conduct the secret lunacy hearing on Gull.

Did Knight ever know of Dr Benjamin Howard's 1896 letter of repudiation? He did, although well after he'd worked out his own conspiracy line involving Howard. But still not too late to do something about it. So how did he react? He simply brushed the letter to one side; it was obviously part of the great cover-up. As he put it: 'Dr Howard would hardly have admitted that he had become drunk and broken the solemn oath binding him to secrecy about the Masonic lunacy commission proceedings. I find it perfectly credible that Howard would deny this betrayal of Masonic secrets most vehemently.' But if the story *was* true, it would have been far too late by 1896 for Howard to make a denial. If Howard had been in Frisco at the time, if he had really broken an oath, if he had really told all, then the Masons would already have marked him down as the only possible culprit. *If* the story was true.

Knight, though, will allow no doubts about the truth. He even asserts that Howard's club, the St George's, ran the hospital at 367 Fulham Road where Annie Crook died. This allowed them to keep her under control and surveillance until her end. This is Knight's fabrication. The directories for 1888 to 1920 show that the St George's Infirmary at 367 Fulham Road was never connected with any private West End club. It was in fact no more than the infirmary of the Union Workhouse run by the Board of Guardians.

Maintaining the truth of that story allows Knight to say: 'The physician Howard described was undoubtedly Gull. From clues contained in Lees's story it can be seen that the doctor he spoke of was also Gull. That both men independently described different but overlapping episodes in the same drama strengthens this argument . . . both stories fit in perfectly with established facts and with Sickert's narrative . . .' In this fashion Knight is able to comfort and delude himself: three stories, all complementing each other! It never dawned on him that there was only *one* story and an exceedingly tall one at that. As ever, zeal warped his judgement, allowing him to find support where it didn't exist. Added to that was an exciting find that would have ousted scepticism, had he felt any.

In a file at Scotland Yard Knight discovered an item that made his head swim. On reading it, he concluded that the Lees story

> . . . had a wide circulation, in London at least, as early as July 1889 – only nine months after the murders. This is confirmed by a note in the *Letters* file at Scotland Yard. Admittedly this is from a crank who signed himself 'Jack the Ripper', but the writer's state of mind is immaterial. Only his knowledge counts . . . The letter, received at the Yard on 25th July 1889, says: 'Dear Boss, You have not caught me yet you see, with all your cunning, with all your "Lees" with all your blue bottles. Jack the Ripper.'

How deeply satisfying this must have been for him. He was now able to reason: 'For the story to have gained this sort of acceptance as early as July 1889 means it must initially have been told (or leaked out) a few weeks after the murder of Kelly . . .'

Again we have an eager, convenient mis-reading. This letter has no bearing on the 1895 Lees story. It doesn't even refer to Lees as an individual. The wording 'all your "Lees" ' refers to a group, not to one man: the inverted commas, the plural use show the name to be nothing but a handy collective term for all those people who were hot on the psychic trail. They were on the fiend-hunt from the early days in 1888 and doubled their efforts after the murder of Alice McKenzie in July 1889, that is to say just a week before this letter was written. Lees's name was chosen to brand the lot because he was by far and away the best known of the coterie. His regular propaganda meetings in London, both indoors and out, made certain that everyone knew of him, and I don't doubt that at some of these meetings he hinted mysteriously that the psychics 'were on to something', that more was known than could be revealed.

I'm certain that Knight would still have used the Lees saga even if he had never found this 1889 letter. It was inevitable, for as I've shown, the American hoax is the essential key to all the theories involving 'the London physician of high standing'. Even so, in order to use the story to best advantage, Knight had to indulge in some dubious wangling. In common with Woodhall, Morton and Spiering, he juggled around with the events in order to make them more acceptable. Of course, he was able to make a superficially plausible case for his actions, claiming that he was justifiably able to tidy things up because of the help given him by a great-niece of Lees, a Mrs Emily Porter of Wembley.

We are never told exactly what Mrs Porter had to say, which is a shame; but armed with 'fresh knowledge' Knight comes up with what he terms 'the original and unblemished story told by Lees.' It's original certainly – but only because it alters the geography of London's West End.

In the primary yarn of 1895, Lees is depicted spotting the Ripper walking south from Marble Arch down Park Lane. At the Duke of Wellington's old home, Apsley House, which stands on the corner of Park Lane and Piccadilly, the alarmed Ripper jumped into a cab and sped off eastwards along Piccadilly. Geographically that makes sense.

Now compare that with Knight's new version. In it he has the Ripper walk eastwards from Marble Arch along Oxford Street. Half-way along the street – which would land him near Oxford Circus – he reaches *Apsley House*, and in a nervous state jumps into a cab and is driven off *down Piccadilly*. How on earth does he do it? Apsley House is over a mile south-west of Oxford Circus by the shortest diagonal route.

Yet if the route is absurd, so is Knight's acceptance of this Ripper

The place 'where the Ripper took flight'.

sighting. It implies that Lees, a working journalist, a man supposed to have close contact with the court, a friend of Gladstone and Disraeli, had never once seen Sir William Gull before and had never even spotted one of Gull's photographs or popular portraits. But Gull was often photographed and drawn: he counted as one of the famous faces of that period. Not to Lees, though, if you go along with the yarn.

Repeatedly Knight returns to the Lees account to indict Gull, asserting: 'Though Lees did not name the doctor . . . the fact that Lees was plainly describing the same physician as Howard, who *was* accusing Gull, makes it certain that he too was saying, "Sir William Gull was Jack the Ripper".' At this point he spies a problem – a clash between the Stowell and the Chicago versions. Stowell reported that Lady Gull had given non-committal replies to the medium. Knight, however, needed to believe that Gull had been *unmasked* at the confrontation. How could the clashing accounts be harmonized? Easy. The Hidden Hand suggested sleight of hand.

Knight now suggested that Stowell was only pretending to point a finger at the Duke of Clarence. Viewed in that light, 'Old Stowell's final emphatic statement that he had not even *thought* Eddy was the Ripper takes on a new significance . . . Stowell's whole article is clearly intended to create the *impression* that Eddy was his suspect. But the only evidence he produced pointed the finger at Gull.' So what lay behind all this subterfuge? What else but – Freemasonry?

Stowell, you see, was a Royal Arch Freemason, a member of Corubria Lodge. Therefore he knew the Masonic secrets surrounding Gull and for some peculiar reason wanted to make them public. But he dare not do so in any forthright way. The knowledge had to be veiled. Stowell worked this stunt by building quaint clues into his article, hoping to reveal the facts and yet escape blame from his Masonic elders. Remember, this is Knight's grand theory, not mine. So let Knight summarize. After mentioning the alleged sighting of Gull in Whitechapel, he says:

> The inescapable conclusion is that Stowell, in making a deliberately inaccurate statement about a man who had never been publicly mentioned in connection with the Ripper, was in fact accusing that man.

Right up until his final chapter Knight accepted the original line-up described by Joseph Sickert: Gull was the crazy master-mind, Netley his slimy assistant and apprentice butcher, and Sir Robert Anderson was the hunter and look-out man. Then, in his final chapter, he introduced his own amazing twist. Anderson was rejected as the third man. The policeman may have been a liar and his conduct may have been suspicious, but even so nothing tied him in directly with the murders. The third man had to be none other than Walter Sickert himself.

From his new position, Knight still held that everything Walter Sickert had said about Prince Eddy, Annie Crook, little Alice, Mary Kelly, Sir William Gull and the murders themselves was true. But Sickert knew far too much for an outsider; the knowledge he displayed was far too deep and accurate. It had to be the knowledge of someone personally involved at all stages of the crimes. His involvement was supposed to have ended at the Cleveland Street kidnap but for Knight, this just wouldn't wash. Sickert was lying. He must have been involved from start to finish. Only this personal involvement could account for old Sickert's obsession with the case. His need to talk about the murders was so great he invented Anderson's role in order to be able to expound on them without betraying his own involvement. That is Knight's reasoning. But did he have any evidence to justify this leap into a new dimension? Most certainly. Just two hours after he had decided that Sickert was involved in the actual murders, Knight came on a passage in McCormick's *The Identity of Jack the Ripper*. It read: 'Yet another suggestion made is that Walter Sickert, the painter, was Jack the Ripper. The reason for Sickert being suspected is that he was believed to have made sketches and paintings of the Ripper crimes...' Once more Knight's mind reeled. With excitement he wrote:

> Someone had already pointed an accusing finger at Sickert. But who? In the fifteen years that had elapsed since McCormick wrote his book, his notes on Sickert had been lost. But the fact remains that Sickert had been accused...

As a flight of fancy this is in the Schneider Trophy class. This earlier involvement of Sickert Senior is based on nothing more than the faulty retelling of already garbled accounts. Strangely enough, Knight was fully aware of one of the seminal accounts that became garbled, the passage in Dr Robert Emmons's *Life of Sickert*, which reads: 'He used to go nightly to music halls and walk home from Hoxton, Shoreditch, Canning Town or Islington, across Primrose Hill and so to Hampstead. He wore a loud check coat, long to the ankles, and carried a little bag for his drawings. One night in Copenhagen Street a party of young girls fled from him in terror, yelling, "Jack the Ripper, Jack the Ripper!" ' It was this basically innocent anecdote that became distorted to portray Sickert *posing* as the Ripper, one version of which appears in Denys Sutton's *Walter Sickert*. It reads: 'There's an odd story, quite in keeping with his theatrical nature, that one night a party of girls, who came across him in Copenhagen Street, fled in terror when he said to them that he was "Jack the Ripper, Jack the Ripper".'

The girls in the Emmons story had very probably been visually primed by the striking illustrations on the front pages of the popular *Illustrated Police News*. The Ripper with his long coat and bag starred on the cover of the 27 October issue of 1888, a close-up of his black bag and contents was thrown in for good measure. Two more Ripper studies graced the front of the 24 November issue; now the coat was even longer and the bag had shrunk to a longish parcel. These motifs were again repeated on the cover of the 8 December number. But Knight was blind to the obvious, insisting that the girls reacted because the public image of the Ripper was actually based on eye-witness descriptions of Sickert himself.

Another twisted story had once involved Walter Sickert's name with the murders. He was supposed to have painted a portrait of Jack the Ripper somewhere around 1906. But this is simply a confusion between the East End murders and the Camden Town murder of 12 September 1907. At that time Emily Dimmock was found with her throat cut. A young artist, Robert Wood, was charged with the crime and later acquitted.

This case was of special interest to Sickert, who then lived in Camden Town and knew Wood. In following the trial, Sickert made a number of studies involving the murder. These were at times wrongly thought of as Ripper studies, and Sickert's impish and macabre sense of humour may have led him to play up to such fanciful errors. In fact, he always got a kick out of elaborate leg-pulling, as Edith Sitwell reports: 'Walter Sickert had a sense of fun that could be disconcerting, as Wyndham Lewis found out when he went to dine with Osbert and Sachie at the same time as

Walter Sickert as 'A Man with Secrets';
inset: Mary Kelly's last alluring smile.

Sickert. Sickert invented a character supposedly out of one of Lewis' novels, and asked him at length about him. Lewis thought he would get the better of Sickert by carrying on the pretence, and a long conversation ensued about a character who never existed. Neither Lewis nor Sickert gave up.'

Yet another tale links Sickert's name with the Ripper, the famous one involving the young veterinary student lodger, but none of these stories points to anything more than an understandable curiosity about a mystery which had touched him first in Copenhagen Street, and later enveloped him when he called on his close friend, George Moore, in July 1889. Moore was later to devote a chapter of his *Conversations in Ebury Street* to Sickert, but in that summer of 1889 he was more preoccupied with the effrontery of the *New York Herald*. The damn paper had sent a reporter to interrupt him just when he was engrossed in correcting the manuscript of a novel. For some unfathomable reason, the *Herald* wanted *his* views on the 'Ripper murder' of the previous day, and his views on Jack the Ripper's driving motives.

On 18 July the *Herald* reported the encounter thus:

Mr Moore was ignorant of the awful crime with which London was ringing, and at first did not seem disposed to talk about it, casting longing glances at his manuscript, and at first answering rather grumpily to the questions inflicted on him. At last, making a virtue out of necessity, he gave his views. '. . . I should say it was the same man . . . I made up my theory almost from the first, and still believe in it. The utter absence of the motives, which generally lie at the root of the murder is very remarkable. These crimes are not committed for gain. That at least is certain. They are not, I think it is equally certain, committed for revenge.

'My theory is that they are the work of some weak-brained zealot of the "purity" class. Just as Eroticism culminated in the Marquis de Sade, the horror of sex and all things sexual from which a large class is now suffering has culminated in Jack the Ripper. Perhaps this unspeakable wretch thinks that by creating a panic among the poor women of the class he preys on, he may frighten them from their profession. An insane idea, of course, but a conceivable one. It is a sort of vulgar Torquemada, murdering as Torquemada burned, to frighten evil-doers, and perhaps also save the souls of his victims. He is a loathsome outcome of the Puritanism of the day. That is my idea.'

Following on this, it is not hard to imagine the warm exchange of theories and counter-theories between Sickert and Moore, yet it was never more than an intellectual exercise. Despite that, it gave the Ripper case plenty of extra colour and it registered well in Sickert's mind, so much so that after the Camden Town murder, where again the killer was never discovered, he developed a fascination with unsolved crimes. It was an interest that lasted for the rest of his life, as his friends confirmed. Marjorie Lilly, for one, has this to say: '. . . He dwelt at length on some famous murder trials. We were more interested in his dramatic exposition of the subject than the actual crime; he told his story with deadly effect, waving his hands to mark his points by the eerie glow of his lantern. Only unsolved crimes detained him, for the solution of which he had endless plausible theories.'

In her entertaining book, *Sickert, the Painter and his Circle*, Marjorie Lilly shows how the Whitechapel murders and the Camden Town murder became intertwined in Sickert's psyche, recording that 'He had two fervent crazes at the moment, crime and the princes of the Church; crime personified by Jack the Ripper, the Church by Anthony Trollope.' When he dropped into his crime mood his studio became a '. . . robbers' lair, illumined solely by the bull's eye lantern'. In ecclesiastical mood, when reading Trollope, the place became '. . . the Dean's bedroom, complete with iron bedstead, quilt and bookcase.' These two interchangeable moods led to a slight clash of decor: 'The ecclesiastical flavour so uncongenial to him was somewhat marred by the red Bill Sykes handkerchief dangling from the bedpost.'

Sickert made use of this handkerchief as an aid to reverie and concentration. As Lilly says, '. . . it was an important factor in the process of creating his picture, a lifeline to guide his train of thought, as necessary as the napkin which Mozart used to fold into points which met each other when he too was composing.' It was at this time that Sickert was grappling with one of his Camden Town murder pictures, '. . . and while reliving the scene he would assume the part of a ruffian, knotting the handkerchief loosely around his neck, pulling a cap over his eyes and lighting his lantern. Immobile, sunk deep in his chair, lost in the long shadows of that vast room, he would meditate for hours on his problem.'

Using her artist's eye, Lilly has beautifully observed a process dear to many artists and writers – the use of a significant object or objects, as an aid to creativity. In Sickert's case, when his handkerchief had served its initial purpose '. . . it was tied to any doorknob or peg that came handy to stimulate his imagination further, to keep the pot boiling. It played a necessary part in the performance of the drawings, spurring him on at crucial moments, becoming so interwoven with the actual working out of his idea that he kept it constantly before his eyes.'

A red handkerchief fairly obviously ties in with bloody murder, in this case the Camden Town affair, yet what is obvious for most people eludes Stephen Knight. In his hunt for anything that would place Sickert on the streets of Whitechapel, this handkerchief becomes the very one worn by the Ripper when Sickert took the role. You have to remember that Knight saw Jack as three men, not one:

> It was so vital to him because this was the handkerchief he had worn on the nights he was Jack the Ripper. Unless this is true, that Sickert was the man with the red handkerchief seen by two independent witnesses on the nights of two Ripper murders, what explanation is there for his obsessive connection of the article *with murder*?

Such *curious* reasoning. Had Knight really forgotten an elementary connection – the colour of blood? Did he fail to recall that Elizabeth Stride had a blood-soaked silk handkerchief wrapped round her slashed throat? As for the red handkerchiefs spotted in Whitechapel, of what importance are they? There is not one jot of proof that they were owned by the Ripper. In any case, such handkerchiefs were widely used. Knight's statement that '. . . red is an unusual colour for a handkerchief . . . it was even more so in the conservative days of Victoria' is simply perverse.

Having cast Sickert as Ripper Mark 3, Knight reached out, it seems, for anything that could be misconstrued. He found three episodes that bore 'the singular mark of Sickert'. They were: '. . . the careful placing of rings and coins at Chapman's feet, the writing of the chalk message on the wall and the planting of grapes in Stride's hand.'

Properly understood, they all pointed at the Masons, while the grapes actually gave a lead to the Masonic madman Dr Gull, who stupefied his victims 'with poisoned grapes'. The writing on the wall had been real enough, but what had it to do with Sickert? Knight argues that '. . . the careful copy of the writing on the wall in the Home Office file, bears a certain resemblance to Sickert's handwriting.' This is sheer self-delusion. The copy does no more than show the layout of the original and its odd use of capitals. Any resemblance between the handwriting and Sickert's is wishful thinking, something by now to be expected of Knight. Only a talented professional copyist would have had the skill to make a copy close enough to the original to allow handwriting comparisons to be made. No one of that calibre visited the site of the writing before it was wiped off.

As for the careful placing of rings and coins and tell-tale grapes – are we dealing here with realities, or with newspaper exaggerations? The various accounts are in collision with each other and little importance should be invested in these trivialities. Especially when we realize that Knight was all along the dupe of a clever hoaxer.

18
The Jester Laughs Last

'Sickert writes very cleverly, but one never knows what he is going to say, or what view he will take on any subject . . . his course is always so zig-zag that when I hear that he is writing an article I seek the most incongruous opinion I can think of as being the very one he will be most likely to uphold . . .' Years ago Henry Tonks said that of Walter Sickert. Today, we can apply almost the same words to his son Joseph, for Joseph was responsible for the incongruous, zig-zagging hoax that gave rise to Knight's *Final Solution*. Ironically, it proved to be a hoax that rebounded on its creator, for when Knight published, out went Joseph's third Ripper, Anderson, and in came Joseph's beloved father to fill the vacancy. There's an old proverb about spitting into the wind . . .

Many different ideas were woven together to create the Sickert hoax. Some were consciously chosen, others may have been dredged up from forgotten stories lodged in Joseph's subconscious. His artist's skill and his facility with words allowed him to compose a coherent and undreamed of solution to one of the great crime mysteries, except that Joseph involved real people and even tied in part of his own family history to lend it conviction. As fiction it would have been acknowledged as a grand synthesis, but it swept to fame as truth, and as truth it has dazzled people for over ten years. Its quietus is now well overdue.

Cleveland Street is the key. For Joseph Sickert, that street was of abiding significance, because his grandmother Annie had lived and worked there, and her unrecorded liaison there resulted in the birth of his mother Alice in 1885. So the place acquired an importance for him.

The only other event of any importance that happened in Cleveland Street was the male brothel scandal of 1889. The scandal came to light in July, when Constable Hanks called at the General Post Office in St Martins-le-Grand to question messenger-boy Charles Swinscow. Some small sums of money had been stolen and Swinscow had been unusually flush of late, at one time reportedly carrying some eighteen shillings on him, a sizeable amount then. When the fifteen-year-old boy was questioned he protested that he had only had the smaller sum of fourteen shillings, and he'd earned it. But where did it come from? It was payment for private work done for a gentleman named Hammond, he said, a man who lived at 19 Cleveland Street. What kind of work paid that well? PC Hanks was quite unprepared for the answer.

'I got the money from Mr Hammond for going to bed with gentlemen at his house.' At that, the constable closed his notebook and sped back to report to his superior officer, returning promptly with fresh instructions to take a full statement from the boy. Other boy messengers were implicated, among them two lads with the appropriate names of Newlove and Thickbroom. By the end of that afternoon, all the accused were suspended from their work and by the next day the Metropolitan Police had been brought in. By the end of the week Newlove had made a statement that put the inquiry on a completely unexpected level.

'Why should I get in trouble,' asked Newlove, 'while men in high position are allowed to walk about free?' He then named some of the high-placed men; they included Colonel Jervois; Lord Arthur Somerset, and the Earl of Euston.

In the end there were trials, accusations of a cover-up, and newspaper editor Ernest Parke landed in jail after publishing an attack on Lord Euston. The whole affair is immensely fascinating, but these events are of importance for Joseph's hoax only because they linked Prince Eddy's name to Cleveland Street for the first time.

Eddy became involved almost by a process of osmosis. No one ever produced any direct link between the prince and the brothel, but there was always the suggestive link through Lord Arthur Somerset. Somerset had long been an intimate of the Royal Family, and if he enjoyed strange fruit, perhaps he'd offered a bite or two to impressionable young Eddy. Since Somerset fled the country he escaped cross-questioning, but he left behind him a welter of rumours.

The British press were traditionally discreet; no rumours linking Eddy and Cleveland Street reached its columns. On the other hand, the American press suffered from no such inhibitions. After Eddy left for his royal tour of India, American columnists began to wonder why: was it to distance him from the storms brewing at home? In New York an article about the scandals even carried a portrait of the prince, with hints so strong that the Tory MP Louis Jennings wrote to the *New York Herald* in an attempt to smother rumour: 'Over and over again it has been whispered about that Prince Eddy would shortly be recalled from India under circumstances peculiarly painful for himself and his family . . . It may, however, put some slight restraint upon the gossip-mongers to be

Clarence, a man born to be King, now reviled without reason.
Right: Lord Arthur Somerset, the real link between Eddy and Cleveland Street.

informed in a semi-official manner that the arrangements in connection
with the young Prince's visit to India will not be altered in any way, and
that he will return at the time originally fixed, and not before.'

Rumour has an ugly habit of becoming hard fact. The whispers about
Eddy were never stilled. In 1910, for instance, Aleister Crowley claimed
that he owned compromising letters from the prince to a boy named
Morgan, whose home had been in Cleveland Street. Just possibly this
may have been the son of Mrs Morgan who ran the tobacconist's shop at
No 22, opposite the male brothel, the shop at which Annie Crook worked.
Sixty years later the link between Eddy and the scandal was pointedly
made by two writers. Montgomery Hyde was the first, with *Their Good
Names*; closely followed by Dr Stowell in his *Criminologist* sensation of
1970. A potential hoaxer couldn't have asked for a better ally.

Given these Cleveland Street 'connections', it's easy to see how the
germ of Joseph's hoax developed. Could Eddy and Annie have met at
some time? What if they'd been drawn to each other? What if their first

162

meeting had been well before the scandals? Perhaps as early as 1884? In that case, Eddy could have fathered Alice Crook.

There were useful historical precedents to draw on. The Duke of Clarence prior to Eddy had been famous for his liaison with a commoner: his romps with actress Mrs Jordan had bequeathed her a brood of Fitzclarences, one of whom was the tragic Earl of Munster. Earlier still, another royal prince had 'fallen for a shop girl': George III, when Prince of Wales, was said to have been smitten with love for the fair Quakeress, Hannah Lightfoot; they married secretly in a private chapel and there was offspring. Some versions of the tale relate that one day a royal coach dashed up, Hannah was hurried into it by the attendants and carried off at high speed. As John Timbs put it: 'Where she was taken to, or what became of her was never known.'

Further royal gossip helped strengthen Joseph's ideas. Eddy was supposed to have given Sarah Bernhardt a son, and Eddy's brother George was alleged to have contracted a secret marriage in 1890 with the daughter of Admiral Sir Michael Culme-Seymour while on a visit to Malta. Once again there were children. This libel was actually printed in the *Liberator* issued in Paris and in 1911 it led to a celebrated court case with the English agent for the journal ending up sentenced to twelve months in prison.

All these titillating scandals, whether true or not, helped a royal escapade seem eminently believable. What's more, they weren't obscure items from forgotten archives. On the contrary, they were revived and given fresh life in the 1930s, thrown into relief by the trauma of the Abdication. In 1937, in dealing with its background, Compton Mackenzie brought the Hannah Lightfoot story into fresh prominence, and in 1939 Mary Pendered and Justian Mallett gave the story in fuller detail in their *Princess or Pretender?*

Given all these possibilities, *how* had Eddy come to find himself in such an unlikely place as Cleveland Street? The answer to that could lie in Walter Sickert's habit of acquiring studios dotted around London. Just suppose he had had such a place in Cleveland Street. Suppose there was a good reason for Eddy to visit him there, such as Annie. It would all come together as a believable set of sequences.

But Walter's records were unobliging: he had never had a studio in the street. Still, that was easily resolved since he had had a studio in parallel Fitzroy Street. So, 15 Fitzroy Street was mentally moved sideways and became 15 Cleveland Street. *Now* the story could be given its full development.

At first, Stowell's indictment of Eddy as the Ripper was a handicap, but this, too, was resolved by some brilliant twists. Eddy was involved, certainly, but only as a helpless pawn. All the evil could be invested in Eddy's doctor and his henchmen. Joseph's story began to gain momentum, and bit by bit, the sections of the hoax were assembled. The secret, private-chapel marriage of the Lightfoot legend became the secret, private-chapel marriage at St Saviour's Infirmary, while the Infirmary name, with its Kelly and Ripper connections, was borrowed from McCormick's book. Undoubtedly Joseph knew of the book: he is a well-read man, especially in this field which intrigued him hugely, partly because of his father's well-known dabblings in Ripper-myths.

The idea of three Rippers – a doctor and two accomplices – had already formed part of the story outlined by William Le Queux in 1925 and repeated by McCormick in 1959. This, too, was lifted and adapted. Even the choice of a Scotland Yard man as one of the Rippers wasn't original: years before Joseph had hauled in Sir Robert Anderson as Ripper No 3, W.S. Baring-Gould had nominated an Inspector Athelney Jones of the Yard as the elusive Jack. He was just playing around, though; there was no long-term decision to deceive.

Originality came in with Joseph's Masonic Conspiracy. This was an inspired touch, yet even this presented no great problems. For many years, anyone in London seeking local colour could have listened to tales of Masonic intrigues and of the Hidden Hand in high places. A strange little man, with a hairless face and more than his fair share of speech defects, used to hold forth weekly at Speakers' Corner, Hyde Park. He had scars across his throat which he claimed were caused when a Mason tried to execute him. His crime? An unforgivable one, for he was a renegade Mason prepared to tell all. And tell all he did. Then, when he'd finished his revelations, he'd nip outside the park gates and sell copies of the Masonic rituals, revealing all the secret signs and passwords. All these were laboriously printed on his home-made press 'to avoid Masonic suppression'.

Apart from this solitary battler there were other, far more sinister characters around, forever pushing pamphlets with such titles as *The Growing Menace of Freemasonry, The Hidden Hand, Race and Politics: A Counterblast to the Masonic Teaching of Universal Brotherhood*. These diatribes were sold along with companion pamphlets with the give-away titles of *Why the Jews Are Hated, Jewish Press Control, Jewish Ritual Murder, The Jewish Question*, and of course, Stephen Knight's prized document, *The Protocols*.

Perhaps even more brilliant than the Masonic touch was Joseph's pretence that clues to the murders had been built into his father's paintings. Knight really fell for that line. At one stage he solemnly went along with the idea that the picture 'La Hollandaise' shows Kelly mutilated on her death-bed. He peered at it and saw that '. . . her face is quite unrecognisable, and the difficulty presented in trying to discern her features is similar to that experienced in studying the Scotland Yard photograph of Kelly's mutilated face. The nose . . . seems to have been cut off, like Kelly's . . .' A pity Knight didn't look at a wider selection of Sickert's paintings; for example, the portrait of Hugh Walpole, 'Le Tose', and 'The Studio'. Had he done so, he would have found that the blurry, indeterminate nature of faces was simply a Sickert mannerism present in a number of his works.

This amazingly erratic research on Knight's part is typical. Ages were spent chasing minor points, but major stumbling blocks were hastily skipped over. To digress from Joseph's hoax for a moment: when Knight began his quest, he sensed rightly the importance of the Lees story, yet he never once checked on it in the essential places. It was a tale about paranormal powers, so the obvious people to consult were bodies studying in that field like the Society for Psychical Research and various spiritualist organizations like the Spiritualists' National Union, the Spiritualist Association of Great Britain, the College of Psychic Studies and so on. Had he checked with them, Knight would have discovered Dr Donald West's SPR interview with Eva Lees. This in itself would have warned him that he was taking heed of a fantasist. He would also have located at the SAGB's Stansted Hall, Lees's own diary for 1888, and would have learned that the police regarded him as just another nuisance. Finally, he would have discovered Lees's own special version of the Ripper episode, a version which kills stone-dead the famous episode involving the omnibus and the tracking and unmasking of an unknown man.

The Lees story was printed in the Autumn 1970 issue of *Light*, the long-established quarterly published by the College of Psychic Studies. It was related by Cynthia Legh, who had known Lees since 1912. Her mother had been so enthusiastic about the medium's book *Through the Mists* that she went to visit him in Ilfracombe. Cynthia went too, and following that visit Lees became a frequent visitor at their home, Adlington Hall in Cheshire. But let Cynthia unfold the story:

> Often when interested friends came over to see him, to ask about his Healing work and his many fascinating experiences, they might say 'What is the real story about Jack the Ripper?'. I therefore heard the story myself at least half a dozen times and hope that I may omit nothing of real interest.
>
> To keep strictly and briefly to the point, I must say first that Queen

Victoria had upon several occasions sent for Mr Lees and she had told him he could at any time ask for an audience with her . . . When the first murder occurred the public was naturally shocked and horrified. Mr Lees and his wife had previously done a good deal of rescue work in the East End of London, and he knew something of its underworld and could move amongst them unharmed. When the second murder was being planned one of his guides told Mr Lees to go and see the head of Scotland Yard. Neither of them of course, expected him to believe what he had to say, but this was the pattern he must follow. They had met before . . . all pleasant, but nothing to be done! However said Mr Lees, I had to come and tell you. and will you please make a note?

The second similar murder took place! The third time his guide spoke, Mr Lees went back again: 'Were we right last time or not?' 'Yes, you were, but that was a coincidence, quite extraordinary, but I can't take action on this kind of "chance".'

The third murder took place! Here I regret that I cannot be sure whether a fourth followed or not – but it was at this point that his guide told Mr Lees to go to the Queen.

He was given a long private audience, at the end of which Queen Victoria gave him a letter to hold until, and if, a further murder should be planned; this was to take with him to the Chief.

The occasion unfortunately arose, and every possible facility was put at his disposal. He took with him a man of authority from Scotland Yard. They went together to a house in London and rang the bell; a man servant answered it. Yes, the 'Doctor' was at home . . . he was alone in his surgery. Mr Lees walked in and greeted him; the doctor looked at him with some surprise and said, 'Well, James! I didn't think it would be you who would come for me.' These words stayed in my memory, for James Lees himself felt so infinitely sad, for the case of this man was the most complete example of Jekyll and Hyde he ever came across. I think he described him as a 'charming fellow ordinarily'. Late that same evening the doctor was taken (privately) to a place of detention and care, where he died a number of years later.

The Queen had asked Mr Lees to leave London with his family for all events five years, and for this period he received from her a pension, as it entailed leaving his job.

People were so disturbed about the murders, and were asking so many questions, she felt they might find themselves in a very difficult situation; also it was a terrible position for the doctor's wife as she held a position at Court.

On this same memorable day a beggar died in the Seven Dials area, where people in those days often died unrecorded; his body was brought into the house during the night, he had a superficial resemblance to the doctor and was much the same height and weight and took his place in the coffin at the funeral. The following day the newspaper reported that Doctor . . . had had a sudden heart attack and had died during the night at his home.

This lurid play could have unhinged a doctor's
mind – so some thought.

How refreshing to encounter a story that has the ring of truth about
it. Its substance may be nonsense, but its recollection is convincing.
There is no pretence of complete recall, but the vital few words that
stayed in the memory – 'Well, James . . .' – have all the hallmarks
of a denouement that would make an unforgettable impact. Cynthia
Legh's recollections destroy completely any possible link between
Lees's own claims and Sir William Gull. Lees insisted that *his* doctor
was publicly buried within days of the last murder, but the records
show that Gull died in January 1890.

So there were, all along, at least three documents warning of the grand
deception, yet Knight saw only what he longed to see: Gull, Netley and
Sickert. Only after his book had appeared did he once face the possibility
of a hoax. Even then he had to be forced to face it, for on 18 June 1978
Joseph Sickert finally confessed. In an interview with David May of the
Sunday Times he said: 'It was a hoax; I made it all up . . . As an artist I
found it easy to paint Jack the Ripper into the story I had been told about
Prince Albert Victor and my grandmother by my father when I was six

years old.' He then explained that he wished to confess because things had got out of hand: 'I want to clear the name of my father. I didn't think that much harm would come from it at the time because I thought the story was just going to appear in a local paper. As far as I am concerned Jack can go back to the Ripperologists.'

Stephen Knight's reactions were contained in a letter printed in the *Sunday Times* on 2 July 1978. In part it read:

> I am not surprised that Mr Joseph Sickert himself whose story provided the basis for my research has now tried to denounce the contents. He threatened to do this after I told him his father, Walter Sickert, had been directly involved in the killings . . . I interviewed him in September 1973. At that stage I was unconvinced by his story . . . I spent 18 months in research, and almost every aspect of the Sickert story proved true. Every aspect except one . . . It is certain that he had spoken the truth about Gull and Netley, but I show in my book that he had lied about Anderson. Walter Sickert himself was the third member of the Ripper party.
>
> It is this fundamental deviation from Walter Sickert's original story that has so incensed and troubled Joseph Sickert . . . he had first begged me not to publish my findings about his father. I had to refuse. He told me then he would find some way of exonerating him even if it meant denying the whole story. I had been prepared for this, and before showing him the last chapter I had secured a signed statement from him that I had recounted his father's original story with complete accuracy. Beyond that, of course, the new evidence I had uncovered spoke for itself . . . his story was confirmed in astonishing detail – for example, the statement in the Home Office file by the only man ever to see a Ripper murder take place tallied in every detail with the description of the third Ripper murder given by Walter Sickert. Until I was given access to the Home Office file that statement had never been made public.
>
> I knew then that Joseph Sickert was merely repeating the words of a man who was without doubt deeply involved in the case.

It was a last-ditch defence. The 'astonishing detail' in the Home Office file is a statement about the Stride murder made by Israel Schwartz. He mentioned seeing two men and a woman in Berner Street at 12.45. Sickert had said that *two* of the Rippers were in the street to carry out the killing. So, Knight argued, the men were independently describing the same events. But the Schwartz description had been secret until published in 1976, so Sickert's tale could not have been second-hand: it had to be that of a genuine participant. Knight reaches this satisfying conclusion by side-stepping contemporary statements which show that a number of men were around in Berner Street at the time, including witnesses William Marshall and James Brown. Differing accounts of a man seen with Stride led to the possibility that two clients were involved, which is why the *Police Gazette* published two different descriptions. The Sickert tale is simply based on this old, published information.

In making his defence, Knight little dreamed of the many absurdities that were waiting to be brought to light, but together they prove the truth of Joseph Sickert's confession. Even if Joseph had stayed tight-lipped, his deception could have been exposed beyond challenge. Indeed, had some basic documents been looked at in 1973, the deception would have been unmasked from the very start. Those documents involve Cleveland Street.

Remember that in April 1888 Annie Elizabeth Crook was said to have been abducted from her basement at 6 Cleveland Street. She then spent 'one hundred and fifty-six days in Guy's Hospital' before being released 'a harmless wreck, broken in body and spirit, abandoned in the streets . . . unable to support herself.' From then on she drifted from workhouse to workhouse.

It's all very touching, but the rate-books for Cleveland Street tell a completely different story. They show Elizabeth Cook living in the basement of No 6 for the whole of 1888. What's more, she was still there in 1889 and for *every year* up until 1893. So much for the abduction nonsense.

As for the house at No 15, the place where Walter Sickert 'had his studio' for years, the place where Annie and Eddy met, the very place from which Eddy was escorted on that black abduction day: that didn't even exist as a house. The rate-books show that Nos 15 and 17 were demolished in Michaelmas 1886 and that the gap stayed as a bustling building site throughout the greater part of 1887. Then, in mid-November, a new building incorporating Nos 15 and 17 opened. It was the Middlesex Hospital Trained Nurses' Institute. It remained as such in 1888 and for years beyond.

It's the old story. The wrong questions were asked. The questioning stopped too soon. A false pedigree was issued – and the *Final Solution* emerged in full glory. It made Stephen Knight rich. It impoverished everyone who confused it with history and reality.

19
The Magician From the Mists

The necromancer must outrage and degrade human nature in every way conceivable. The very least of the crimes necessary for him . . . to commit to attain the power sought is actual murder, by which the human victim essential to the sacrifice is provided.

Tautriadelta

The inescapable question now has to be faced. Does the Ripper *have* an identity? When I examined the contending theories, I ended up by rejecting each one, accepting that the killer was probably someone unknown and unsuspected. He stayed as a faceless, anonymous blur for a very considerable time, but that image was slowly pushed out of the reckoning by the emergence of a bizarre creature who could not be ignored or sidestepped.

In the end I was forced to conclude that of all the many candidates and fringe-players in this drama, only one cried out for reassessment. In truth, only one man can rightfully be seriously considered as Jack the Ripper. That man is Doctor Roslyn D'Onston. He alone of all the suspects had the right 'profile', the opportunities, the motives and the ideal cover. His background, his personality, his skills, his frame of mind, all fitted him for the fateful role.

Roslyn D'Onston was born plain Robert Donston Stephenson on 20 April 1841 in Charles Street, Sculcoates, near Hull in Yorkshire. Until recently, it was believed that his birthplace was a humble one, that his claim to be the scion of a well-off yeoman family was mere fantasy. But in 1841 Charles Street housed wealthy manufacturers, and D'Onston's father was, in fact, a mill-owner, co-proprietor of Dawber and Stephenson, bone- and seed-crushers, and linseed oil manufacturers. There was money, too, on his mother's side, for she was one of the Dawbers.

D'Onston's family money secured him a good education, though where he gained this education is not certain. From his writings, it seems the most likely place was in Munich. What is certain, though, is that his early driving interests were in all subjects leading to a medical career. He did eventually claim medical degrees based on studies in France and in the

United States. This orthodox learning, though, was paralleled by studies on a very different plane, for D'Onston was fascinated by all aspects of magic: not the magic of the stage-illusionist but the 'real magic' alleged to be understood and practised by small bands of initiates in every country.

D'Onston has left an account of the evolution of his fascination. He wrote:

> I was always, as a boy, fond of everything pertaining to mysticism, astrology, witchcraft, and what is commonly known as 'occult science' generally; and I devoured with avidity every book or tale that I could get hold of having reference to these arts.
>
> I remember, at the early age of fourteen, practising mesmerism on several of my schoolfellows, particularly on my cousin . . . As a medical student, however, my interest in the effects of mind upon matter once more awoke, and my physiological studies and researches were accompanied by psychological experiments. I read [Lytton's] *Zanoni* at this time with great zest, but I'm afraid with very little understanding, and longed excessively to know its author; little dreaming that I should one day be the pupil of the great Magist, Bulwer Lytton – the one man in modern times for whom all the systems of ancient and modern magism and magic, white or black, held back no secrets.

In 1862 D'Onston had the good fortune to meet Bulwer Lytton's son in Paris; this led to a meeting with the idolized writer in the following spring, when D'Onston was presented as '. . . an earnest student of occultism'. Luckily Sir Edward Lytton warmed to him. D'Onston records:

> I suppose Sir Edward was attracted to me partly by my irrepressible hero-worship of which he was the object, and partly because he saw that I possessed a cool, logical brain: had iron nerve; and above all, was genuinely, terribly in earnest.

After a brief period D'Onston won complete acceptance. Sir Edward directed him to a secret place and his training began. He says: 'I entered, he was standing in the middle of the sacred pentagon, which he had drawn on the floor with red chalk, and holding in his extended right arm the baquette, which was pointed towards me. Standing thus, he asked me if I had duly considered the matter and had decided to enter upon the course. I replied that my mind was made up. He then and there administered to me the oaths of the neophyte of the Hermetic lodge of Alexandria – the oaths of obedience and secrecy.'

D'Onston remained tight-lipped about the many things he learned and did as a lodge member, but in talking about an Italian 'witch' he says this: '. . . I knew all this from the books of "Black Magic" I had studied under Lytton. Hermetics have to *know* all the practices of the "forbidden art" to enable them to overcome the devilish machinations of its professors.'

D'Onston was more open about his other romantic ventures: he had panned for gold in the United States, witnessed devil-worship in the Cameroons, and hunted for the authentic rope-trick in India. For a while he had even courted danger as a surgeon-major with Garibaldi's army. But by the late 1860s he seemed to have settled down for some time in his native Hull. His job there he described as 'almost a sinecure'. There follows a strange gap in his history. He broke with his family and home town; the safe job was forsaken, and his fortunes spiralled downwards, downwards to seamy rooms in uncaring London.

By the 1880s D'Onston displayed all the characteristics of the traditional black sheep. He never once mentioned his family connections and only used the family name, Stephenson, on the rare occasions that official protocol dictated – on application forms and sworn statements. Yet some sort of private allowance surely came his way, meagre, but enough to allow him to live in genteel poverty, eking out this pittance with freelance journalism.

D'Onston's newspaper writings are packed with deception; biographically, they are of limited use and his tales of magic in Europe, Asia and Africa are just too exaggerated to be true. But then, they were never meant to be swallowed whole by everyone. D'Onston admired Lytton's attempts '. . . to teach the world many new and important truths under the veil of fiction' – so he set out to emulate his Master. He gave fair warning that this was his intention. In his *Pall Mall* article on 'Obeeyahism' (African magic) he promises that he will go into the subject in a forthcoming book: '*Sube, the Obeeyah*, a work of professed fiction. Its readers will have to decide for themselves how much is absolute matter of fact – whether all or none – and how much imagination. It will not be my part to give any clue to the student of occultism; it may convey many new ideas, and indicate the true lines on which his investigations should proceed; to the holiday maker and the simple novel reader it will certainly give a fresh and hitherto unexperienced sensation . . .'

Unfortunately, most of D'Onston's writings for the popular press are unsigned and untraceable; perhaps they were only run-of-the-mill reports. But those that can be traced are significant and revealing: they deal with black magic and with the Whitechapel murders.

At the time of the murders D'Onston was lodging in Whitechapel. For over 25 years he had pursued the chimera of a great magical happening, something that he himself would initiate with his intense combination of will and skill. He had read every magical tome and scribble he could lay hands on. He had talked with magical practitioners at all levels, risked his life to observe African wizardry and endangered his health touring India in search of esoteric knowledge. And, after all that, he'd landed up in London's East End, unenlightened, unhonoured and unrewarded, with only an assortment of unrecognized newspaper articles to show for this life-time search.

One can only make inspired guesses at the trigger factors that set D'Onston's feet on the left-hand path to ritual murder. The burden of a wasted life; the irrational leaps of a drug-stimulated mind; the perverse allure of the unknown and untried. All these things may have united to push the lonely searcher into his hideous experiment.

But why *ritual* murder? The answer lies in the phantasmagoria that the magical frame of mind can generate. This belief in magic is a burden inherited from the childhood of Man, a retrograde view of the Universe and of Man himself employing the dreads and yearnings of the child, and dressing them up with heady symbolism, and the language of a spurious wisdom. All magic deludes by promising unrealizable control, by offering entry into halls of hidden and terrible knowledge. In its menacing black form it operates not by violating the laws of nature, but by violating the minds of its dupes.

Black magic has results only because its devotees are willing to act out their fantasies. It allows hidden desires to become justified and rationalized. At its extreme, aided by drugs and mind-sapping ceremonies, it can lead to murder. We have only to think back to the Charles Manson case: there his cultists brutally killed seven people, including pregnant actress Sharon Tate. In Victorian Whitechapel in 1888 there was a warped magician infinitely more learned, controlled and determined than Manson, a man fully capable of carrying out his own executions.

The concept of a black magical drive behind the killings is by no means new. Aleister Crowley advanced the idea in 1969 in his *Confessions* and later expanded on it in his essay 'Jack the Ripper'. In the 1930s, crime reporter Bernard O'Donnell, a friend of Crowley, had reached the same conclusion, but quite independently, and others at that time thought the same.

Bernard O'Donnell once pressed Crowley to name the Magician-Ripper, long before the *Confessions* were published. Irritatingly, Crowley deflected the question with a studied vagueness: 'He was just another magician . . . I didn't get on very well with him. He had no sense of humour.' That was the most O'Donnell could drag out of him except for confirmation of something the reporter already knew: that Crowley had once owned a box 'belonging to the Ripper'.

The tell-tale box was literally stumbled upon by Betty May, the artists' model who had posed for Epstein. She had married Raoul Loveday, an Oxford graduate, who promptly dragged her into a cloying relationship with Crowley and his circle. May stayed at the magician's 'Abbey of Thelema' in Sicily in the 1920s and had this story to tell:

> . . . one day I was going through one of the rooms in the abbey when I nearly fell over a small chest that was lying in the middle of it. I opened it and saw inside a number of men's ties. I pulled some of them out, and then dropped them, for they were stiff and stained with something. For the moment I thought it must be blood. Later I found the Mystic and asked him about the ties. He was in one of his kindly moods. 'Sit down,' he said, 'and I will tell you about them.' He then went on to say that these were the relics of one of the most mysterious series of murders that the world had ever known. They had belonged to Jack the Ripper! 'Jack the Ripper was before your time,' he went on. 'But I knew him. I knew him personally, and know where he is today. He gave me those ties. Jack the Ripper was a magician. He was one of the cleverest ever known and his crimes were the outcome of his magical studies. The crimes were always of the same nature, and they were obviously carried out by a surgeon of extreme skill.
>
> 'Jack the Ripper was a well-known surgeon of his day. Whenever he was going to commit a new crime he put on a new tie. Those are his ties, every one of which was steeped in the blood of his victims. Many theories have been advanced to explain how he managed to escape discovery. But Jack the Ripper was not only a consummate artist in the perpetration of his crimes. He had attained the highest powers of magic and could make himself invisible. The ties that you found were those he gave to me, the only relics of the most amazing murders in the history of the world.'

The typically Crowleyian clap-trap should be suffered with good humour. But why the evasions? Why hold back the name? For in his volume of *Confessions*, he is quite open. There he gives the past history of the trunk and names its former owner, and in his 'Jack the Ripper' he features the trunk once more, and again names its owner. It was D'Onston's trunk. Crowley's other fine details can't be relied on. In *Confessions* there were seven ties but in his revised 'Jack the Ripper' essay these had diminished to five.

By contrast, the story told by the occultist Vittoria Cremers is much more consistent and convincing, but then she had the advantage of speaking of first-hand experiences. She not only knew D'Onston but had lived in the same house with him and Mabel Collins.

Cremers gave her account in the late 1920s to O'Donnell, the only investigator really to sense that D'Onston had to be taken seriously. Unfortunately O'Donnell was hampered in his search. He never discovered D'Onston's real name; some of his information was faulty, and he had no chance to read the police files on D'Onston. So his live-wire energy was short-circuited, and his findings were shelved. But, though never published by him, his notes survived. They tell of the quaint relationship between Mabel Collins, Vittoria Cremers and the sinister Dr Roslyn D'Onston.

Mabel Collins was a novelist, a devoted follower of Madame Blavatsky, and associate-editor of the Theosophical Society's magazine *Lucifer*.

Dr Roslyn D'Onston. Steel-nerved, dead of eye, heartless.
In person – unmemorable. As a master of terror – unforgettable.

Collins was beautiful, impressionable and vulnerable. Vittoria Cremers was the very opposite. In his *Moonchild* Crowley describes her:

> . . . squat stubborn figure . . . clad in rusty-black clothes, a man's except for the skirt; it was surmounted by a head of unusual size, and still more unusual shape, for the back of the skull was entirely flat, and the left frontal lobe much more developed than the right; one could have thought that it had been deliberately knocked out of shape, since nature, fond as it may be of freaks, rarely pushes asymmetry to such a point.
> 'The face was wrinkled parchment, yellow and hard; it was framed in short, thick hair, dirty white in colour; and her expression denoted

175

that the utmost cunning and capacity were at the command of her rapacious instincts . . . in her eye raved a bitter hate of all things, born of the selfish envy which regarded the happiness of any other person as an affront upon her. Every thought in her mind was a curse – against God, against man, against love, or beauty, against life itself. She was a combination of the witch-burner with the witch; an incarnation of the spirit of Puritanism, from its sourness to its sexual degeneracy and perversion.

She hardly seems like a companion to love, treasure and hold, but Mabel Collins became captivated by her. Like Blavatsky, Cremers had a powerful personality, and exquisite Mabel was too frail to resist its strident pressures. But there were complications. While Cremers was away in America, Collins made contact with Dr D'Onston.

She had been excited by one of his articles in the *Pall Mall Gazette*, dealing with African magic. An enthusiastic letter, care of the editor, brought a reply from the London Hospital: regrettably, Dr D'Onston was too ill to write at length, but they could meet as soon as he was well. They met. And when Cremers returned to England, in March 1890, she found that Collins had moved to Southsea, was busy on a new novel, and was bedded-down with the doctor-journalist.

Mabel Collins was glowingly infatuated with D'Onston: 'He's a marvellous man, Vittoria. A great magician who has wonderful magical secrets.' Cremers' view was understandably a little more detached. She described D'Onston as 'a tall, fair-haired man of unassuming appearance. A man at whom one would not look twice.'

Two weeks after this initial meeting, all three were united in a joint business venture. They took premises in Baker Street and set up The Pompadour Cosmetique Company: the ladies provided the money and D'Onston his secret recipes for beauty creams and rejuvenating salves. Adjoined to the offices were useful living quarters; Cremers occupied the third-floor flat, while D'Onston took a first-floor back room. So, for over a year and a half, Cremers and D'Onston were in almost daily contact.

During this period Mabel's infatuation waned and was replaced by revulsion and fear. She was never fully explicit about her fears but she did tell Vittoria: 'I believe D'Onston is Jack the Ripper.' She refused to go further, saying only that it was 'something he said to me. Something he showed me. I cannot tell even you, but I know it, and I am afraid.'

Cremers was not content to have her questions unanswered. If Mabel would not speak, then she herself would discover the truth about this unwelcome male intruder. In his room she had noticed a large black enamelled deed-box. She'd never seen it open, so perhaps it held private, revealing papers. Cremers waited until D'Onston was away from Baker

Street, then entered his room and tried odd keys in the deed-box lock.

Her venture paid off. One of her keys sprung the lock and inside she found a few books and some black ties with ready-made knots machined into them. When she picked out the ties she noticed that each one had dull stains at the rear. And they were stiff and hard, as if some thick fluid had soaked in and congealed. Was it blood? At the time she wasn't sure. Later, she was certain of it.

This certainty came after D'Onston commented on a newspaper report suggesting that the Ripper was about to start fresh operations. D'Onston laughed at the idea and said emphatically: 'There will be no more murders.' He then continued:

> Did I ever tell you that I knew Jack the Ripper? Just after the last of the murders I was living in the Whitechapel neighbourhood . . . I was taken seriously ill and had to go into hospital. It was there that I met him. He was one of the surgeons, and when he learned that I had also been a doctor we became very chummy. Naturally, we talked about the murders . . . One night he opened up and confessed that he was Jack the Ripper. At first I didn't believe him, but when he began to describe just how he had carried out the crimes I realised he was speaking from actual knowledge.
>
> At the inquests it was suggested that the women had been murdered by a left-handed man. All those doctors took it for granted that Jack the Ripper was standing in front of the women when he drew his knife across their throats. He wasn't. He was standing behind them. The doctors at the inquest made a point of mentioning that the women did not fall but appeared to have been laid down. This is about the only thing right about their evidence. Everybody was on the look-out for a man with bloodstained clothing, but, of course, killing the women from behind, my doctor friend avoided this. When he took away those missing organs, he tucked them in the space between his shirt and his ties. And he told me that he had always selected the spot where he intended to murder the woman for a very special reason. A reason which you would not understand.

To Cremers, this was D'Onston's safe way of boasting about his Autumn of Terror, and it threw light on the strange signature he had used for one of his articles in *Lucifer*. The article, yet another on African magic, was signed 'Tautriadelta'. When she asked why he had chosen such a name, he agreed it was 'A strange signature indeed, but one that means a devil of a lot.' It was devised from the Hebrew letter Tau, once written as a cross; the Greek word Tria, or three; and Delta, the Greek letter D written in triangular form. The composite word then signified 'Cross-three-triangles'. Having explained that, D'Onston refused to go further, saying: 'There are lots of people who would be interested to know why I use that signature. In fact the knowledge would create quite a sensation. But they will never find out – never.'

Could it be that the name embodied a specific reference to the Whitechapel murders? One thing is certain, the name was never used *before* the murders, only afterwards. And then just twice.

How reliable is Cremers' memory? Is her retelling of D'Onston's Ripper tale simply the invention of a bitter, jealous rival? There are identifiable errors in her reminiscences but these are trifles. By contrast, her summary of the Ripper tale is flawless. That can be said with complete confidence, since her words are confirmed by a statement actually written by D'Onston and filed at Scotland Yard.

If we take it that D'Onston was referring to himself, what lies behind his cryptic reference to the 'very special reason' for the choice of the murder spots, 'a reason which you would not understand'? The answers, even if incomplete, are to be found in an article in W. T. Stead's *Pall Mall Gazette* of 1 December 1888, the first to voice the theory of a black magical origin to the Whitechapel murders.

This seminal, unsigned article was wrongly ascribed to the Earl of Crawford and Balcarres, due to a slip of memory by Cremers. The piece, however, is one of D'Onston's, for which he was paid £4.00. Four pounds for an article which is at once a veiled confession and a tantalizing exercise in mis-direction, with more substance to it than the complete portfolio of Jack the Ripper letters.

With typical D'Onstonian flourishes the article is headed 'Who Is the Whitechapel Demon? (By One Who Thinks He Knows)'. The first section deals with the notorious writing on the wall and the attempt to implicate the Jews. Having dealt with that, and opened up a false trail – that the Ripper was a Frenchman – D'Onston (the man with a French name) then asks 'What is the motive?' He continues:

> . . . in endeavouring to sift a mystery like this one cannot afford to throw aside *any* theory, however extravagant, without careful examination, because the truth might, after all, lie in the most unlikely one.
>
> There seems to be no doubt that the murderer, whether mad or not, had a distinct motive in his mutilations; but one possible theory of that motive has never yet been suggested. In the nineteenth century with all its enlightenment, it would seem absurd, were it not that superstition dies hard, and some of its votaries do undoubtedly to this day practise unholy rites.
>
> Now, in one of the books by the great modern occultist who wrote under the nom de plume of 'Eliphaz Levy,' *Le Dogme et Rituel de la Haute Magie*, we find the most elaborate directions for working magical spells of all kinds. The second volume has a chapter on Necromancy, or black magic, which the author justly denounces as a profanation. Black magic employs the agencies of evil spirits and demons, instead of the beneficent spirits directed by the adepts of *la haute magie*. At the same time he gives the clearest and

fullest details of the necessary steps for evocation by this means, and it is in the list of substances prescribed as absolutely necessary to success that we find the links which join modern French necromancy with the quest of the East-end murderer. These substances in themselves are horrible and difficult to procure. They can only be obtained by means of the most appalling crimes, of which murder and mutilation of the dead are the least heinous. Among them are strips of the skin of a suicide, nails from a murderer's gallows, candles made from human fat . . . and a preparation made from a certain portion of the body of a *harlot*. This last point is insisted upon as essential and it was this extraordinary fact that first drew my attention to the possible connection of the murderer with the black art.

Further, in the practice of evocation the sacrifice of human victims was a necessary part of the process, and the profanation of the cross and other emblems usually considered sacred was also enjoined. In this connection it will be well to remember one of the most extraordinary and unparalleled circumstances in the commission of the Whitechapel murders, and a thing which could not by any possibility have been brought about fortuitously. Leaving out the last murder, committed indoors, which was most probably not committed by *the* fiend of whom we speak, we find that the sites of the murders, six in number, form a perfect cross. That is to say, a line ruled from No.3 to No.6, on a map having the murder sites marked and numbered, passes *exactly* through Nos.1 and 2, while the cross arms are accurately formed by a line from No.4 to 5. The seventh, or Dorset-street murder, does not fall within either of these lines, and there's nothing to connect it with the others except the fact of the mutilations. But the mutilations in this latter case were evidently not made by any one having the practical knowledge of the knife and the position of the respective organs which was exhibited in the other six cases, and also in the mutilated trunk found in the new police buildings, which was probably the first of the series of murders, and was committed somewhere along the lines of the cross, the body being removed at the time. Did the murderer, then, designing to offer the mystic number of seven human sacrifices in the form of a cross – a form which he intended to profane – deliberately pick out beforehand on a map the places in which he would offer them to his infernal deity of murder? If not, surely these six *coincidences* (?) are the most marvellous event of our time.'

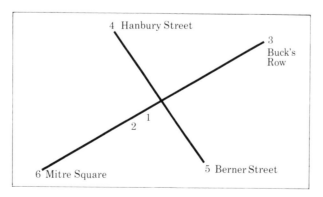

There we encounter D'Onston in a mocking and arrogant mood. Under the guise of explaining a newly-arrived-at theory he discloses the real impetus behind the killings; then steers suspicion away by including the Tabram killing, and eliminating Kelly from the list. Again, he pretends that the sacrificial trappings set out by Levy are new to him, but from his later disclosures in 1889 and 1896 we know that he had studied all aspects of black magic for well over 20 years.

Black magical rites may have endless permutations, but the sought-after ends are limited. They usually involve power-seeking, domination and erotic experiences. All three were uppermost in the Ripper's thoughts, coupled with the illusion of attaining the pinnacle of supreme magical powers. This point of glory had to be reached by dominating and eliminating scarlet women at the moment of orgasmic release. This ritual orgasm was supposed to unleash tremendous psychic energy which could be harnessed for the Great Work. On paper it looks so infantile and incredible. Put into practice it created a terrible atmosphere of fear and a lasting legend.

Did D'Onston escape suspicion at the time? Not completely. In 1896, editor W.T. Stead wrote this of him: 'He is one of the most remarkable persons I ever met. For more than a year I was under the impression that he was the veritable Jack the Ripper; an impression which I believe was shared by the police, who, at least once, had him under arrest; although, as he completely satisfied them, they liberated him without bringing him into court.' The police records are woefully incomplete, so I have no details of the incident Stead mentioned, but they do contain some documents showing how D'Onston worked an extremely cunning trick. He talked and wrote about his crimes but projected them on to another doctor, creating the impression that he was indulging in paranoiac fantasies. It nullified suspicion. In the eyes of the police it made him a man to greet with a yawn, a blank stare, and a goodbye.

In November 1888, D'Onston, from his hospital bed, had pestered W.T. Stead for an assignment, with financial backing, to hunt down the Ripper. It would have been a supreme irony if Stead had agreed: the Ripper chasing his own tail, and paid to do it. But Stead had his doubts about D'Onston and refused to co-operate. So on his release from hospital and after his misleading article of 1 December 1888, D'Onston launched the second stage of his campaign of misinformation. He met George Marsh, an impressionable man with time on his hands and the comfortable delusion that he had the makings of an amateur detective.

D'Onston fed Marsh lurid tales combining fact with fiction. Marsh fell for it all and became so excited that on Christmas Eve 1888 he visited

Scotland Yard and dictated this statement to Inspector J. Roots:

About a month ago at Prince Albert public house, Upper St Martin's Lane, I met a man named Stephenson and casually discussed the murders in Whitechapel with him. From that time to the present I have met him there two or three times a week and we have on each occasion discussed the murders in a confidential manner. He has tried to tell me how I could capture the man if I went his way to work. I simply told him I should go my own way about it and sooner or later I'd have him. I told him I was an amateur detective and that I had been for weeks looking for the culprit. He explained to me how the murders were committed. He said they were committed by a woman hater after the forthcoming manner:-

The murderer would induce a woman to go up a back street or room and to excite his passion would 'bugger' her and cut her throat at the same time with his right hand, holding on by the left.

He illustrated the action. From his manner I am of the opinion he is the murderer in the first six cases, if not the last one.

Today Stephenson told me that Dr Davies of Houndsditch (I don't know the address although I have been there and could point it out) was the murderer and he wished me to see him. He drew up an agreement to share the reward on the conviction of Dr Davies. I know that agreement is valueless but it secured his handwriting. I made him under the influence of drink thinking that I should get some further statement but in this I failed as he left to see Dr Davies and also to go to Mr Stead of the *Pall Mall Gazette* with an article for which he expected £2. He wrote the article in the *Pall Mall Gazette* in relation to the writing on the wall about Jews. He had £4 for that. I have seen letters from Mr Stead in his possession about it; also a letter from Mr Stead refusing to allow him money to find out the Whitechapel Murderer.

Stephenson has shown me a discharge as a patient from the London Hospital. The name Stephenson is obliterated and that of Davies is marked in red ink. I do not know the date.

Stephenson is now at the common lodging house No.29 Castle St., St Martin's Lane, WC and has been there three weeks. His description is: Age 48, height 5ft 10in, full face, sallow complexion, moustache heavy – mouse coloured – waxed and turned up, hair brown turning grey, eyes sunken. When looking at a stranger generally has an eyeglass. Dress, grey suit and light brown felt hat – all well worn; military appearance: says he has been in 42 battles: well educated.

The agreement he gave me I will leave with you and will render any assistance the Police may require.

Stephenson is not a drunkard: he is what I call a regular soaker – can drink from 8 o'clock in the morning until closing time but keep a clear head.

The tongue-in-cheek agreement referred to reads as follows: 'I hereby agree to pay to Dr R D'O Stephenson (also known as 'Sudden Death') one half of any or all the rewards or monies received by me on a/c of the conviction of Dr Davies for wilful murder.' It should be noted that this was

181

one of the rare occasions when D'Onston used his real family name and that the nickname 'Sudden Death' is by no means a reference to the murders. It simply refers to one of D'Onston's tall stories about the evil eye, the glance that could kill men and animals instantly.

Having prepared the ground, D'Onston then made his own trip to Scotland Yard, and there, on Boxing Day 1888, he wrote the following five-page statement:

> I beg to draw your attention to the attitude of Dr Morgan Davies of . . . , Houndsditch, E. with respect to these murders. But, my suspicions attach to him principally in connection with the last one – committed indoors.
>
> Three weeks ago, I was a patient in the London Hospital, in a private ward . . . with a Dr Evans, suffering from typhoid who used to be visited almost nightly by Dr Davies, when the murders were our usual subject of conversation.
>
> Dr Davis [sic] always insisted on the fact that the murderer was a man of sexual powers almost effete, which could only be brought into action by some strong stimulus – such as sodomy. He was very positive on this point, that the murderer performed on the women from behind – in fact, *per ano*. At that time he could have had no information, any more than myself, about the fact that the post-mortem examination revealed that semen was found up the woman's rectum, mixed with her faeces.
>
> Many things, which would seem trivial in writing, seemed to me to connect him with the affair – for instance – he is himself a woman-hater. Although a man of powerful frame, &, (according to the lines on his sallow face) of strong sexual passions. He is *supposed*, however, by his intimates, never to touch a woman. One night, when five medicos were present, quietly discussing the subject, & combatting his argument that the murderer did not do these things to obtain specimens of uteri (wombs) but that – in his case – it was the lust of murder developed from sexual lust – a thing not unknown to medicos, he acted (in a way which *fairly terrified* those five doctors) the whole scene. He took a knife, 'buggered' an imaginary woman, cut her throat from behind; then, when she was apparently laid prostrate, ripped and slashed her in all directions in a perfect state of frenzy.
>
> *Previously* to this performance I had said: 'After a man had done a thing like this, reaction would take place, & he would collapse, & be taken at once to the police, or would attract the attention of the bystanders by his exhausted condition?' Dr D— said 'NO! he would recover himself when the fit was over & be as calm as a lamb. I will show you!' Then he began his performance. At the end of it he stopped, buttoned up his coat, put on his hat, and walked down the room with the most perfect calmness. Certainly his face was as pale as death, but that was all.
>
> It was only a few days ago, after I was *positively* informed by the Editor of the *Pall Mall* Gazette that the murdered woman *last* operated on had been sodomized – that I thought – 'How did *he* know?' His acting was the most vivid I ever saw. Henry Irving was a fool to it. Another point. He argued that

the murderer did not want specimens of uteri, but grasped them, & slashed them off in his madness as being *the only hard* substances which met his grasp, when his hands were madly plunging into the abdomen of his victim.

I may say that Dr Davies was for some time House Physician at the London Hospital Whitechapel, that he has lately taken this house in Castle St., Houndsditch; that he has lived in the locality of the murders for some years; & that he professes his intention of going to Australia shortly should he not quickly make a success in his new house.

Roslyn D'O Stephenson

PS I have mentioned this matter to a pseudo-detective named George Marsh of 24 Pratt St., Camden Town NW with whom I have made an agreement, (enclosed herewith) to share any reward which he may derive from my information.

There is no record of the inquiries prompted by this statement, but no police action was taken against Dr Davies. The police concluded that the account was no more than the musings of a fevered mind, but that is exactly what they were meant to conclude. D'Onston's visit, however, did prompt Inspector Root to write some interesting notes on the Ripper. Under the heading 'Whitechapel Murders, Marsh, Davies & Stephenson', Inspector Roots says this:

With reference to the statement of Mr George Marsh of 24th inst., regarding the probable association of Dr Davies and Stephenson with the murders in Whitechapel.

I beg to report that Dr Stephenson came here this evening and wrote the attached statement of his suspicions of Dr Morgan Davies, Castle St., Houndsditch; and also left with me his agreement with Marsh as to the reward. I attach it.

When Marsh came here on 24th I was under the impression that Stephenson was a man I had known 20 years. I now find that impression was correct. He is a travelled man of education and ability, a doctor of medicine upon diplomas of Paris & New York: a major from the Italian Army – he fought under Garibaldi: and a newspaper writer. He says that he wrote the article about Jews in the *Pall Mall Gazette*, that he occasionally writes for that paper, and that he offered his services to Mr Stead to track the murderer. He showed me a letter from Mr Stead, dated Nov. 30 1888, about this and said that the result was that the proprietor declined to engage upon it. He has led a Bohemian life, drinks very heavily, and always carries drugs to sober him and stave off delirium tremens.

He was an applicant for the Orphanage Secretaryship at the last election.

These important papers were not unearthed until 1975 and even then their full significance did not hit home until quite recently. Stephen Knight, who first lighted on them, merely used them to illustrate the extremes of the woman-hating mentality, but Knight was well blinded by then by his Gull obsession, and never dug any deeper. 1975 also brought to light the exact form of the famous writing on the wall. It was shown on a police copy made at the time. It runs: 'The Juwes are The men That will not be Blamed for nothing.' In his article of 1 December 1888, D'Onston had employed these words in their correct eccentric order and with the vital eccentric spelling. Yet, as Richard Whittington-Egan has shown, other commentators since that time have used six different variations of the wording – all of them wrong. So all those years ago, D'Onston had demonstrated that he knew more about the writing on the wall than anyone else. His was the confidence of the insider. There are certainly absurdities in that account of D'Onston's. The writing is said to have been '. . . found on the wall in Mitre Square, just above the body of the murdered woman' – that's just one example. But these gaffes are part of an observable pattern: every now and again a deliberate mistake is made, allowing the writer to appear as an outside observer – not the inside perpetrator.

Yet what gave magician D'Onston the ability to melt into the background, to disarm the women's suspicions? The observations of both Crowley and Cremers give us some clues. Crowley spoke of him as having '. . . polished manners . . . his whole behaviour quite gentle and composed; he gave the impression of understanding any possible situation and of ability to master it . . . Now although D'Onston was so charming a personality, although his graciousness was so notable, yet behind this superficial gentleness it was easy to recognize an iron will . . . if he thought anything his duty, he allowed nothing else to stand in the way of performing it . . .'

Cremers diagnosed him as a neutral personality: 'Nil – absolutely nil . . . Gentle, uncannily silent in all his movements, one who would remain calm in any crisis.' Little about him stuck in the mind – except for his eyes. As she put it: 'It was his eyes that impressed me most. They were pale blue, and there was not a vestige of life or sparkle in them. They were the eyes which one might expect to find set in the face of a patient in the anaemic ward of any hospital.' His appearance was shabby but ultra-clean – unmemorable, unalarming.

Imagine such a man on the streets of Whitechapel. In his pockets are letters and receipts from newspaper editors – his cover. As a journalist he is legitimately out and about, hunting for anything fresh on the murders and the latest suspects. He moves silently and swiftly, in iron-willed command of himself. The geography of the area is pictured pin-sharp in his memory. The veteran of the Italian battlefields now plans his moves with military precision.

He's covered all eventualities to ensure that his victims will be compliant, even stupefied. He's an expert on poisons and weakening drugs, including the ones he carries. And he habitually carries a phial of chloroform which can be used when needed. Apart from that, he revels in other techniques of control: since a boy he's studied and practised the art of hypnotism, he knows just the right form of words and gestures needed to lull the pathetic drabs into a sense of false security. This gentlest of gentlemen has a right to ask them questions. He works for the papers, he values their opinions, and he's so soft-spoken and polite, not like some! A harmless, sincere man. A man to trust. And die for.

Over 20 years ago Tom Cullen gave this picture of the Ripper: 'While everything indicates that the Ripper suffered from a split personality . . . he undoubtedly was quiet-spoken, with nothing in his looks or manner to attract attention, let alone to raise alarm . . . Here was someone who knew how to approach prostitutes without arousing their suspicion, who could talk their language, catch them off guard. And it should be remembered that the whores who worked in Whitechapel were in a state bordering on hysteria . . . He had studied the terrain as a general might study a situation map.' Without knowing it, Cullen has accurately described D'Onston.

In 1980, Richard Gordon, novelist, doctor and anaesthetist, added something extra. He saw the Ripper as a medical man who chloroformed his victims first, because that would slow down the heartbeat, stifle cries and lead to a less bloody murder. Again this is D'Onston's profile. He was in a constant state of sub-acute alcoholism, so he carried various potions to stave off delirium tremens, among which was his bottle of chloroform. This was used legitimately to make one of the remedies of the time, spirits of chloroform: one part of the anaesthetic to nine of alcohol. The police knew he carried such things, so no suspicion would be roused by them. This heartless man had thought of everything.

Yet if D'Onston was a man without heart, why did the killings stop? Perhaps one reason was the complete worthlessness of the gory ritual. Neither heaven nor earth moved. No magic entered his life. Nothing but pain and anguish visited him, for following the murder of Kelly, D'Onston was struck down with a serious illness and his next few weeks were spent in a private ward in Whitechapel's London Hospital. As a student, he had suffered from a bout of 'brain fever' (the popular parlance for encephalitis), which can often lead to personality changes and brain damage. So perhaps in November 1888, he had another bout. Then, within three weeks of being released from hospital, he was struck down once more. From then on, his stamina flagged and his health gradually declined. He was in no fit state to plan or execute any type of crime.

D'Onston's promised book on Obeeyahism was never published. The man who had embraced the black arts was dramatically shattered, and changed utterly. Like Saul on the road to Damascus, he experienced the anguish and relief of religious conversion. Had his health been robust enough he would have sought redemption by submerging himself in a remote leper colony. Instead, he devoted the rest of his life to a study of the Christian revelation.

For years D'Onston toiled away to produce his slim volume of atonement, *The Patristic Gospels*. It was published by Grant Richards of London late in 1904. To produce it, D'Onston had collated texts from 120 of the Greek and Latin fathers from the second to the tenth century; from the 26 old Latin versions of the second century; from 24 Greek uncials and some cursives; from the vulgate; the Syriac, the Egyptian and other ancient versions; all the Greek texts from 1550 to 1881; plus all English versions from Wiclif to the American Baptist version of 1883; to which he added every commentator who had ever suggested a practicable rendering. It was the sort of work that few people would read and even fewer would buy.

D'Onston conducted this act of penance over eleven tormented years. Of that period and his work he said: '. . . most of [this] time has been one long fight against pain and paralysis; and nothing but the undeniable aid of the Holy Spirit could have enabled them to have been completed single-handed, and without assistance whatever from anyone.'

Shortly after his book appeared Dr D'Onston simply vanished. The man of secrets stayed secret until the end. Did he quietly settle in some foreign part? Was he drawn back to old student haunts in Paris or Munich? Did the lost comradeship of the battlefields lure him back to Italy? The questions stay as questions. Of D'Onston's fate no man is certain, so graveyard ghouls must remain thwarted; nothing tangible exists for them to gasp and gape at. But if his grave is ever brought to light, let us earnestly hope and pray that no one was misguided enough to have chiselled on his stone the traditional inscription: RIP.

Endpiece

Since this book was completed fresh evidence has come to hand which allows me to state categorically that Stephen Knight was not an innocent dupe; he knew that his elaborate conspiracy theory was based on hoaxes and deliberately concealed facts that would have destroyed his case. Not only did he invent material in order to make his story plausible, but he was presented with proof of his errors – his duplicity – by at least two independent researchers. Knight made vague promises about being willing to issue a form of recantation but avoided taking any action; naturally to have done so would have affected the sale of his Ripper book and of future books.

Specifically, I can now state that I supplied Knight with documentation showing that his case was pure fiction, and now Simon Wood, in his new magazine *Bloodhound*, has revealed that he too did the same.

Simon Wood reviews the information on Annie Elizabeth Crook given to Knight by Alan Neate of the Greater London Records Office. He shows that these records alone proved that the Annie Elizabeth Crook living at 6 Cleveland Street in 1885 was not the same person as the Elizabeth Cook who rented the basement flat at 6 Cleveland Street in 1888 and right through to the end of 1893.

This had been clear to me from the fact that in January 1889 Annie Crook had been admitted to the Endell Street Workhouse while Elizabeth Cook had remained as a stable rate-payer in Cleveland Street. Now, Mr Wood shows, the records demonstrate that, in 1889, Annie Crook had in fact been living at 9 Pitt Street, Tottenham Court Road. In addition, the records show her religious creed as Church of England, thus destroying the Roman Catholic element in the conspiracy theory.

These things, and more, were made known to Knight. As Simon Wood attests: 'A few years ago I met Stephen Knight and dismantled his theory. He listened intently and remained smilingly unrepentent . . .' He later repeated his fictions in his book on the Freemasons.

The Women Who Died

'Fairy Fay': 26 December 1887.
Emma Smith: 3 April 1888.
Martha Turner,
   also known as Tabram: 7 August 1888.
Mary Ann Nichols: 31 August 1888.
Annie Chapman: 8 September 1888.
Elizabeth Stride: 30 September 1888.
Catherine Eddowes: 30 September 1888.
Mary Jane Kelly: 9 November 1888.
Alice McKenzie: 17 July 1889.
Frances Coles: 13 February 1891.

The women's names, like many of the other characters in the drama, are often found with sundry variations which I have retained: Nichols is often spelt Nicholls, Mary Kelly is at times Marie Kelly, McKenzie is Mackenzie, etc. Not all these were victims of Jack the Ripper, but in the public view they *had* to be, for in time the Ripper became more a state of mind than reality.

Whitechapel as it is Today

There are still streets in Whitechapel that the Ripper might have sped along, yet none of the murder sites now remains. Two of the murder landmarks, however, are worth noting. Still standing and hardly changed is the old Spitalfields Church, meeting place of the local drabs described by the *New York Herald*. Then, just twenty feet or so away from the church, is the sole memorial to the victims of the killer, the ancient 'Jack the Ripper' pub. This Truman-Watney house, hosted by Ernie and Yvonne Ostrowski, is more than just a focal point for those who are intrigued by the mystery. Under its earlier name 'The Ten Bells', it was used by all the local ladies of the street. Every one of the Ripper's victims knew it well, indeed it was the very place where Annie Chapman took her last drink.

Select Bibliography

Adam, Hargrave Lee: *Trial of George Chapman*. Hodge (London) 1930.

Anderson, Sir Robert: *Criminals and Crime*. Nisbet (London) 1907.

Anderson, Sir Robert: *The Lighter Side of My Official Life*. Hodder & Stoughton (London) 1910.

Arlen, Michael: *Hell! said the Duchess*. William Heinemann (London) 1934.

Barnard, Allan (Ed): *The Harlot Killer*. Dodd Mead (New York) 1953.

Barnett, Henrietta Octavia Weston: *Canon Barnett*. 2 vols. John Murray (London) 1918.

Beaumont, F. A.: *The Fiend of East London. The Fifty Most Amazing Crimes of the Last 100 Years*. Odhams (London) 1936.

Camps, Professor Francis E. and Barber, Richard: *The Investigation of Murder*. Michael Joseph (London) 1966.

Crowley, Aleister: *The Confessions of Aleister Crowley*. Jonathan Cape (London) 1969.

Cullen, Tom A.: *Autumn of Terror: Jack the Ripper, his Crimes and Times*. Bodley Head (London) 1965, Fontana (London) 1973.

Deacon, Richard: *A History of the British Secret Service*. Muller (London) 1969.

Deacon, Richard: *A History of the Russian Secret Service*. Muller (London) 1972.

Dew, Walter: *I Caught Crippen*. Blackie (London) 1938.

Douglas, Arthur: *Will the Real Jack the Ripper*. Countryside Publications (Chorley, Lancs.) 1979.

Emmons, Robert: *The Life and Opinions of Walter Richard Sickert*. Faber & Faber (London) 1941.

Farson, Daniel: *Jack the Ripper*. Michael Joseph (London) 1972.

Griffiths, Arthur George Frederick: *Mysteries of Police and Crime*. Cassell (London) 1898.

Halsted, Dennis Gratwick: *Doctor in the Nineties*. Johnson (London) 1959.

Harrison, Michael: *Clarence: the Life of the Duke of Clarence and Avondale*. W. H. Allen (London) 1972.

Knight, Stephen: *Jack the Ripper: The Final Solution*. Harrap (London) 1976, Treasure Press (London) 1984.

Leeson, Benjamin: *Lost London: The Memoirs of An East End Detective*. Stanley Paul (London) 1934.

Le Queux, William: *Things I Know About Kings, Celebrities, and Crooks*. Nash & Grayson (London) 1923.

Lilly, Marjorie: *Sickert: The Painter and His Circle*. Elek (London) 1971.

MacLeod, C. M.: 'A Ripper Handwriting Analysis.' *Criminologist* (London) August 1968.

Macnaghten, Sir Melville L.: *Days of My Years*. Arnold (London) 1914.

Marjoribanks, Edward: *The Life of Sir Edward Marshall Hall*. Gollancz (London) 1929.

Matters, Leonard W.: *The Mystery of Jack the Ripper*. W. H. Allen (London) 1948.

McCormick, Donald: *The Identity of Jack the Ripper*. Jarrolds (London) 1959; John Long (rev. edn.) (London) 1970.

Moore-Anderson, Arthur P.: *Sir Robert Anderson and Lady Agnes Anderson*. Marshall, Morgan & Scott (London) 1947.

Pearsall, Ronald: *The Worm in the Bud*. Weidenfeld & Nicolson (London) 1969.

Rumbelow, Donald: *The Complete Jack the Ripper*. W. H. Allen (London) 1975, Star Books (London) 1979.

Simpson, Colin; Chester, Lewis; Leitch, David: *The Cleveland Street Affair*. Little, Brown & Co., (Boston, USA) 1976.

Smith, Sir Henry: *From Constable to Commissioner*. Chatto & Windus (London) 1910.

Spiering, Frank: *Prince Jack*. Doubleday & Co. (New York) 1978.

Stewart, William: *Jack the Ripper: A New Theory*. Quality Press (London) 1939.

Stowell, Thomas E. A.: 'Jack the Ripper – A Solution?' *Criminologist* (London) November 1970.

Symonds, John: *The Great Beast: The Life and Magick of Aleister Crowley*. Macdonald (London) 1971.

Wagner, Gillian: *Barnado*. Eyre & Spottiswoode (London) 1980.

Whittington-Egan, Richard: *A Casebook on Jack the Ripper*. Wildy & Sons (London) 1975.

Winslow, Forbes: *Recollections of Forty Years*. Ouseley (London) 1910.

The Protocols of the Learned Elders of Zion

The literature on the *Protocols* is extensive. An excellent bibliography can be found in Professor N. Cohn's *Warrant for Genocide*. Eyre & Spottiswoode (London) 1967.

Gwyer, John: *Portraits of Mean Men*. Cobden-Sanderson (London) 1938. Also has a useful bibliography.

The all-important Lees story is to be found in the following:

Chicago *Sunday Times-Herald*. 28 April 1895.

Daily Express, London. 7, 9 & 10 March 1931.

Fifty Strangest Stories Ever Told. Odhams (London) 1937.

Light. (London) Autumn, 1970.

Prediction. (London) January 1937.

Two Worlds. (London) 21 February 1959.

Archer, Fred: *Ghost Detectives*. W. H. Allen (London) 1970.

Hill, William Boyle: *A New Earth and A New Heaven*. Watts (London) 1936.

Neil, Charles (Ed): *The World's Greatest Mysteries*. Neil (Australia) 1936.

Saxon, Peter: *The Man Who Dreamed of Murder*. Sexton Blake Library (London) November 1958.

Woodhall, Edwin T.: *Crime and the Supernatural*. John Long (London) 1935.

Woodhall, Edwin T.: *Jack the Ripper: Or When London Walked In Terror*. Melifont (London) 1937.

The known writings of Roslyn D'Onston:

'Who Is The Whitechapel Demon? (By One Who Thinks He Knows)'. *Pall Mall Gazette*. 1 December 1888. Unsigned.

'The Real Origin of "She". By One Who Knew Her'. *Pall Mall Gazette*. 3 January 1889. Signed R. D.

'What I Know Of Obeeyahism. By the Author of the Original of "She".' *Pall Mall Gazette*. 15 February 1889. Signed Roslyn D'Onston.

'African Magic'. *Lucifer*, November 1890. Signed 'Tautriadelta'.

'A Modern Magician'. *Borderland*, April 1896. Signed Tautriadelta.

The Patristic Gospels. Under the name Roslyn D'Onston. Grant Richards (London) 1904.

Though the autobiographical material in *Borderland* was published in 1896, it was not written in that year. Two lengthy sections were written in 1889 and the rest was most probably written in 1892 or 1893. We know for certain that some time in 1892 D'Onston supplied W. T. Stead with biographical anecdotes. One of these was later included in the 1931 edition of the Rev. Charles Tweedale's *Man's Survival After Death*, Richards (London) pp.156–8. The Tweedale book is long out of print, but the D'Onston story is reprinted in my *Sorry You've Been Duped*

(1986) and *Investigating the Unexplained* (USA). My comments on D'Onston's piece show clearly that at one time (1983) I did not take D'Onston seriously. Indeed, I then described him as a man '. . . whose whole life was make-believe. His background was a humble one, not the well-off one he had boasted about. His medical qualifications were bogus.' When I wrote that, I was concerned only with a single story of his which scarcely justified extra research, and my summing up of D'Onston had to rest on the scanty information derived from O'Donnell. But O'Donnell's details were erroneous, as I was later to prove.

Those wishing to read the whole of the *Borderland* material should note that the copy in the British Library Reading Room is incomplete. When it was delivered to me, I discovered that the vital page on which W. T. Stead tells of his suspicions about D'Onston had been torn out; on the back of it had been the only known photograph of D'Onston.

Did D'Onston himself remove this hateful reminder of what he had once been? The question is not as far-fetched as it might at first seem. In 1930 Bernard O'Donnell needed to check on D'Onston's writings. *Lucifer* and *Borderland* were then easy to come by, either in bound volumes or single copies, so he had no need to consult the British Library. But the *Patristic Gospels* was a rarity and meant a visit to the Reading Room. In the Author's Catalogue there, O'Donnell noticed that alongside the printed listing of the *Patristic Gospels* someone had added in ink the letters MD after the author's name. When he mentioned this to the Superintendent of the Reading Room it was suggested that only D'Onston himself would have had an interest in adding that information. A man who was prepared to alter a catalogue in his favour was certainly capable of mutilating a book that is not just unfavourable but, in a way, damning . . .

KATE EDDOWES THE MITRE SQUARE VICTIM

SKETCH OF THE MAN WHO VISITED Mc LUSK

THE WHITECHAPEL MYSTERY.